Sexual Abuse

Incest Victims
and Their Families

Sexual Abuse

Incest Victims
and Their Families

Jean Goodwin
with contributions

PSG PUBLISHING COMPANY, INC.
LITTLETON, MASSACHUSETTS

Library of Congress Cataloging in Publication Data

Goodwin, Jean, 1946-
  Sexual abuse.

  Bibliography: p.
  Includes index.
  1. Incest—United States. I. Title. [DNLM:
1. Incest. WM 610 G656s]
HQ71.G66   306.7   81-16300
ISBN 0-7236-7012-9   AACR2

Published by:
PSG PUBLISHING COMPANY, INC.
545 Great Road
Littleton, Massachusetts 01460, U.S.A.

Second Printing

Printed in the United States of America.

International Standard Book Number: 0-7236-7012-9

Library of Congress Catalog Card Number: 81-16300

Dedication

To my fathers and mothers

Robert Bergman, MD
Adjunct Associate Professor
Department of Psychiatry
University of New Mexico
  School of Medicine
Albuquerque, New Mexico

Catherine G. Cauthorne, PhD
Clinical Psychologist
Albuquerque, New Mexico

Peter DiVasto, PhD
Assistant Professor
Department of Family, Community,
  and Emergency Medicine and
  Department of Psychiatry
University of New Mexico
  School of Medicine
Albuquerque, New Mexico

Carol Geil, MD
Assistant Professor
Department of Pediatrics
University of New Mexico
  School of Medicine
Albuquerque, New Mexico

Jean Goodwin, MD, MPH
Director of Joint Programs
Medical College of Wisconsin and
  Milwaukee County Mental
  Health Complex
Milwaukee, Wisconsin

Rebecca Jackson, MD
Assistant Professor
Department of Family, Community,
  and Emergency Medicine
University of New Mexico
  School of Medicine
Albuquerque, New Mexico

Teresita McCarty, MD
Resident
Department of Psychiatry
University of New Mexico
  School of Medicine
Albuquerque, New Mexico

Julie Ortiz y Pino, MA
Caseworker
Family Resource Center
Team III
Albuquerque, New Mexico

John Owen, MA
Staff Psychologist
Family Resource Center
Team III
Albuquerque, New Mexico

Richard T. Rada, MD
Professor
Department of Psychiatry
University of New Mexico
  School of Medicine
Albuquerque, New Mexico

Lydia Roybal, MD
Fellow
Department of Child Psychiatry
University of New Mexico
  School of Medicine
Albuquerque, New Mexico

Doris Sahd, PhD
Clinical Psychologist
Albuquerque, New Mexico

Anita Willett, MD
Resident
Department of Family, Community,
  and Emergency Medicine
University of New Mexico
  School of Medicine
Albuquerque, New Mexico

Mary Simms Zouhar, RN
Chief Nurse
Jail Crisis Unit
Bernalillo County Mental
  Health Center
Albuquerque, New Mexico

CONTENTS

Introduction

I Evaluation and Treatment Planning

II The Sequelae of Incest

INTRODUCTION

In this book "intrafamilial sexual abuse" and "incest," are used interchangeably to mean the sexual exploitation of a child by an older person in a parental role.

The term "sexual abuse" connects sexual exploitation by parents to "physical abuse" by parents and conveys the recent and revolutionary determination of society to protect children from these parental behaviors. To appreciate the radical nature of this redefinition, one needs only to review Sigmund Freud's 1905 unfinished psychoanalysis of "Dora," (see Chapter 2). That work conveys no sense that the teenage patient might require protection from the family friend who was attempting to seduce her, or that her father might be remiss in refusing to believe her complaints, or in continuing to insist that she meet with his friend. Freud shares no worries about the possibility that "Dora" might contract syphilis or be impregnated should the seduction succeed. Of course, Freud knew that "Dora" was an unusually tough and stubborn young woman. However, he was also thinking of the situation in terms of "seduction," rather than of "sexual abuse." He, and his society, had not yet defined these behaviors as "abuse."

I have used the word "incest" as well, even though it is an old word with many contradictory, legal, genetic, and psychiatric definitions. "Incest" conveys, in a few syllables, the fact that, in almost all of the cases to be described, the perpetrator was a family member. Another useful attribute of this old-fashioned word is that it connects the families that I treat to a larger body of explanatory, rule-making, and literary attempts to cope with a universal and recurring human problem. People in other times and in other cultures have called these problems "incest"; the families currently in new versions of that crisis because of incest can learn from their experience.

The clinical problems described are those I have encountered in working with over 300 incest victims and their families. Many of these patients have been referred to me by protective service agencies, either because of ongoing sexual abuse of a child in the family or because the mother or father in the abusive family had been previously sexually abused in childhood. Other former and current victims have been referred from psychiatric clinics because of suicide attempts, from prenatal clinics because of ambivalence about a pregnancy, from psychiatric hospitals because of delusions about incest, from general hospital clinics because of somatic symptoms, and from rape counseling centers after a rape subsequent to the incest.

My experience as a psychiatrist and, more specifically, as a consulting psychiatrist to a child protective agency, has shaped my point of view. I see the extreme and the difficult cases, and must rely on friends and colleagues, as well as on certain patients, for an understanding of those incest situations that leave minimal scars. Because I tend to be called in crises—suicide attempts, pregnancy or venereal disease in victims, runaways, recurrences of the incest—I tend to focus on the recognition, prevention, and treatment of these extremities, rather than on the day-to-day support of the family. An underlying goal in all of my research has been to remoralize the often demoralized social workers, physicians, and therapists with whom I work. Like the incest family, we professionals can become numb to the hurt, fear, and anger in the incest situation unless we are helped to remain hopeful that these feelings can be survived and resolved. In moments of despair after a therapeutic disaster, I will usually ask, "But what can we learn from this?" This question has been the source of much of the work described in this book.

The book's first section guides the reader through the first weeks of talking with a family after an incest accusation has been made. Chapter 1 reviews a case in order to alert the reader to the important diagnostic questions, the evaluative strategies, and the pitfalls to be avoided in investigating an allegation of incest. Chapters 2 and 3 give examples of errors that professionals dread in these cases; that is, that one will incorrectly diagnose sexual abuse when the actual diagnosis is something else (childhood neurosis, maternal psychosis—pinworm and dogbite are examples given); or alternatively, that one will be seduced by the family into overlooking actual incest. Chapter 4 reviews the necessary medical examination for the child incest victim and illustrates how this can provide the foundation for long-term medical care for the entire family. Supportive medical care can be therapeutic and growth-promoting for many incest victims and their parents. Chapters 5 and 6 examine direct quotations from family members and drawings done by victimized and nonparticipant children as clinical clues to the family's inner realities. Chapter 7 describes how the needs of incest victims vary with the victim's age at the time of the report. Incest victims at a particular developmental stage, and their families, will tend to present with developmentally determined symptoms and will require developmentally appropriate supports.

The middle section of the book focuses on some of the late sequelae of the incest experience. These chapters describe girls and women whose incest experiences usually were not recognized or treated in childhood, but who came to medical attention months or years later with complaints that could be understood as delayed reactions to incest. The chapters are arranged in a developmental sequence beginning with those sequelae that appear earliest in childhood. Chapter 8 describes a syndrome of simulated neglect that we observed in 9-year-olds who had been physically and sexually abused before age five. The abused girls recreated in adoptive homes a pattern of denigration and deprivation reminiscent of Cinderella's plight in the fairytale. Chapter 9 describes a symptom cluster of hysterical seizures, runaways, promiscuity, and suicide attempts in teenage incest victims, and compares clinical observations to Navajo and Anglo-European folk-beliefs that connect these symptoms with incest. Chapter 10 examines more closely the occurrence of suicide attempts after incest is revealed. In our sample most attempts occurred in adolescents aged 14 to 16 whose accusations had not been believed by the mother and whose families had not remained intact. Chapter 11 presents a case report of a victim of mother-daughter incest whose temporary homosexual adjustment in adolescence seemed to be a result of the incest experience. Chapter 12 reviews the genetic hazards of first-degree incestuous matings and describes the clinical problems that develop when teenagers become pregnant by fathers, stepfathers, or uncles. Chapter 13 describes adult incest victims whose children are now being physically or sexually abused. In the last two chapters clinical material is used to explore more general questions. Chapter 14 asks whether or not physicians should report child abuse. We argue that the example of sexual abuse indicates that increased reporting can reduce morbidity for the victim, for her parents, for her siblings, and perhaps for her children. In Chapter 15 I ask if my clinical observations of incest victims are similar to data that tribal leaders and storytellers have used to construct the taboos and legends about incest that exist in all cultures. New versions of medieval folktales about incest are appended to this chapter and can be helpful in providing metaphors to children who need to talk about sexual abuse.

Maintaining confidentiality is an inevitable concern when one is presenting numerous case examples. Names or initials have been invented for some complex cases simply to make the case histories readable. These invented names bear no relationship to the names or initials of real families. When a detailed case history has been required, I have followed a policy of altering one or several nonessential details, such as making an uncle into a second cousin, or a family of four into a family of five. This should foil any attempt to match a particular case history with a real family. My anxieties about confidentiality have diminished as I have seen more and more cases of incest and have come to believe more fully that the patterns are repetitive and compulsive. Former patients who believe they recognize themselves in an example should pause to wonder if there was not another case with a similar pattern, or another dozen cases. The uniqueness of each family's experience will have to wait for expression in the books that the patients themselves will write.

Several chapters have been adapted from some of my previously published papers. I wish to acknowledge and thank the following journals for their kind permission in allowing my adaptation for this book: *The Bulletin of the American Academy of Psychiatry and Law* (Chapter 2), *Child and Youth Services Review* (Chapter 5), *The American Journal of Psychiatry* (Chapter 8), *The American Journal of Orthopsychiatry* (Chapter 9), and *Child Abuse and Neglect* (Chapters 10, 11, and 13).

Financial support for much of my clinical work (Chapters 4, 5, 6, 10, and 13) with incest victims has come from a sexual abuse demonstration grant from the National Center for Child Abuse and Neglect to the Family Resource Center. The general Clinical Research Centers Program, through the University of New Mexico Hospital, funded the screening of parents in incest families for emotional and medical problems.

The list of contributors includes much of my own support system. I would like to thank Wayne Holder of the Child Protection Division of the American Humane Association for getting me into this morass of child abuse. I am also grateful to the faculty and house staff of the University of New Mexico for sharing their patients and their knowledge with me, and to Ellen Stuart and the other staff members of the Department of Psychiatry who have helped me to get all this down on paper.

Jean Goodwin, MD, MPH

SECTION I
Evaluation and Treatment Planning

1

Helping the Child Who Reports Incest:
A Case Review

Jean Goodwin

When a child reports incest, the family and the professionals involved often enter a confusing and upsetting atmosphere of accusation, denial, and blame.

A typical incest accusation is reviewed in this chapter, together with the responses to the accusation of the family and the community. In this case, the lack of response to the child's complaint is in striking contrast to the overresponse that so many families and professionals fear. The father was not imprisoned; the child was not removed to a foster home or an orphanage. A more typical response occurred[1]: The child was not believed.

This case review illustrates some sources of professional unresponsiveness to incest accusations: 1) lack of experience with actual incest cases, 2) fear of being fooled by an incest hoax, 3) the difficulty of working with the family without joining the family's system of blaming and recrimination, and 4) failure to keep in focus the health and interpersonal problems in the child and in the family that predate the accusation of incest.

The Case Example

An 8-year-old girl is brought to the office by her grandmother. The grandmother has noticed a discharge on the girl's panties and says that the girl's father has raped the child. The child is interviewed alone. She says, "My daddy did it to me. Grandma told you. Daddy pulled my pants off and would not let me go. He sat me on his lap and put his bird through my legs. He French-kissed my privates. He had my brother spy to make sure we did not get caught. That was when I was six. This is my third year now."

Physical examination reveals a mixed vaginal infection, not gonococcal, an intact but stretched hymen, and no bruises, tears, or other evidence of genital trauma. The parents are contacted and deny the accusation of incest. Interviewed together, the parents tell you that their daughter lives in a fantasy world, lies, and reads pornography. The child's teacher confirms that the child tells lies. According to the parents, the grandmother has been trying to break up their marriage for years and is repressive and moralistic about sexuality. The girl's father is unemployed because of chronic back problems. The parents say their daughter is very bright, but that her grades have fallen in the past year. Psychological testing of the child reveals an IQ of 127 and shows that she uses fantasy extensively. The parents refuse psychological testing for themselves. A judgment is made that the child has invented the incest story, although she persists in saying that she is telling the truth. The parents refuse a recommendation that the child receive play therapy. Two weeks later, the grandmother calls back to say that the parents have moved to another city and have left the child in the grandmother's care. The family was lost to follow-up.

Was this actual incest? Was it a hoax? Each reader's biases will provide an answer. What is important to realize is that there is not enough information in this investigation to make a definite judgment. In five years of searching for documented cases of false accusations of incest[2] I have been referred to many similar cases as examples of *false* accusations. "The family left town." "The parents refused to be interviewed." "The child has a history of lying, and is manipulative." "The child is too psychotic (or retarded) to give a coherent history." It is true that such cases cannot always be substantiated as incest, even in the mind of the physician, much less in a criminal court. This does not mean that the child's report was false. Often it means that the caseworker, the physician, the psychologist, and the psychiatrist were unable or unwilling to stay with the disrupted child and family long enough to find answers to the difficult questions.

There remain questions in this case that are no longer possible to answer now that the family has fled treatment. What has made the relationship between parents and grandmother so bitter? Is it true that this 8-year-old reads pornography and, if so, why does she? Why are her grades falling, and in what classes? What has caused her vaginal discharge and how can it be treated? Why is the father still unemployed after his back injury? Has he had adequate medical treatment? Did the injury impair his sexual functioning? What does the brother feel at this time of crisis? Did he actually see his father sexually manipulating his sister? Has he been physically or sexually abused?

Other, more general, questions about this case can be approached in a case review. Is this the way a child talks about actual incest? Is this the way a child lies about incest? Is the child's description typical of what actually occurs in incest situations? Were the results of the physical and psychological examinations correctly interpreted?

These questions can best be approached if the investigator 1) is familiar with the natural history of incest, 2) is not intimidated by the possibility of being duped by the child, 3) can anticipate the pressures the family will place upon her, and 4) can keep a consistent emphasis on the health needs of the child and family.

Patterns of Incest

As used in this chapter, incest means the sexual exploitation of a child by an older person in a parental role. Stepfather-daughter or father-daughter relationships are most commonly reported (70% to 80% of cases), although uncle-niece, brother-sister, father-son, mother-daughter, grandfather-granddaughter relationships also occur.[3] Incest is the most common type of sexual molestation in childhood, with more than 75% of child sexual assaults involving a relative or friend as the offender.[4,5] Mother-son incest is rarely reported. Although cultural exceptions may be allowed in other types of incest, (eg, brother-sister marriage was encouraged in Egyptian, Incan, and Hawaiian royal families to maintain the purity of the line), mother-son incest is never condoned.[6] Avoidance of sexual relationships between mother and son has been observed in the higher primates.[7]

When incest occurs, the relationship includes genital and anal fondling and/or oral-genital stimulation in about 90% of victims under 12 and in 30% of older victims.[8] It is important to remember that oral-genital contact and anal intercourse can lead to gonorrheal infection, so sexual abuse victims need a physical examination, even when vaginal intercourse has not been alleged.[9,10] Physical evidence of force is found in less than 10% of cases, although threats and coercion are almost universal.[6,11] The sexual relationship tends to occur over a prolonged period, three months to 12 years.[12] The child is usually over two years old although there is one report of an infant victim who died from suffocation during attempted fellatio.[13] The modal age for incest is between 8 and 12.[14,15] In at least 30% of families with more than one child, multiple children are involved in the incest.[16] Physical abuse or neglect of one or more of the children, in addition to incest, occurs in 50% of incest cases reported to protective services.[12] In 25% of cases there is a history of incest in one or both parents.[17] The father is alcoholic in about 50% of protective service cases[11,18] and, in at least 5% of cases a suicide attempt will occur in the family after the accusation is made.[19]

Families in which incest occurs often have intense shared fears of family disintegration.[20-22] These are dysfunctional families who tend to isolate themselves from the rest of society.[4] Sexual relations between mother and father are impaired in more than 40% of cases at the time incest is disclosed.[23] The mother has often ceded many of her functions to the daughter. Both parents may seem superficially well adjusted; however, careful life histories will reveal early abandonments of these parents by their own parents, and lifelong ànd extreme inhibitions and confusions about sexuality.[20] On psychological testing, both parents may show signs of paranoia, denial, and rationalization.[24]

Many physicians are unaware of how commonly incest occurs. One in 1000 emergency room visits will report child sexual abuse.[25,26] As many as 30% of women who present for psychiatric treatment will report a history of incest.[27] Five percent of children who present for treatment at a child psychiatric clinic will be experiencing incest.[28] If one examines girls in a juvenile detention home, the percentages are higher; about 50% of female runaways are incest victims.[29] Twenty-five percent of women with three or more illegitimate pregnancies will have histories of prior incest.[30] In studies of prostitutes it has been reported that 50% are incest victims[31] and, in severe drug abusers, over 40% of the women have been found to be incest victims.[32] In women who have been raped three or more times, 30% are incest victims.[33] It has been reported that 74% of men incarcerated for sexual perversions (rape, exhibiting, pedophilia) had been sexually involved with a family member.[34] One wishes that these male and female incest victims could meet in group treatment rather than on the streets in a rape encounter.

When 500 women in the general population were surveyed, we found that 3% reported a prior incest experience, and 1% had been involved in incest with a father.[17] A study of Ivy League freshmen reported a higher frequency; 9% of those women reported a sexual experience with a family member. Almost every known psychiatric syndrome has been reported as a sequel to the incest experience: frigidity, promiscuity, delinquency, suicidal depression, phobia, psychosis, postpartum psychosis, anorexia nervosa, hysterical seizures, and anxiety attacks.[35] In one study of 26 incest victims followed into adulthood, about 40% of victims were either promiscuous or engaged in some form of acting out.[14] Twenty percent complained of frigidity, 20% complained of depression, and 20% had a good adjustment. Another study reports that three fourths of adult incest victims, including many who are promiscuous, have some kind of orgasmic dysfunction.

The child incest victim usually presents with symptoms. In a German study of 70 forensically identified victims, 31% presented with school failure; 25% were having behavior problems, of which lying, promiscuity, running away, and truancy were most prominent; 28% were depressed; 20% had psychosomatic symptoms; and 16% were having severe sleep disturbances.[6] Only about one third of the 70 children were not given a psychiatric diagnosis. Other studies have found that depressive symptoms, school problems, or behavior problems are present in almost all victimized children at the time they complain.[3,20]

The incest experience is often revealed by the child at a point when a new family crisis has emerged, ie, excessive interference of the father with the child's dating, the initiation of a younger child into the incest, or a rebellious conflict between the child and her father based on her view of him as a hypocrite carrying a guilty secret. Many children refuse to speak about the incest; others may show a grim determination to bring the father to justice, and may describe what happened with "brazen poise."[11,37] The family's fears of separation and dysfunctional reactions to those fears—in particular, the parents' search for nurturing from the victim child—undoubtedly contribute to the poor adult adjustment of these victims.

People who grow up as incest victims may experience developmental advantages as well as impediments. The Grimms' fairytale, *Thousand-furs,* describes a daughter who must run away to escape her father's determination to marry her.[38] However, she takes with her the three beautiful gowns and the fur cloak which her father has given her and which represent the precious aspects of the relationship. These she uses to build a new relationship with her chosen prince. Lewis Carroll's young friends whom he often photographed nude experienced the specialness of being his *Alice in Wonderland*[39,40] as well as the confusion about his sexual preoccupations. Incest victims in real life can express an ambivalent appreciation for the special attention and affection that may have been part of the experience.

Individual reactions to an incest event are myriad and continue through a lifetime of development. One case report describes an 81-year-old woman who began to have panic attacks at night after the death of her husband. In treatment it emerged that she had been sexually assaulted at age six. Although the incident had been consciously forgotten, it seemed to have shaped the expression of this woman's sense of loneliness and vulnerability after her husband's death.[36]

False Accusations and False Denials

If we return now to the case which opened this chapter, it is clear that the review of the literature about patterns of incest has brought us to firmer ground. The 8-year-old is at a typical age for incest to be revealed. The description of the two-and-one-half year duration of the relationship is typical, as is her description of penile rubbing between the girl's legs, a technique which will not usually leave physical signs. The caseworker, naive about this sexual technique, believed the child was describing intercourse when she said, "He put his bird between my legs," and thought that the intact hymen proved the child was lying. The parents' feeling of being put upon and in danger of being separated is what would be expected in a dysfunctional family where fears of separation are prominent, and where defenses are few. The child's lying and school failure would be expected in an incest victim, and her brazenly graphic description of the sexual activities is not atypical.

However, even at this point, many physicians will still be concerned about the question of whether this child is simply fantasizing. Since Freud, physicians have been terribly cautious about being misled by accusations that are actually expressions of incestuous fantasies. Freud, himself, despite warning of this possibility, never described such a case in detail. It is important to remember that Freud believed that the frequency of actual incest was less than one case per million population.[4] It is, in fact, quite difficult to find any well-documented, well-investigated case of an incest hoax in the literature. Such situations are probably quite rare. In one study of 64 emergency room visits where the chief complaint was sexual abuse of a child, it was found that sexual assault had not occurred in only four of the 64 cases.[36] Less than 4% of sexual abuse referrals in our experience involved a child making a false report of a sexual experience with a parent.[2] Some false reports have come from children who have actually experienced sexual abuse with another family member in the past and who have major psychiatric problems such as retardation or psychosis that interfere with reality testing. Only very rarely do we see a child who is telling an opportunistic lie in making the false accusation. In almost all of these atypical situations a simple question to the child in a private interview (as, "Is this something that actually happened or is this something that you thought about?") will elicit a confession from the child. This is especially true if the child realizes that the interviewer is interested in her problems and will continue to help even if the child retracts her accusation.

More common than the incest hoax perpetrated by a child are false retractions of valid incest accusations by a child who is terrified by the impact of her action on her family. These false retractions have, in the past, been counted as incest hoaxes and form much of the (false) experiential basis for believing that children invent incest stories. A typical pattern is that the victim, after talking to a social worker, a physician, a law enforcement officer, and then to her family, will come back the next day and say that she lied about everything. Again, empathic questioning focusing on the child's worry about the family's reaction to her confession will often elicit an admission by the child that the retraction is a lie.

Lie detector testing can be useful in certain cases. In other situations, the inappropriate emotions of the girl as she tells the retraction (often the affect is wooden), a coached quality, or an inconsistency in the retraction, can be clues that it is the retraction that is the lie and not the previous accusation of incest. For example, a 6-year-old who spoke perfect English made her retraction in the broken English used by her mother. There were bizarre inconsistencies in her story. At one point the child said that an evil neighbor had held a gun on her and forced her to tell her story to the police; at another point she said the weapon had been a knife.

The confirmed incest hoax is more likely to be the work of a parent than of a child. In our experience, false accusations by a parent outnumber false accusations by a child by two to one. We have seen several custody battles in which each parent falsely accused the other of incest with the child. Another pattern of false accusation is seen when a schizophrenic mother, as part of her delusional system, alleges incest.[2] Since actual incest can also occur in the often disorganized families of these psychotic women, such accusations have to be carefully investigated, much as one has to investigate a new complaint of pain in a hypochondriac. The answer comes easily in some cases. One psychotic woman told a plausible and circumstantial tale of her husband's incestuous relationship with her daughters. Investigation revealed that all of her children had been removed to foster care years before, and that this incest complaint was the inevitable prodrome in this patient to a recurrence of her psychosis. In another situation a woman who alleged that almost all family members were involved sexually with her daughter launched into a long diatribe during the court hearing about how the psychologist who had examined her was having incestuous relationships with his daughters; in fact, this man had no daughters. One usually has to wait in such cases for the mother's psychosis to remit in order to understand the meanings of her false accusation.

Guidelines for Talking with the Family

Members of a family where incest has been alleged anticipate criticism, condemnation, and punishment from the outside world. The physician or other professional can easily be swept along by these expectations and can be misled into trying to be a prosecutor or a defender of the family instead of remaining focused on the job of healing and soothing wounds without rendering additional harm. The panic in these families cannot be overestimated. In a German study of fathers actually convicted of incest, over 80% denied the allegation throughout the criminal process.[6] It has been reported in another study that 75% of mothers did not act to end the incest once it had been revealed.[11] Far more rare than the incest hoax is the situation in which it is the father who brings the incest situation to the attention of any kind of therapist. One treatment program for incestuous parents estimates that about 50% of parents will still be denying that incest occurred at the end of treatment despite having made significant gains in treatment.[41] In our experience, parents fluctuate in their ability to acknowledge the incest situation. The pressure on the victim is intense. It was estimated in one study that one third of victims seriously consider withdrawing and retracting the accusation they have made.[42]

The first step should be to bring the whole family together and to confront the family with what the child has alleged. This is not an easy maneuver and is best done by a skilled person who has already interviewed all family members individually. It has been our experience that families with significant strengths are able to use this family meeting to open up hidden fears. For example, the uninvolved siblings often have a great deal of information and many questions about these incest secrets. Such a family meeting can help the father to confess and can begin the process of reintegrating him into the family on the basis of an understanding of what actually happened.

Many families cannot do this. In fact, many families cannot pull themselves together to appear at such a meeting. This can be helpful information diagnostically as well as prognostically. In an actual incest hoax, the accused perpetrator is usually eager to explain the mistake. In actual incest, the accused perpetrator is often quite elusive.

When the family cannot talk about the incest in this first session, the interviewer can continue to work on clarifying and redefining the family's situation. It is almost always helpful for the interviewer to state clearly that it seems that nobody really understands yet what has happened, but that something has to be seriously wrong or the child would not have said what she said. This approach can establish an alliance with the family to find out what is wrong even if they are not ready to form an alliance to understand and stop the incestuous relationship. At this point, further interviewing can be scheduled.

Offering physical examination to parents who have chronic physical complaints or hidden physical fears can often be the key to establishing trusting relationships. Treatment of a parent's alcoholism can often be initiated more easily in the context of a medical examination than in a psychotherapeutic relationship. The family will want to talk about who is to blame. The physician must persist in refocusing on what care is needed. Behind the family's preoccupation with blame are often fears that whoever is to blame will be cast out, destroyed. The family needs to talk about these fears and they need information and modeling from the interviewer that can help them to realize that there are alternatives other than blindly denying all problems or losing everything valuable in the family. What alternatives are available? Can the mother protect the child with the father remaining in the home? Can the child protect herself now if she has outside support? Should the child stay with friends or relatives for a few days? Is hospitalization indicated for the child, or for the alleged perpetrator? Is the perpetrator so out of control that the police need to be involved? It may be necessary to explain to the family concretely and with statistical data that the child's allegation does not mean that she will be removed and does not mean that the perpetrator will be imprisoned.

This kind of intervention is intense and draining. The investigator needs to set firm limits. At times these families flee even before diagnostic tests are completed. If the investigator is to be in touch with the family's fear of exposure, fear of loss, and despair about finding nondestructive ways to be closer, the investigator must come to terms with those feelings herself. It is rarely possible to handle a situation like this singlehandedly. The group of professionals working on the case, like the family involved, needs to be able to stop its members from arguing and blaming and to refocus on 1) the family problems which require care, and 2) the painful feelings that underlie the family's battles and the therapeutic battles which can succeed them.

The Medical, Psychological, and Psychiatric Evaluation of the Child Victim

One problem in the case that began this chapter was that too much reliance had to be placed on the physical examination of the child. The parents refused follow-up family interviews, refused personal psychological testing, and refused medical examinations. The investigator was left with a medical examination of the child, which was negative, and a psychological evaluation of the child that indicated extensive use of fantasy. A judgment was made that the child had been lying.

Do the data warrant such a judgment? Negative physical findings are consistent with the sexual contact described by this child. What if the hymen had not been intact? This is seen in 20% to 40% of girls who have never had intercourse.[43] In our series of substantiated cases of incest, the physical examination was completely negative in 40% of cases. Other studies report that physical evidence of trauma is found in less than 25% of cases.[15]

The few cases of hoax that we have seen coincided with psychological evaluations that showed mental retardation, psychosis, and/or extreme anxiety and depression, not with extensive use of fantasy play. An increase in fantasy is the normal response of a latency age child to trauma.[44] To make a judgment solely on the basis of these data from the child is to overstrain the power of the tests.

The medical examination of the child is not an efficient way to "reveal the truth." This must at times be explained to parents who bring in a frightened child and demand an immediate examination. Often, much can be gained by simply talking with the child and doing part of the physical examination on that first traumatic day and postponing the forensic pelvic examination. For example, a 6-year-old child alleges that her father forced her to perform fellatio with him, and says that the last occasion was six days ago. She is frightened of being examined and will not allow the physician to touch her. One approach to such a child would be to promise not to undress her below the waist level until a second examination to be scheduled the next day. A throat swab can be done immediately to determine if she has a pharyngeal gonococcal infection. Blood can be collected for a serologic test for syphilis. If she is not frightened of the physician, she is much more likely to return for the follow-up treatment necessary if she does have an infection. Vaginal washings for sperm and vaginal/rectal cultures for gonorrhea are unlikely to be positive, unless she is minimizing the extent of the sexual contact. If she is minimizing it, time spent playing and talking with the physician may uncover this fact. Combing of head hair (for samples of the perpetrator's pubic hair) and the collection of swabs from behind the premolars and under the tongue (for microscopic examination for sperm cells) can be done unobtrusively as part of the preliminary pediatric examination.

The physician can help the family to develop by making it clear that she is not preoccupied with "finding the truth" but is giving the child a careful head-to-toe physical examination in order to identify any problems. The physician will usually ask about school, hobbies, siblings, physical illness before asking about sexuality. Some parents need to be present for at least part of the examination to observe this for themselves. Other parents must be excluded, either because they cannot be dissuaded from being punitive with the child or because they are obviously seeking voyeuristic gratification from the examination. We have worked with several parents who repeated the pelvic examination later with the child at home in ways that became part of the sexual abuse ritual.

The physician needs to create an environment of matter-of-fact acceptance of sexuality and of the genitals. This can be a therapeutically surprising experience for many victims and their families. To create such an experience takes time, and it is best to schedule two or three hours for such an examination. Helpful questions are: Do you think you will ever marry? Do you think you will ever have children? What do you know about how babies are made? Who explained that to you?

After the child takes off her panties, the physician needs to ask her if she has names for those parts of her body. Drawings or a model may be used to teach medical names. Once a common vocabulary has been established, one can ask, "Has anyone ever touched you there? Have you ever seen a naked boy or man? Do you ever touch your own body? Where? What does it feel like?"

The sexual ignorance of even late pubertal incest victims and of their mothers is a continual source of astonishment. One must often remind oneself to give basic information, such as describing what will happen to the child as pubertal development progresses, what menstruation is, what masturbation is, and so on.

When a vocabulary for talking about sexuality has been devised, one can begin to sketch in the history of the present complaint. With a young child, the interview might go like this:

> Somebody touched you? Can you draw me a picture of the person who did that? (Discuss the picture.) Where were you two when that happened? Can you draw me a picture of your house so I can see where? Were you living in this house when you went to first grade?

The questions of who, what, where, how, and why can be difficult to establish. A child younger than eight or nine will usually not have a formal mastery of concepts like duration.[44] What can be helpful is to construct an event calendar which may be illustrated. This "calendar" will have in sequence birthdays, other special days, grades, and schools attended, family moves, and other major family events. The child can often mark on this sequential list the point where the first sexual contact occurred.

The medical history of the event includes the child's reactions, both internal and external. The physician needs a complete school history including grades and absences. We have seen several incest victims who had been misdiagnosed as having mental retardation. Careful review of school records showed that the decline in school performance coincided with the initiation of sexual contact. For some of these children, "being dumb" was the only strategy they could find to comply with the perpetrator's nonverbal demand that they should not understand the meaning of the sexual contact. While some children can maintain the school as their only safe place, others displace fears from home to school. One 9-year-old presented the problem of serious truancy. Underlying the truancy were fears that she would be blinded or cut into pieces by her classmates. Not only were her own guilty fears about the prior incest with her father expressed in this symptom, but her truancy became the focus of family fights, so she could believe that her parents were angry with her because of her school failure, not because of the incest. The work history in these children should include listing jobs at home. This last is often extensive and inconsistent with the child's "scapegoat" reputation as lazy and unreliable.

In the review of systems, onset of physical symptoms can also be correlated with the onset of sexual contact; examples are, recurrent sore throat in a child involved in fellatio, or abdominal swelling in a child whose father had explained that he was trying to make her pregnant. Sleep disturbances are common, particularly nightmares. If a child says she does not remember any nightmares, one might say, "Then tell me about a good dream you have had." One child, at this point, drew a picture of a girl in a wedding dress and talked of fearing that her mother would die if the incest accusation led to divorce.

A child's fantasies reveal the child's fears. Several simple strategies can open the door to this inner life. "If you had three wishes, what would you wish for?" Incest victims often wish for help for the mother. "Draw a picture of the inside of your body as if your skin were transparent and you could see right inside." The drawings of incest victims with somatic symptoms often reveal concerns about the symptomatic organ's having been harmed in the sexual contact. "Will you get married when you grow up?" "Will you have children?" Incest victims often say no and may also begin to talk about feelings of revulsion toward men or about fears that they may not be able to bear children.

The physical examination should be thorough but gentle. The child will be sensitive to anything resembling assault, so she needs to stay in control whenever possible: taking off her own clothes, watching the genital examination in a mirror, telling you when she needs you to stop for awhile. Be alert for signs of physical abuse. The speculum examination can be deferred in a child with an intact hymen and without signs of perineal or genital trauma. In a small child, a test tube may be substituted for the speculum. A careful rectal examination should be done to check for trauma around the anal sphincter. Pharyngeal, vaginal, and rectal cultures for gonorrhea should be taken, as well as the blood test for syphilis. Four percent to 10% of incest victims have gonorrhea.[9,10]

The pregnancy test needs to be done even in a midpubertal girl who has not yet menstruated. The incest relationship, unlike rape, will have a long history at the time of disclosure. Several studies have reported a 10% to 20% incidence of pregnancy (see Chapter 12). We have seen one 11-year-old girl who had never menstruated whose incest pregnancy was not recognized until the sixth month.

PROGNOSIS

Families that choose incest as a defensive strategy tend to resist outside intervention. The investigator or physician who sees the family first needs to be aware that her diagnostic maneuvers may be the only treatment the family will allow. Most treatment interventions tend to be helpful: supportive treatment for the mother, play therapy for the child, group treatment for the father in a fathers' group. Treatment for the child is often most acceptable to the parents, and other treatment recommendations can spin off from this focus on the child's adjustment. Family therapy may be seen at first as threatening, until it can be linked to specific goals, ie, improving the parents' sexual relationship, improving the child's school performance, increasing the mother's homemaking skills.[45] Specific time-limited contracts for treatment may be more acceptable to the family than a more general recommendation for psychiatric care. If the gynecologist or pediatrician who sees the child initially develops a good relationship with the family, that physician may elect to follow through with brief therapy for the child or for a parent with consultation from a psychiatrist or psychologist.

The careful physician will develop a long list of goals for the incest family. These might include: getting a dental bridge for the battered wife, improving the child's school performance; helping the family to develop a bedtime ritual for the insomniac victim that is more age-appropriate than genital fondling by the father; getting medical treatment for the father's impotence, which might include alcohol detoxification and films on nongenital and genital pleasuring; involving the victim's married sister in an adult victims' group. For certain of these goals, the prognosis is bound to be fair or good.

In terms of the central goals of protecting the child and her siblings from further abuse and from further sequelae, the most secure situation is one in which at least one family member, and preferably more than one, has learned to call for help. The investigator who has responded appropriately to felt needs is most likely to be called.

The program designed by Henry Giaretto [46,47] in Santa Clara County, California, has given us the best data on prognosis. In this program, which is part of the perpetrator's probation, each family member participates in group, individual, or family therapy for three months or more. Ninety percent of fathers confess under this treatment regimen, and the recurrence rate for incest is less than 1%. Eighty-five percent of the marriages remain intact and over 90% of the victims return to live with one or both parents. There is some evidence[48] that full disclosure of the incest to a monitoring agency will stop the incest in most cases, even without involving the courts; however, the exceptions to this rule are alarming.[11] In a system that cannot legally enforce treatment recommendations, the percentage of victims living away from the parents is likely to rise, as is the percentage of divorces in incest families, and the recurrence of incest with the identified child or a sibling.[48,49]

In the incest situation it is easy to confuse the goals and methods of the forensic system with those of the medical system. A forensic decision that no incest occurred will not cure a child's gonorrhea or prevent the mother from becoming infected if the medical incest is not treated. If medical evidence leads to forensic decisions that lead to incarceration of the father, this may leave the inadequate mother and the guilty daughter even more in need of treatment than before. Physicians sometimes try to set themselves apart from the legal system by refusing to become involved at all in the legal aspects of incest. The risk here is that the family

14

will experience the physician as making the same sort of "bargain with the devil" that the father and the rest of the family have already made. "We are too weak and the dangers are too great. We cannot follow the rules that everyone else follows." If the physician is seen to join too closely with the family's position, the opportunity to help change the family may be lost. Maisch, in his study of incest families, found one father who reported the incest himself.[16] He gathered the entire family around him, told everyone what he had done, and told them that he did not know what would happen when they told the authorities but that he thought this had to be done to make things right again. The approach of this father is one of the best blueprints we have found for how the professional can talk with the family when a report must be made, without blaming the family, without giving them the message that they are being abandoned to a forensic system, and without entering into a devil's bargain which tells them it is impossible to change.

REFERENCES

1. Forward S, Buck C: *Betrayal of Innocence*. Los Angeles, J.P. Tarcher, 1978.

2. Goodwin J, Sahd D, Rada R: Incest hoax: False accusations, false denials. *Bull Am Acad Psychiatry Law* 6 (3):269–276, 1979.

3. Nakashima I, Zakus G: Incestuous families. *Pediatr Ann* 8:300–308, 1979.

4. Weinberg SK: *Incest Behavior*. New York, Citadel, 1955.

5. Tsai M, Wagner NN: Incest and molestation: Problems of childhood sexuality. *Resident Staff Physician:* 129–136, 1979.

6. Maisch H: *Incest*. New York, Stein & Day, 1972.

7. Bourgeois M: Shunning of incest in human and nonhuman primates. Preliminary note. *Ann Med Psychol* (Paris) 137:1008–1020, 1979.

8. Gebhard PH, Gagnon JH, Pomeroy WB et al: *Sex Offenders: An Analysis of Types*. New York, Hoeber Medical Books, Harper & Row, 1965.

9. Goodwin J, Fried J: Rape. *N Engl J Med*. 298:167, 1978.

10. Greenberg N: The epidemiology of childhood sexual abuse. *Pediatr Ann* 8:289–299, 1979.

11. Meiselman K: *Incest*. San Francisco, Jossey-Bass, 1978.

12. DeFrances V: *Protecting the Child Victim of Sex Crimes Committed by Adults*. Englewood, CO, American Humane Association, 1969.

13. Sgroi SM: Sexual molestation of children. *Child Today* 4:18–21, 1975.

14. Lukianowicz NE: Incest: Paternal incest. *Br J Psychiatry* 120:301–313, 1972.

15. Finkelhor D: Psychological, cultural and family factors in incest and family sexual abuse. *J Marriage Family Counselors* 4:41–49, 1978.

16. Tormes Y: *Child Victims of Incest*. Englewood, Colorado, The American Humane Association, 1968.

17. Goodwin J, McCarty T, DiVasto P: Prior incest in abusive mothers. *Child Abuse Neglect* 5:1–9, 1981.

18. Virkunnen M: Incest offences and alcoholism. *Med Sci Law* 14:124–128, 1974.

19. Goodwin J: Suicide attempts in sexual abuse victims and their mothers. *Child Abuse Neglect* (to be published).

20. Kaufman T, Peck AL, Tagiuri CK: The family constellation and overt incestuous relationships between father and daughter. *Am J Orthopsychiatry* 24:266–279, 1954.

21. Lustig N, Dresser J, Spellman SW: Incest: A family group survival pattern. *Arch Gen Psychiatry* 14:31–40, 1966.

22. Gutheil TG, Avery NC: Multiple overt incest as a family defense against loss. *Family Process* 16:105–116, 1977.

23. Weiner I: Father-daughter incest: A clinical report. *Psychiatr Q* 36:607–632, 1962.

24. Sahd D: Psychological assessment of sexually abusing families and treatment implications, in Holder W (ed): *Sexual Abuse of Children*. Englewood, Colorado, The American Humane Association, 1980, pp. 71–86.

25. Brant RST, Tisza VB: The sexually misused child. *Am J Orthopsychiatry* 47:80–90, 1977.

26. Eaton AP, Vastbinder E: The sexually misused child. A plan of management. *Clin Pediatr (Phila)* 8:438, 1969.

27. Rosenfeld AA: Incidence of a history of incest among 18 female psychiatric patients. *Am J Psychiatry* 136:791–795, 1979.

28. Browning DH, Boatman B: Incest: Children at risk. *Am J Psychiatry* 134:69–72, 1977.

29. Kempe CH: Sexual abuse, another hidden pediatric problem. The 1977 C. Anderson Aldrich Lecture. *Pediatrics* 62:382–389, 1978.

30. Malmquist C: Report on females with three or more illegitimate pregnancies. *Am J Orthopsychiatry* 36:476–484, 1966.

31. Flugel J: *The Psycho-Analytic Study of the Family*. London, Hogarth Press, 1926.

32. Densen-Gerber J, Benward J: *Incest as a Causative Factor in Antisocial Behavior: An Exploratory Study*. New York, Odyssey Institute, 1976.

33. Miller J, Moeller D, Kaufman A, et al: Recidivism among sex assault victims. *Am J Psychiatry* 135:1103–1104, 1978.

34. Hammer EF: Symptoms of sexual deviation: Dynamics and etiology. *Psychoanal Rev* 55:5–27, 1968.

35. Finkelhor D: Risk factors in the sexual victimization of children. *Child Abuse Neglect* 4:265–273, 1980.

36. Peters J: Children who are victims of sexual assault. *Am J Psychotherapy* 30:398–421, 1976.

37. Bender L, Blau A: The reaction of children to sexual relations with adults. *Am J Orthopsychiatry* 7:500–518, 1937.

38. Manheim R (translator): Grimms' Tales for Young and Old. New York, Doubleday, 1977.

39. Greenacre P: "It's my own invention." A special screen memory of Mr. Lewis Carroll, its form and its history, in Greenacre P (ed): *Emotional Growth, Volume 2*. New York, International Universities Press, 1971, pp 438–478.

40. Gattegno J: *Lewis Carroll: Fragments of a Looking Glass*. New York, Crowell, 1974.

41. Gottlieb B, Dean J: The co-therapy relationship in group treatment of the sexually mistreated adolescent. Read before the Second International Congress on Child Abuse and Neglect, London, September 12–15, 1978.

42. Nakashima I, Zakus GE: Incest: Review and clinical experience. *Pediatrics* 60:696–701, 1977.

43. Underhill RA, Dewhurst J: The doctor cannot always tell. *Lancet* i :375–376, 1978.

44. Sarnoff C: *Latency*. New York, Jason Aronson, 1976.

45. Berlin IN: A developmental approach to work with disorganized families. *J Am Acad Child Psychiatry* 18:354–365, 1979.

46. Giaretto H: Humanistic treatment of father-daughter incest, in Helfer RE, Kempe CH (eds): *Child Abuse and Neglect in the Family*. Cambridge, Ballinger, 1976.

47. Giaretto H, Giaretto-Einfeld A: Involving the community in the treatment of incest. Read before the Third International Congress on Child Abuse and Neglect. Amsterdam, April 21–25, 1981.

48. Cormier BM, Kennedy M, Sangowicz J: Psychodynamics of father-daughter incest. *Can Psychiatr Assoc J* 7:203–216, 1962.

49. Molnar G, Cameron P: Incest syndromes: Observations in a general hospital psychiatric unit. *Can Psychiatr Assoc J* 20:373–377, 1975.

2

False Accusations and False Denials of Incest: Clinical Myths and Clinical Realities

Jean Goodwin
Doris Sahd
Richard T. Rada

In the psychiatric literature the definition of incest ranges from the narrow requirements of consanguinity and sexual intercourse to the more inclusive definition of child sexual abuse by an adult or older child in a parental role.[1] The purpose of this chapter is to discuss clinical aspects of false accusation or false denial of incest using case examples and to suggest guidelines in the clinical investigation of such cases. Our case examples conform to the broader definition of incest and include examples of father- and stepfather-daughter incest accusations.

Despite the recent increase in research on incest, the question of false accusation has been largely neglected in the psychological and psychiatric literature. A search of psychological abstracts from 1968 to 1978 yielded only one report, a Hungarian paper,[2] which dealt with the problem of false accusation. We reviewed 88 psychiatric papers on incest published between 1973 and 1978. Two papers present surveys of the historical importance of false accusations of incest,[1,3] and four papers contain individual case reports of false retractions of valid incest accusations.[4-7] We were unable to find a recent case report of a false accusation of incest. Macdonald[8] implies that false accusations are an important forensic problem; however, most of his case examples are drawn from a book published in 1913.[9]

Although reported false accusations of incest are rare, legal and mental health professionals tend to be suspicious of incest accusations. This may be explained, in part, by the continued influence of Freud's conclusion that many reports of incest were based on fantasy.[10-12] However, it is interesting to note that, to our knowledge, Freud never reported a detailed case example of false accusation of incest. Furthermore, he confirmed some of the accusations by interviewing family members.[13-15] The case of Dora documents his approach to an accusation of seduction, which the family alleged to be a lie, but which Freud validated as an actual event.[16,17] Some writers[18,19] believe that Freud overstated the importance of fantasy as the basis for incest accusations, and that the therapist's assumption that an accusation is fantasy may drive victims out of treatment and into psychosis.

Only one published article documents the relative frequency of false accusations of child sexual abuse. Peters[3] studied 64 children seen at a hospital emergency room with a complaint of sexual assault and found four cases in which the staff concluded that no sexual assault had occurred. However, the actual relationship between the alleged offender and victim is not indicated, and the 64 cases included offenders who were not living within the family nor related to the victim.

False Accusation by the Daughter

The medicolegal literature on incest contains only a few reported cases in which a daughter falsely accuses the father or stepfather of incest. In one of these a teenager accused a hated stepfather of incest to shield the boyfriend who had impregnated her. In another a girl was coaxed and bribed with candy to make the accusation. Both girls ultimately admitted that they had lied.[8,9]

False accusations of incest by children appear to be opportunistic lies rather than symptoms of a specific hysterical or delusional state. A desperate child decides the benefits of the lie outweigh the risks and has, at hand, the information necessary to fabricate an incest story.[20] In the reported cases the child usually has an adult confederate, and the child readily admits the lie on direct questioning.[9] Where the child has made more than one false accusation, more specific pathology may be found.[8,21]

Cases 1, 2, and 3 illustrate false accusations of incest by the daughter:

Case 1 A 13-year-old girl had become jealous, disobedient, and depressed after her mother's remarriage. Both parents were achievement-oriented professionals who tended to ignore their daughter's concerns as she became more symptomatic. The girl finally ran away from home and stayed with a girl friend whose father was a policeman. As the other family members questioned her about why she had run away, the girl elaborated a vague account of having been sexually seduced by the stepfather. When interviewed individually, she readily admitted that she had concocted the story from a book about incest. She focused with angry despair on her isolation in the family. Brief individual and family therapy successfully reintegrated her into the family unit. The incest accusation in this case apparently expressed the girl's wish to be included in her parents' relationship as well as an attempt to gain revenge.

Case 2 A pathologically jealous mother, who had recently married a man fifteen years younger than she, dreamed that her new husband raped her 10-year-old daughter. Several weeks later she noticed a rash in the daughter's genital area. Mother questioned the daughter angrily, using very specific questions derived from her recent dream. The daughter answered each question in the affirmative. Physical examination of the girl showed an intact hymen. The stepfather was eager to be interviewed and seemed appropriately angry. In an individual interview, the daughter said that she had supported her mother's explanation of the rash in order to conceal the masturbation which the child believed had caused the rash. Psychological testing showed that the child saw herself quite literally as an extension of her mother's body. The mother had chosen a young husband whose age was exactly intermediate between her own age and the age of the daughter. The girl's sense of fusion with mother made it more difficult for her to admit an independent sexual exploration than to admit to a sexual experience with mother's mate.

Case 3 Maria is a 13-year-old girl who complained to her school counselor that her stepfather was "beating" her. During the interview, it became clear that the stepfather was shadow-boxing with her in a teasing way, and that it was the teasing that alarmed and angered her. She said that the night before, he had come into her room and "fondled" her. As she spoke, she became more panicked and distraught, saying that her mother would never love her again. When the parents were interviewed, Maria's mother said that Maria had been upset by the mother's remarriage three months before. Maria had known her new stepfather as a neighbor long before he met her mother. Maria felt that their marriage had ruined her special relationships with each of them. The stepfather said that on the night in question he had been very drunk and had gone into the wrong room of their small apartment. He had taken off his clothes, then "groped around" for the bed. When Maria began screaming, he became so confused and frightened that he made a hole in the wall in his attempt to get out of the room. The mother said that Maria had seemed to understand at the time that he had come into the room by mistake. By this time, however, Maria was so agitated that the family agreed to have her placed until she could feel more comfortable at home. Physical examination of Maria revealed a pneumonia with a high fever and hyperventilation. After treatment of the pneumonia in the hospital, Maria's panic about her stepfather resolved and she said that she knew he had not been sexually attacking her. However, because of her refusal to accept her mother's remarriage, the family decided that she should live with other relatives.

Case 1 illustrates the most simple but also the most rare type of false accusation—the opportunistic lie. In Case 2 the child's need to lie to avoid disclosing her masturbation practices was abetted by her mother's delusional conviction that her new husband was sexually betraying her. In Case 3 an actual incident was misinterpreted by the child, in part because of the wish to be included and the desire for revenge described in Case 1, and in part because the child was near delirium from pneumonia and could not clearly distinguish fantasy from reality.

Maternal Delusions of Incest

Lustig et al[22] report a mother who had an encapsulated delusion that incest was taking place between her husband and her daughter. In that case, actual incest eventually did occur, possibly provoked and unwittingly engineered by the sick mother. Another case reported a psychotic mother who eventually murdered her husband because of a delusion of incest.[8] Case 4 is illustrative.

Case 4 Mrs. *W* is a 35-year-old housewife with a long history of hospitalization for schizophrenia. Previous psychotic breaks had been associated with the birth of her first child and with the marriage of her father to a much younger woman. She had recently delivered her second daughter, and during the pregnancy her father died. Despite this, she appeared stabilized on phenothiazines. When her baby was four months old, Mrs. *W* complained to her psychiatrist that her husband was sexually abusing her daughters by fondling their genitals. Her psychiatrist believed the accusation, referred the family to a protective services agency, and helped Mrs. *W* initiate divorce proceedings.

Mr. *W* was cooperative with the child protection agency and denied sexual abuse. He admitted tickling his daughters and said he had cleaned the baby's vulva several times at Mrs. *W*'s request. He gave a complete sexual history and was concerned that recent increased sexual experimentation in the marriage may have upset his wife. The 9-year-old daughter was interviewed and denied that her father had touched her genitals. Projective testing of father and daughter showed that both had excessive and overt sexual concerns. Mr. *W* said that when his wife was psychotic, her sexual preoccupations upset everyone in the family.

Two months after her initial accusation, Mrs. *W* was hospitalized with florid schizophrenic symptoms. She said God was telling her to have sex and that her husband was trying to make her homosexual. She gave a history of intercourse since age nine and blamed her father for having let her run wild.

The investigating agency made a judgment that Mrs. *W*'s accusations of sexual abuse were delusional, based on displaced anger at her father who had allowed her to have intercourse as a child and who had married a woman young enough to be his daughter. Father's death had revived these issues.

The judgment was not communicated to Mrs. *W*'s treating psychiatrist, who continued to discourage visits by Mr. *W* and encouraged the patient to proceed with divorce. Mrs. *W*'s psychosis continued to worsen until she was transferred to another hospital and another psychiatrist. On recovery, she said that nothing sexual had happened between her husband and her daughters.

This case shows how expressed fantasies about incest can be as devastating to a family as actual incest.[23] The delay in fully exploring the mother's accusation and the precipitous overreaction to a charge which did not even involve intercourse probably interfered with prompt and appropriate treatment of her psychosis. The antagonized father was unwilling to accept a recommendation that he and his daughter receive psychotherapy.

In more severe cases, failure to recognize a maternal delusion of incest may place the child at risk for physical abuse by the psychotic mother. The following case is illustrative.

Case 4A Mrs. *O* brought her 7-year-old daughter to the emergency room saying that the child had been sexually abused by her uncle, Mrs. *O*'s brother, and that the sexual relationship had been ongoing for many years. She kept shouting to her daughter, "Tell them the truth; tell them what happened." The child began to cry, saying, "That's why I got the spanking." In an individual interview, the child convincingly denied any sexual contact. The only positive physical finding was the presence of bruises on the child's arms and buttocks inflicted by the mother when she beat the child with a belt buckle to make her "tell the truth." The child was placed with her godparents, and the mother was psychiatrically hospitalized. Further investigation revealed that the mother had been sexually involved in childhood with the same brother that she falsely accused of assaulting her daughter.

False Denial of Incest

Several cases have been reported in which a child victim falsely retracts an allegation of incest because of threats from the father, infatuation with the father, or guilt about upsetting the family.[24] In these instances, the child's lie is in the service of covering up a sexual assault that actually occurred. Refusal to talk or testify about the incest is more common than false denial and may occur on the part of as many as 30% of victims.[6]

Case 5   Eleven-year-old Veronica and 9-year-old Melissa ran away from home, saying their stepfather was beating them. While the charge of physical abuse was being investigated, one of the girls hinted that sexual abuse had also taken place. Physical examination of Veronica showed a ruptured hymen and a wide vaginal canal. In a tearful interview Veronica described a year-long sexual relationship with the stepfather that had begun while mother was in the hospital having a baby. The relationship was rationalized as sex education and Veronica colluded in it because she enjoyed intercourse. Veronica decided to expose the relationship because the stepfather had recently begun the sexual education of the younger sister. Melissa confirmed this. Veronica was heavily made-up and appeared much older than eleven.

The mother was most concerned with her own mother's insistence that she leave the stepfather because of the girls' accusations. Mother revealed that as a teenager she had been involved in incest with her own father. Mother said that she would not leave the stepfather even if she believed her daughters' accusations. The stepfather would not agree to being interviewed, even by telephone, but the mother said he denied having had sex with the girls. The stepfather was chronically unemployed and both parents drank heavily.

At the next family interview, the mother and both daughters said the accusation was a hoax. They said the girls had been coached by unidentified older girls to accuse the stepfather in the hopes that this would make mother leave him. Veronica repeated this story woodenly in the individual session but refused to elaborate on it. Melissa began weeping in the individual session and admitted that the retraction was a lie invented by the mother.

DeFrancis[24] cites data which indicated that untrained interviewers often accept false denials of incest at face value, and speculates that this is one factor that has led to the underestimation of the incidence of incest and to the assumption that many accusations are false.

DISCUSSION

Verification of an accusation of incest is often technically difficult. Frequently, however, a thorough psychiatric examination of the family indicates a firm diagnosis and suggests appropriate intervention strategies.

Where such psychiatric investigation is indicated, we have found the following guidelines to be useful.

1. The investigator must be aware of his biases. Teenagers, schizophrenics, and self-dramatizing women can elicit strong irrational reactions, both positive and negative. Excessive horror of incest can lead to precipitous action.

2. The investigator should take the position that he does not yet know what really happened. The family often adopts this attitude of suspended judgment, which allows family members to alter and elaborate on prior statements without loss of face. At this point, interim treatment plans can be made and an extensive diagnostic workup scheduled.[25]

3. The investigator should see individually every family member directly involved. The supposedly uninvolved siblings should also be interviewed to clarify family dynamics, to rule out other incestuous partnerships, and to identify psychopathology or behavior problems. Open lines of communication should be maintained, and family members should be confronted with the puzzling fact that stories do not tally and should be asked for their opinions and feelings about this. The investigator's insistence on clarity can be therapeutic, especially in chaotic families with poor reality testing. The incest victim herself may be eager to avoid facing the truth, using familiar family defenses such as denial, projection of blame, or even withdrawing into a hypnoid state where repression can obliterate the reality and exchange it for fantasy.[25]

4. A detailed sexual, psychosocial, and family history should be obtained from each parent.

5. The affective responses of each family member should be carefully noted. This is not the place for the traditional child guidance approach where family members are interviewed by different therapists. Decisions about whether a person is lying are subtle and subjective.[21] If multiple interviewers are involved, each interviewer should see all available family members.

6. The investigation should not be made more traumatic for the family than the alleged sexual abuse.[27-29] This cannot be overemphasized. In some cases the alleged victim should have a pelvic examination. Projective testing of family members can be helpful, especially in the case of the father who may have very subtle paranoid symptoms.[30,31] We have found kinetic family drawings particularly useful in identifying family pressures that may be motivating the daughter. Children who have experienced incest have great difficulty drawing the perpetrator, and their drawings often reflect fears of men or of being in their own houses.

Other specific investigative techniques should be considered. Hypnotic age regression has been helpful in eliciting detailed descriptions of the alleged incestuous events.[2] Polygraph testing in one of our cases confirmed our clinical impression that a child's retraction of an incest accusation was false. However, patients interviewed with amobarbital or hypnosis may make statements about sexual events that combine fact with fantasy.[32]

7. The investigator should know the typical family profile in pater-

nal incest, but should use the knowledge flexibly and be alert for exceptions.[33-35] In the typical pattern, the father is rigid, moralistic, and patriarchal; he is unlikely to engage in extramarital relations, other perversions, or other antisocial acts. However, he may have chronic problems with alcohol abuse or with unemployment. The mother, typically, has relinquished many maternal functions to the child victim. The child victim tends to be pseudomature and very protective toward the mother.

8. The investigator should keep in mind that actual paternal incest is fairly common in psychiatric patients (about 5% in women and girls[34]) and that incest delusions and hoaxes are probably quite rare. Our findings and one prior study[2] indicate that a small percentage of incest accusations are false. Increased enforcement of child abuse laws has made false accusations a more potent manipulative weapon for children and teenagers. For this reason, if for no other, questionable accusations should be carefully investigated.

On the other hand, the judgment that an accusation is false should be made positively and not by inference or exclusion. For example, lack of physical evidence of criminal penetration and persistent denial of the accusation by the parents may occur in cases of actual incest where the sexual contact has been limited to fondling or to oral intercourse.[33] If an incest accusation is false, thorough investigation will reveal precipitants of the hoax, psychodynamic explanations for this behavior, and the step-by-step development of the hoax.[36]

SUMMARY

Expertise in investigating incest accusations is essential for psychiatrists, because the law requires the reporting of sexual abuse of children. Persistent and methodical investigation in such cases tends to yield a consensually credible view of what really happened without resorting to special forensic techniques of truth-finding. In order to make a diagnosis of incest hoax, the investigator must thoroughly understand the mechanics of the hoax and the psychodynamics of the perpetrator. Failure to recognize a delusional hoax can delay treatment for the perpetrator of the hoax. Failure to recognize a child's fabrication can subject the family to unnecessary legal action and unwittingly support the use of a similar manipulative technique by other susceptible children. Failure to recognize the false retraction of an incest accusation may leave the victim in danger of further sexual abuse or of physical punishment for having revealed the secret.

We would like to thank Robert Duncan, PhD, Richard Harris, PhD, and Samuel Roll, PhD, for their help in preparing this chapter.

REFERENCES

1. Rosenfeld AA, Nadelson CC, Krieger M, et al: Incest and sexual abuse of children. *J Am Acad Child Psychiatry* 16:327–329, 1977.

2. Majlath G: On the veracity of injured juveniles and on the general possibilities of drawing up an adequate psychological expertise in cases of deprivation and incest. *Pszichologiai Tanulmanyok* 2:623–640, 1968.

3. Peters JJ: Children who are victims of sexual assault and the psychology of offenders. *Am J Psychother* 30:398–421, 1976.

4. Parker G: Incest. *Med J Aust* 1:488–490, 1974.

5. Huntington D: Forensic gynaecology. *Practitioner* 216:519–528, 1976.

6. Nakashima I, Zakus GE: Incest: Review and clinical experience. *Pediatrics* 60:696–701, 1977.

7. Brant RS, Tisza VB: The sexually misused child. *Am J Orthopsychiatry* 47:80–90, 1977.

8. MacDonald JM: *Rape: Offenders and Their Victims.* Springfield, Ill, Charles C. Thomas, 1971.

9. Thoinot L, Weysse AW: *Medicolegal Aspects of Moral Offenses.* Philadelphia, Davis, 1913.

10. Freud S: *Correspondence with Wilhelm Fliess.* London, Imago, 1954 (Letter of September 21, 1897).

11. Freud S: My views on the part played by sexuality in the aetiology of the neuroses (1905), in: *Standard Edition* 7:274–276. London, Hogarth, 1963.

12. Freud S: On the history of the psychoanalytic movement (1914), in *Standard Edition* 24:17–18.

13. Freud, S: Heredity and the aetiology of the neuroses (1896), in *Standard Edition* 3:152–156.

14. Freud, S: Further remarks on the neuropsychoses of defense (1896), in *Standard Edition* 3:163–166.

15. Freud, S: The aetiology of hysteria (1896), in *Standard Edition* 3:203–208.

16. Freud, S: Fragment of an analysis of a case of hysteria (1901, 1905), in *Standard Edition* 7:3–124.

17. Erikson EH: Reality and actuality: An address. *J Am Psychoanal Assoc* 10:451–474, 1962.

18. Ferenczi S: Confusion of tongues between adults and the child. *Int J Psychoanal* 30:225–230, 1949.

19. Litin EM, Giffen ME, Johnson AM: Parental influence in unusual sexual behavior in children. *Psychoanal Q* 25:37–55, 1956.

20. Burton RV: The generality of honesty reconsidered. *Psychol Rev* 70:481–499, 1963.

21. Selling L: The psychiatric aspects of the pathological liar. *Nervous Child* 1:358–388, 1942.

22. Lustig N, Dresser JW, Spellman SW, et al: Incest: A family group survival pattern. *Arch Gen Psychiatry* 14:31–40, 1966.

23. Heims LW, Kaufman I: Variations on a theme of incest. *Am J Orthopsychiatry* 33:311–312, 1963.

24. DeFrancis V: *Protecting the Child Victim of Sex Crimes Committed by Adults.* Englewood, CO, American Humane Association, 1969.

25. Molnar G, Cameron P: Incest syndromes: Observations in a general hospital psychiatric unit. *Can Psychiatr Assoc J* 20:373-377, 1975.

26. Silber A: Childhood seduction, parental pathology and hysterical symptomatology, the genesis of an altered state of consciousness. *Int J Psychoanal* 60:109-116, 1979.

27. Bender L, Blau A: The reaction of children to sexual relations with adults. *Am J Orthopsychiatry* 7:500-518, 1937.

28. Eaton AP, Vastbinder E: The sexually molested child: A plan of management. *Clin Pediatr* 8:438-441, 1969.

29. Henriques B, Wells NH: Sexual assault on children. *Br Med J* 2:1628-1633, 1961.

30. Weiner IB: Father-daughter incest: A clinical report. *Psychiatr Q* 36:607-632, 1962.

31. Cavallin H: Incestuous fathers: A clinical report. *Am J Psychiatry* 122:1132-1138, 1966.

32. Glenn TJ, Simonds JF: Hypnotherapy of a psychogenic seizure disorder in an adolescent. *Am J Clin Hypn* 19:245-249, 1977.

33. Kaugman I, Peck AL, Tagiuri C: The family constellation and overt incestuous relations between a father and daughter. *Am J Orthopsychiatry* 24:266-279, 1954.

34. Henderson JD: Incest: A synthesis of data. *Can Psychiatr Assoc J* 17:299-313, 1972.

35. Lukianowicz N: Incest: Paternal incest. *Br J Psychiatry* 120:301-313, 1972.

36. Goodwin J, Sahd D, Rada R: Incest hoax: False accusations, false denials. *Bull Am Acad Psychiatry Law* 6:269-276, 1979.

3 Physical Conditions That May Be Mistaken for Sexual Abuse

Carol Geil
Jean Goodwin

Physicians working in the area of physical abuse have described several physical findings that can be mistaken for physical abuse, ie, organic syndromes which cause easy bruising, physical conditions which cause failure to thrive,[1] and cultural practices such as coin-rubbing in southeast Asia,[2] which may leave bruises but are not experienced as abuse. Until recently, the problem of underdiagnosis of sexual abuse has been so extreme,[3] that there have been few diagnostic errors of this type. In this chapter five cases are described in which physical findings caused by infection, congenital defect, or trauma were mistakenly attributed to sexual abuse. Although the error led to legal action in only one of these cases, in all cases the physician's patience and persistence in looking beyond the possibility of sexual abuse were critical to the care of the child.

Timely and appropriate diagnosis of sexual abuse is important for the involved child and her family.[4,5] Although many cases of bona fide sexual abuse are associated with *no* physical findings and must be diagnosed by history alone,[6,7] the child who has been sexually abused may also be brought to medical attention with a definite complaint referable to the genital system. It is important to consider sexual abuse when a young child presents with vaginal discharge or bleeding[7,8] or when there are suspicious lesions around the genitalia. However, not all situations suggesting sexual abuse on first encounter will ultimately have this diagnosis. For the pediatrician or family practitioner who does not deal frequently with sexual abuse, such situations may present perplexing problems. It is important neither to minimize the problem nor to "panic." Keeping an open mind to differential diagnostic possibilities, utilizing the skills of other disciplines and, at times, observing physical findings over a period of time may all be helpful in arriving at an accurate impression of whether or not a particular situation is sexual abuse.

Case Examples

Case 1 Sally, an 8-year-old girl, was seen in a pediatric clinic for evaluation for possible sexual abuse. She had a history of vaginal bleeding and discharge of approximately four years' duration. Over this period of time she had had extensive evaluations by many different physicians; workups had included pelvic examinations, cystoscopy, vaginoscopy, and bimanual pelvic examination under anesthesia. She had no clinical or laboratory evidence of precocious puberty. She had responded to empirical treatment with gantrisin. However, on discontinuation of the antibiotic, she again developed vaginal discharge and bleeding. The mother had confided to a social worker that the child was sleeping with the father. The child was brought for examination because it was felt that recurrent sexual abuse was the most likely cause of her symptoms.

The family constellation included Sally, a 4-year-old brother, the father aged 37, and mother, 26. The family seemed stable. The mother was cooperative although not medically sophisticated. Sally, although cooperative, was clearly embarrassed by the vaginal discharge and bleeding and the attention being focused on it. Both mother and child, interviewed separately, denied the possibility of sexual contact.

On examination there was yellowish, bloody, foul-smelling discharge. The hymenal ring appeared intact. Vaginal, throat, and rectal cultures were negative for gonococcus. Sally was again empirically placed on gantrisin and referred for follow-up to her private pediatrician.

Approximately a month later she was again examined under anesthetic by her pediatrician and a gynecologist. The examination revealed gross bleeding from an inflamed cervix, and the smear revealed *Enterobius vermicularis* (pinworms). Sally was treated with one dose of pyrantel pamoate and has since remained asymptomatic.

Case 2 Wendy was a lively, attractive 6-year-old who performed at a superior level in school. Her mother brought Wendy to the family physician when Wendy returned with a vaginal discharge from a visit with her father, the mother's former husband. Wendy's mother was concerned that something sexual had happened, but did not want to question the child for fear that the questioning might be traumatic. The child's pediatrician was convinced that the discharge resulted from sexual abuse.

In a joint psychiatric interview with Wendy and her mother, Wendy stated that she hoped the discharge would go away soon and that she thought it had been caused by germs. She readily understood the interview questions about whether she had been frightened by an adult or touched under her panties by someone. She answered with a thoughtful no and said if that did happen she would tell her mother or her teacher. She said that if no one else were available she would even tell the psychiatrist, but that would be a little embarrassing since it was not a person she knew well. Wendy's mood and manner did not change when her mother left the room. She was able to draw her father and talk about him and her sadness about the divorce in an unrestricted, matter-of-fact way. She denied masturbating. When freed from diagnostic tasks, she built a fort and had the interviewer help her to defend it from imaginary Indians.

Further medical workup in this case revealed a monilial infection and a family history of diabetes.

Case 3   A 6-month-old boy, Eddie, was being followed in a maternity and infant care clinic. At several weeks of age he had had a severe ulcerated diaper rash so that the perineal area could not be adequately inspected. There were concerns on the part of the clinic staff and public health nurse regarding the care he was receiving from his young, unwed mother. He was subsequently brought in by his paternal grandmother who had assumed the role of primary caretaker. At this time he was noted to have an unusual rash in his perineal area, which the grandmother said she had not noticed before. There was a purplish semicircular lesion which superficially resembled a "hickey" or "love bite" between the base of his scrotum and his anus. Sexual abuse was considered. However, as the infant was observed over several weeks, the lesion remained absolutely unchanged. A diagnosis was made of hemangioma in an unusual location.

Case 4   At five months of age, Patsy was seen in pediatric clinic with bruises on her buttocks, left lower leg, and face, as well as evidence of vaginal bleeding. Examination revealed a 1 cm tear of the posterior vaginal fourchette. A diagnosis was made of physical and sexual abuse but protective service workers could not be certain of the identity of the perpetrator. The social situation was dysfunctional. Patsy was being cared for by her teenage mother, Betsy, her teenage father, Richard, and a friend of his. Both of the young men were working as projectionists in a pornographic movie house. A protective service worker attempted to work with the family, but the situation remained in turmoil. At eight months of age the infant was placed in protective custody with the grandmother. Following involvement of both the baby and her mother in a therapeutic preschool program, plans were made for gradual return of the child to the parental home.

At one year of age, following an overnight visit to her parents, Patsy was noted to have a 1 × ½ in. purpuric area on her right labia majora. This was felt initially by the pediatrician to represent evidence of new sexual abuse. Concerns about the father's refusal to participate in therapy and about the young mother's slow progress in treatment crystallized around this physical "evidence" of recurrent sexual abuse. However, on continued examination the area remained unchanged and it finally became clear that this was a birthmark rather than a bruise.

Case 5 A 1-year-old toddler was brought to the hospital in critical condition after being attacked by a dog. Physicians became concerned about the accuracy of the history because: 1) the boy had an unusual type of circumferential anorectal tear which had been reported previously only in small children who had been sodomized, and 2) because the bite marks were slit-like and relatively symmetrical, almost as if they had been made by a knife in the hands of a sadist, rather than by a dog. A forensic pathologist was asked to investigate the case (J. Weston, personal communication). Unfortunately, the case was referred for prosecution and publicized as a case of child abuse before this investigation was completed. The investigator made the following observations: 1) there were reliable witnesses who saw the boy being attacked by the dog, and 2) the dog in question was a wolf-shepherd cross bred as a watch dog and not fully grown. The animal was subsequently sacrificed and autopsied, and his teeth were examined by a forensic dentist. The thin, pointed teeth of this immature half-wild dog matched the slit-like marks on the child, but were quite different from the bite marks of mature domestic dogs which are more familiar to physicians. A veterinary pathologist, expert on animal attacks on humans, was consulted about the pattern of wounds. Apparently, wild dogs tend to attack prey first on one side and then the other, leaving a symmetrical pattern of wounds. They will often lunge for the animal's rump, taking a deep bite, so they can flip their prey into the air.

A diagnosis was made of trauma secondary to attack by a mixed domestic and wild dog.

DISCUSSION

Both pinworms and foreign bodies can be causes of chronic vaginal discharge in young girls.[8] In Case 1 several facts mitigated against the diagnosis of sexual abuse: 1) there were no definite behavioral indicators of sexual abuse, either in this child or in her mother, and 2) the family seemed genuinely concerned about the vaginal bleeding and discharge and had gone to great lengths to have the child evaluated for it, with no hints of any "secrets" to hide. The key to this case was a thorough examination which included the differential diagnostic possibility of pinworms. It was also helpful to document that there was no evidence of vaginal penetration. The pediatrician who routinely examines a child's genitals as part of the physical examination can be authoritative when the question arises as to what is normal and what indicates probable penetration. It was also important to have obtained cultures for gonococcus, since the finding of a positive culture would have been strongly suggestive of sexual abuse.[9]

Psychiatric evaluation of the child may be sought in some of these ambiguous situations to confirm the physician's clinical impression that the child is telling the truth when she says she was *not* sexually abused. This is the reverse of the more usual clinical question about whether the child is telling the truth when she says she *was* sexually abused. However, in view of the intense pressures that many children feel to protect the abuser, and because concealment of abuse and false retractions do occur, it is an important clinical question.[3]

In the psychiatric interview reported in Case 2 there were many elements that are simply not seen in a child who is making a false retraction. Wendy was open and trusting with the interviewer, but was also respectful and protecting of herself. There was no change in affect when her mother left the room. Anxiety and aggression were not excessive or intrusive. Wendy did not show guilt about asking for help. She did not minimize her problems. She could talk about her vaginal discharge and other sexual topics, but was obviously much more interested in age-appropriate fantasy play.

In Cases 3 and 4 observation over time convinced the physician that skin lesions which were initially suggestive of bruises that could have been inflicted during sexual contact were, in fact, congenital marks. In Case 4 where recurrent sexual abuse was a distinct possibility this was an especially important diagnostic decision. These examples are akin to the error of mistaking Mongolian spots for the bruises of physical abuse. The appearance is superficially similar, but the lesions do not go through the normal evolution of bruises and they have different pigmentary characteristics.

In Case 5 it was especially tragic that the parents were disbelieved and suspected of concealing or perpetrating a sadistic sodomy on their child at a point when they were having to cope with a catastrophic accident and with their child's critical physical condition. It is of note that in this extreme case the intact family reacted to the investigation with a reasonableness and calm, absolutely uncharacteristic of families where sexual abuse is actually occurring. This case highlights the need for the physician 1) to not panic, 2) to keep an open mind to the diagnostic possibilities, 3) to get the best expert help, and 4) to take time before making a diagnosis.

CONCLUSIONS

As noted initially, in many instances of sexual abuse there are no physical findings and it is important to rely on history.[6] In the examples given above there *were* definite physical findings which could have indicated sexual abuse yet ultimately did not yield this diagnosis. The following suggestions summarize our experience and our advice to the physicians faced with such a problem:

1. Do not panic at the idea of sexual abuse. That will tend to stampede you into either refusing to consider sexual abuse, or into blundering into the diagnosis even when the physical findings do not really support it. Keep in mind the different diagnostic possibilities. In cases where one is not sure it may be appropriate to share this uncertainty with the family—to say, "We have to be concerned about sexual abuse, but there are other possibilities as well." This may provide an opportunity to introduce involvement with a social worker skilled in dealing with sexual abuse.

2. Utilize expert help and creative approaches. As our five cases illustrate, the needed expert may be a psychiatrist, psychologist, or a social worker, but one may also need to call on a veterinary, a forensic pathologist, or an anesthetist.

3. Observation of certain physical findings over time may help to differentiate between a lesion inflicted as part of sexual abuse or some other stable skin finding such as a birthmark. It is, of course, important to assess whether the child is adequately protected while this waiting period occurs.

4. The importance of careful history taking, physical examination, and observation of child and parents cannot be overemphasized. It is the physician's anxiety in these cases that can interfere with completing a standard systematic examination.

It may be misleading to end this chapter with the impression that the pediatrician will always be able to make a diagnosis of either sexual abuse or of some other physical syndrome—infection, birthmark, trauma. We see situations in which both occur—a physical condition affecting the genitals together with sexual abuse. Chronic, mixed bacterial infections are not uncommon in prepubertal girls experiencing sexual abuse. Such children can be as upset by the chronic vaginal discharge as they are by the sexual abuse itself. Just as sexual abuse can cause organic disease, so organic genital problems can lead to sexual abuse. It is not uncommon to find that a child begins to be sexually abused by a family member only after she has been raped traumatically by a stranger. It is as if the crisis generated by the rape shifts a new sexual focus to that child which places her at higher risk for sexual contact within the family. We have noted elsewhere that blind, epileptic, retarded, or other physically special children seem to be at higher risk for sexual abuse.[10,11] Physical problems that affect the genitals may be especially prone to weaken the incest taboo protecting that child. In one of our cases, the child experienced signs of precocious puberty at age two. Symptoms remitted after appropriate treatment, but she was subsequently abused sexually by two different family members.

REFERENCES

1. Schmitt BD, Grosz CA, Carroll CA: The child protection team: A problem-oriented approach, in Helfer RE, Kempe CH (eds): *Child Abuse and Neglect—The Family and the Community.* Cambridge, Ballinger, 1976.
2. Yatman GW: Pseudobattering in Vietnamese children. *Pediatrics* 58:616–618, 1976.
3. Goodwin J, Sahd D, Rada R: Incest hoax: False accusations, false denials. *Bull Am Acad Psychiatry Law* 6 (3): 269–276, 1979.
4. Kempe CH: Sexual abuse. The 1977 C. Anderson Aldrich Lecture. *Pediatrics* 62:382–389, 1978.
5. Stechler G: Facing the problem of the sexual abuse of children. *N Engl J Med* 302:348–349, 1980.
6. Schechter MD, Roberge L: Sexual exploitation, in Helfer RE, Kempe CH (eds): *Child Abuse and Neglect—The Family and the Community.* Cambridge, Ballinger, 1976.
7. Tilelli JA, Turek D, Jaffe AC: Sexual abuse of children. *N Engl J Med* 302:319–323, 1980.
8. Pascoe DJ: Management of sexually abused children. *Pediatric Ann* 8:309–316, 1979.
9. Farrell MK, Billmore E, Shamroy JA, et al: Prepubertal gonorrhea: A multidisciplinary approach. *Pediatrics* 67:151–153, 1981.
10. Goodwin J, Zouhar M, Bergman R: Hysterical seizures: A sequel to incest. *Am J Orthopsychiatry* 49:678–703, 1979.
11. Friedrich WN, Boniskin JA: The role of the child in abuse: A review. *Am J Orthopsychiatry* 46:580–590, 1976.

4 Medical Care for Male and Female Incest Victims and Their Parents

Jean Goodwin
Anita Willett
Rebecca Jackson

When physicians think of incest and child sexual abuse, they usually think about the anxiety-provoking and specialized areas of the forensic pelvic examination and of medical-forensic testimony. However, in more than one half of substantiated cases of incest, the forensic examination will yield absolutely no physical evidence[1] (see also Chapter 1). When there is physical evidence, it will usually be found in the general physical examination rather than in specialized forensic tests; examples are the presence of obvious perineal tears, or of bruises and petechiae.[1] In the majority of incest cases the legal outcome of the case relies not on specific medico-legal evidence, but on the child's testimony, on a confession by the offending parent or, in a children's court, on the assessment of the child's overall functioning and well-being. The aim of this chapter is to refocus physician concern, from the mastery of the forensic pelvic examination, to providing needed medical care to the victim and to other family members. In adult rape cases the forensic pelvic examination is often done in a single visit with no commitment made for longer-term treatment.[2] For the child victim, a more extensive doctor-patient relationship is often indicated, either 1) to allay intense anxiety in the child, 2) to allow the child, particularly the male child, to redefine the event as a treatable physical injury rather than as a moral lapse or sexual perversion, 3) to treat sequelae in the victim, which may include venereal disease, pregnancy, promiscuity, or psychosomatic problems, and 4) to treat physical problems identified in the course of the diagnostic evaluations of the incest victim, of her mother, and of her father. Over 20% of the child victims of sexual abuse will have a coexisting medical disorder; previous abuse or neglect, mental retardation, behavior disorders, and seizure disorders are seen most commonly.[1] Alcoholism in a parent or a parental physical problem which interferes with sexuality can often best be treated in a medical setting.

Using the Initial Forensic Examination to Establish a Caring Doctor-Patient Relationship

Private physicians usually refer the child sexual victim to a hospital center for forensic examination and for evidence collection. In incest victims who may report the problem weeks or months after the last sexual contact, the collection of evidence may not be possible. The pediatrician or family practitioner can consider examining the child in the office after consulting with a physician who is experienced in examining sexually abused children. If a referral for evidence collection is necessary, the child's pediatrician may want to be present and to assist the specialist. In some communities the physicians most experienced in doing the forensic pelvic examinations may have had little experience in treating children, and a physician will need as much support as possible in these cases.

For the physician who feels overwhelmed by the numerous laboratory tests listed in most descriptions of the forensic pelvic examination, it is important to realize that the only procedures necessary in *all* first examinations of child incest victims are:

1. A detailed history of the sexual event
2. A thorough physical examination, including documentation of bruises or other signs of physical injury, and a complete description of the perineal area and of the external and internal genitalia
3. A blood sample for complete blood count, for serology for syphilis and, if indicated, for blood typing
4. Urine sample for urinalysis and, if indicated, for examination for the presence of spermatozoa. In pubertal or older females the urine should be used for a pregnancy test. In males the urine should be tested for the presence of gonorrhea
5. Pharyngeal, rectal, and vaginal swabs for culture for gonorrhea and, if indicated, prophylactic treatment for venereal disease
6. If there is a vaginal discharge or if vaginal penetration is prob-

able, the cervical smear should be stained for Papanicolaou testing as well as cultured for gonorrhea. Aspirates from the vaginal vault should be collected and examined for sperm, acid phosphatase, and pathogenic organisms.

A specific informed consent is required if the physician, in addition to performing a complete medical examination for the benefit of the child, formally collects a forensic evidence kit. In an incest situation the discussion of evidence collection with the child's mother can be a crucial step in treatment. Many incest mothers are desperately interested in knowing whether sexual contact occurred but they may be reluctant to consent to procedures, such as the collection of semen for typing, which might identify the perpetrator. In an emergency, the physician can examine the child and collect evidence even without parental consent.

Evidence collection may not be clinically indicated. If the child has bathed and changed since her last sexual contact, there is no need to collect clothing for evidence of rips or secretions, or to use the Wood's fluorescent lamp to search for dried semen on the child's skin and hair.[3,4] Fingernail scrapings from the child are unlikely to yield the perpetrator's blood or tissue type if the incest victim did not physically resist and if the last contact was remote in time. Samples of the victim's own saliva and blood must be collected for typing only if semen, tissue, or blood possibly traceable to the perpetrator has been found. If contact has occurred within the past week, the child's head and pubic hair should be combed in order to collect hairs from the assailant which may have been caught there. It is only if hair samples have been found in clothing or combings that samples of the victim's head and pubic hair need be collected for comparison.

In general, the child's description of what happened, the readily apparent physical signs, and the presenting symptoms will guide the physician to the appropriate laboratory tests. For example, in cases of forced fellatio, evidence of sperm and acid phosphatase can be detected in swabs from between the molars up to a week after the last incident.[3] The perpetrator's pubic hairs may also be found in combings from the child's head hair. If the child gives hints that sodomy has been part of the abuse, the stool should be guaiac-tested for the presence of occult blood. Swabs from the perianal area can be tested for sperm and for acid phosphatase, as well as being cultured for gonorrhea.

There is little chance of detecting sperm in any orifice if more than 72 hours have elapsed since the last sexual contact. The presence of motile sperm in vaginal aspirates indicates sexual contact within the past 28 hours.[2] This will be found in less than 10% of child victims (see Chapter 1). Acid phosphatase at levels of more than 50 King-Armstrong units in the vaginal aspirate is considered to be definite evidence of recent coitus. If more than 24 hours, but less than 72 hours, have elapsed since the last prior contact, sperm cells may still be identifiable on stained air-dried slides of a cervical Papanicolaou smear or, as mentioned before, in a smear taken from between the teeth.[3]

Concern about venereal disease and pregnancy should override the general rule of allowing history, symptoms, and signs to guide the examination. Even if the child does not complain of penetration, and even if the intact hymen and perineum make it unlikely that intercourse took place, good practice requires vaginal, rectal, and pharyngeal swabs for culture for gonorrhea, the blood test for syphilis, and the pregnancy test if the child is pubertal. This is done simply to prevent the worst possible consequences to the child in case intercourse was attempted and the child is minimizing the extent of the sexual abuse. If the physician is certain of being able to follow-up a child victim, prophylactic treatment for venereal disease need not be given.[1] Venereal disease prophylaxis can be achieved by giving probenecid, 25 mg/kg orally (to a maximum of 1 g) followed by ampicillin, 50 mg/kg orally (to a maximum of 3 g). Tetracycline can be substituted if the child is allergic to penicillin. The dosage is 25 mg/kg at the time of the examination (maximum 1.5 g) and 10 mg/kg (maximum 500 mg) qid for 10 days.[3]

The initial pregnancy test is necessary to document pregnancies which may have occurred prior to the report of sexual abuse. This is especially important in incest victims who will have been sexually involved for many months or years before they report. In incest cases pregnancy prophylaxis should be considered in postmenarchal or menarchal girls who report recent vaginal intercourse and who have a negative pregnancy test. The nausea caused by the drug and the unknown long-term sequelae in children are problematic enough that some physicians recommend monitoring for pregnancy, and then therapeutic abortion, if this is tolerable to the child and her family.[1]

The physician should understand the forensic tests well enough to protect the child from the "rape kit." For example, some physicians routinely pluck pubic and head hairs from the victim, because this procedure is listed in some evidence kits. Samples of the victim's hair are needed for microscopic comparison with hair samples which may have been obtained from combings or clothing. If the last sexual contact occurred several weeks prior to the examination, there is no need either for the combings or for the sample of the victim's hair. Only rarely will roots be needed to compare with evidential samples of the perpetrator's hair. If this does become necessary, samples can be obtained at any time. The morphology of the victim's hair roots will not change. The pulling out of pubic and head hairs can be done later, in a less traumatic circumstance, which does not include a first pelvic examination.

Errors of omission as well as errors of commission can increase the trauma for the child. If the physician forgets to do a wet mount of the vaginal aspirate for *Candida* and for *Trichomonas*, the child with a vaginal discharge may undergo more prolonged symptoms and, in addition, another pelvic examination. If evidential samples of blood from the perpetrator's clothing are obtained and the physician has not obtained the child's blood group status, her blood must be drawn again.

The physical examination begins with the kind of thorough examination that one gives to any child when physical abuse or neglect is suspected. The entire body should be examined for bruises; the size, location, and age of bruises should be noted on a body chart. Informed consent is required if photographs are taken. A complete blood count needs to be done to determine whether the child has anemia on the basis of nutritional neglect, or because of bleeding or bruising.[5]

The genital examination should be made a matter-of-fact part of the head-to-toe physical examination. It is important to explain to the child, preferably while the child is still dressed, what will be done and why. Parents usually must be reassured that the examination will not harm the child and that no damage will be done to the hymen.[6] Ask if the child has questions. Try to let her have as much control over the examination as is possible. Ask her to take off her own clothes and to participate as, for instance, by holding the swabs for you, or by holding a mirror while you examine the external genitalia. Abused children appreciate any comments from the examiner that reassure her that the genitalia are intact, normally developed, and without defect.

The description of the appearance of the external genitalia can sometimes be the key physical finding in sexual abuse. One should look for erythema, for abrasion, for lacerations and for bruises. Often abrasions of the perineum, vaginal, or rectal mucosa are not obvious unless the skin is gently put under tension between the thumb and index finger. The hymen should be described in detail. However, it is important for the physician to be aware that the presence of an intact hymen does not rule out penetration and that the absence of a hymen does not mean that penetration has occurred. The hymen is described as present, absent, intact without scarring, or recently ruptured.[5,7]

If the hymen is intact, secretions should be aspirated from beyond the hymen for laboratory specimens. If the hymen has been lacerated, one can then introduce a small speculum to obtain secretions. Lubricating jelly interferes with some of the laboratory cultures, but warm water may be used to aid insertion of the speculum. After the speculum is inserted, the walls of the vagina and the cervix can be visually inspected for abrasions, lacerations, or bruises. Any vaginal discharge should be characterized as to quantity, color, and odor. The Papanicolaou smear can be examined for signs of *Hemophilus* or herpes infections which may be responsible for a child's vaginal discharge.

Aspirates and swabs from the vaginal vault will be cultured for gonorrhea, wet mounted to detect motile sperm, *Trichomonas*, or *Candida*, assayed for acid phosphatase, and dry mounted for detection of stained sperm. As mentioned above, it is when contact has occurred within the past week that it is worthwhile to make every effort to detect sperm.[8]

A urinalysis should be done on all children. Vaginal penetration can lead to bleeding into the urinary tract or to painful or difficult urination.[3]

In asymptomatic male children the first 10 ml of urine voided can be cultured for gonorrhea by placing two swabs in the urine sample, and then plating onto a Thayer-Martin media. There is better recovery with this method and less trauma than with the urethral swab.[9]

The Medical Setting as a Safe Place for the Male Victim of Sexual Abuse

Boys rarely report sexual assaults, and when they do, they are more likely to describe physical, rather than sexual aspects of the assault.[10] In a survey of New England college students, 9% of the men and 19% of the women reported a sexual assault in childhood.[11] If these figures represent the true frequency, and it is possible that even on an anonymous questionnaire men conceal forced sexual experiences, then one would expect one third of the victims of childhood sexual abuse to be male. In fact, most programs report that 10% to 12% of child victims are male,[1,12,13] indicating that only about one third of the sexually abused males are detected. The following case example illustrates how determined a young boy can be in concealing a sexual assault.[10]

> **Case 1** A 15-year-old boy walked into the emergency room saying that he had been knifed in the back during a fight. He was reluctant to talk, shy, and very embarrassed. An alert physician asked him if anything more had happened. The boy then described having been given a ride by a man who offered to give him drugs. The man had then held the boy at gunpoint for several hours, had forced the boy to fellate him, had forcibly sodomized the teenager, and then had knifed him in the back and in the face. Had this boy not encountered a knowledgeable physician, he might never have admitted the actual circumstances of the injury.

Of male victims identified in our hospital, more than one-third did not mention the sexual assault in their first visit.[10] Male rape victims were significantly more likely to have been severely beaten than were female victims. This may be an artifact of the male tendency to conceal; males may seek help only when associated physical injury forces them to medical attention.

When the sexual abuse is perpetrated by a family member, the offender is likely to be the father. Fathers who sexually abuse their sons often have histories of alcoholism and of family violence and tyranny. The boy victims often have intensely hostile, and even homicidal feelings toward the father.[14] Fear that he may be homosexual, as well as the intensity of actual and threatened violence accompanying the assault, may make sexual abuse more traumatic for a boy victim than for the girl victim.[15,16] However, in families in which both brothers and sisters have been victimized by the father, the females usually receive counseling at some point and the males usually do not.

In the following case it was the pediatrician who identified the sexual abuse and then continued to provide counseling to the boy victim in the medical setting which the victim himself had sought out.

Case 2 Four small children from a large, disorganized family were brought to the clinic for immunizations. The 5-year-old boy looked sad. When brought into the examining room, he began to weep silently. A complete physical examination revealed a urethral discharge which proved to be gonococcal. The pediatrician reassured the child that medicine would cure the problem and that the child would not have to return home if he did not want to do so. The boy described how his stepfather had forced mutual fellatio on him and his two sisters. The child was deeply shamed by what his stepfather had done to him and also by the fact that he had failed to protect his sisters from the stepfather. The pediatrician continued to see this boy weekly in brief sessions which involved reculturing for gonorrheal infection, retesting for syphilis, health questions, conversation, and play with toys. This physician was a stable ally while the child was in foster care with his sisters awaiting placement with relatives.

Long-Term Medical Care for the Victim

As the preceding case illustrates, follow-up medical care is necessary to assure that venereal disease will not be a continuing problem. Children who have received prophylactic treatment should be recultured for gonorrhea in about eight days and retested for syphilis in eight weeks. Children at risk for pregnancy should have the pregnancy test repeated after four to eight weeks.

Some children will need more than this basic follow-up. The following case is one in which medical follow-up was the most effective way to help a sexually abused teenager to reintegrate her life.

Case 3 A 14-year-old girl was seen for a pelvic examination two weeks after she had run away from home because of undressing and mutual masturbation with her natural father. As expected, there were no physical signs of trauma and no signs of venereal disease or pregnancy. At her follow-up visit, she asked to see a woman physician and saw this physician frequently over the next year. Upper respiratory infections were a chronic problem, tending to recur at times of stress, as: 1) when she was formally placed in the custody of her grandmother, 2) when she failed three classes in school, 3) when she was caught stealing, and 4) when she visited her father and stepmother. Other crises led directly to medical contact, as when she and her girlfriend were raped while breaking curfew or when she and her boyfriend "went all the way" and she became afraid that she was pregnant. The physician became involved in crisis intervention, sex education, rape prevention, and family planning.

In many ways this girl used the female physician as a mother substitute; her own natural mother had abandoned her in infancy. She had many conflicts with the other "substitute mothers" in her life, but the structure of the medical visit seemed to help her to preserve this relationship as a constructive one.

The structured and safe touching that takes place in a medical visit has been important in the medical follow-up of many adolescent victims. Any adolescent may feel threatened by impulses to return to the parental hugs and kisses that allayed anxiety earlier in childhood. For the incest victim, such impulses are especially frightening. The physical check-up can be an acceptable way for the victim to get the touching she needs.

Several late-adolescent victims have chosen to leave home for an independent living arrangement rather than for foster or group home care. For these girls, having one's own physician is part of the assumption of adult responsibility. At the same time, this relationship allows the complaints, the voicing of sexual confusion, and the admission of weaknesses that they may be suppressing in other contexts. The following is a case example.

Case 4   A 16-year-old was forensically examined after reporting a long history of intercourse with her father. She had sought help because she believed herself to be pregnant. Close questioning revealed that she had very unclear ideas about how to recognize pregnancy and about how women become pregnant. After reporting the incest, she left home and adopted a homosexual life style. This led her into a good deal of sports and other physical activity and, during this phase, she was seen medically for back pain, knee pain, and muscle pain. Sexual questions were often asked during visits, and the teenager began to talk about her intense self-consciousness around boys. Medical care at this time moved to treatment for acne and for weight control. When she developed a close relationship with a boyfriend, she returned for advice about sexuality and birth control.

The female physician's reliable and concrete support of this teenager's changing developmental needs were critical to the good outcome.

Medical Care for the Parents

Preliminary findings indicate that physical illness is at least as prevalent in adults who present with a sexual abuse problem as it is in adults who present with other kinds of psychiatric symptoms (40% to 60%).[17]

In a study of consecutively substantiated incest families, 37 parents, 25 mothers and 12 fathers, were asked to complete physical screening questionnaires and to be physically examined. Only 19 completed the screening questionnaires and only eight appeared for the free physical examination. However, in all eight of the parents who were examined, previously unrecognized physical problems were found which required treatment. Problems identified in mothers included: alcoholic liver disease, chronic abdominal pain with dyspareunia, cystic breast disease, headaches secondary to osteoarthritis, rheumatic heart disease, and abnormal cervical cytology. Problems identified in fathers included: diabetes mellitus, hypertension, nongonococcal urethritis, obesity, and decreased hearing. On exploration many of these physical problems were found to be creating anxiety or interfering with the marital sexual relationship. Alcoholism, depression, and anxiety were also problems. Of the five fathers and 14 mothers who completed screening questionnaires, two fathers and no mothers scored as alcoholic on the Michigan Alcoholism Screening Test.[18] On the Symptom Questionnaire[19] two fathers and ten mothers scored as clinically anxious. Two fathers and nine mothers scored as clinically depressed.

The treatment in a family practice setting of alcoholism and physical problems has been an effective way to offer concrete help to parents. The following cases trace the course of medical treatment and its influence on counseling goals for the family.

Case 5 A 26-year-old Spanish-American woman brought her sodomized 2-year-old daughter to the hospital saying, "I just cannot believe that my boyfriend did it." She chose to place her child in foster care; the boyfriend refused to be interviewed. Since age 17, she had lived with three different violent and abusive boyfriends. As part of the screening study, she was referred to a family practitioner for physical examination. She was obese and had a family history of diabetes. She admitted to "getting drunk" once a week and her liver function tests were elevated. External hemorrhoids and trichomonal vaginal infection were diagnosed and treated. Intercourse had been painful for her recently, and she had been refusing sexual contact with her boyfriend. Reliable birth control was initiated. Although she had refused counseling or psychotherapy, she enthusiastically accepted a weight reduction plan from the physician. She also accepted the physician's diagnosis of alcoholism and stopped drinking. After several months, she began dating, left her boyfriend, and resumed the care of her daughter.

In several other cases, mothers in incest families have been able to use the support of the family physician to escape a destructive marital relationship. Personal medical care, birth control, and medical care for the children are critical ingredients. In certain cases the physician may be consulted about medical problems in the husband or boyfriend, or may provide antidepressant medication to the mother. Rape, physical assaults, and accidents are recurrent in some families, and these can be better integrated when physician support is available.

Fathers who perpetrate incest are often reluctant to use medical support. In cases in which a father's unemployment has been a precipitant of the incest, the precipitant of the unemployment was often an untreated or partially treated medical disability. One of the many functions of an incestuous relationship can be to reassure an ill father of his power and invulnerability (see Chapter 15). Medical treatment offers a less magical form of reassurance which can become part of the father's entry into more developmentally adult functioning. The following are case examples.

Case 6 A 42-year-old man had begun fondling his daughter when she was four years old. "It was when her baby brother was born. I wanted to keep her from hurting the baby, so I told her where babies come from." Four years later, when his wife found out about the relationship, she left him. He became terrified about being alone. Because of the unusual degree of his panic, psychiatric consultation was sought. In the evaluation he described frequent chest pain. His father had died from a heart attack when about the current age of the patient. At a routine physical examination several years earlier, the patient had been diagnosed as having a cardiac arrhythmia. Although he had been reassured that this was benign, he was frightened whenever he became aware of his heartbeat, particularly during sexual intercourse. His fears about this diagnosis had contributed, together with his lifelong inhibitions about sexuality, to his abandoning all sexual contact with his wife in favor of "less stimulating" fondling and voyeurism with his daughter. His hypochondriacal fears had magnified his anxiety after the family separation because he feared he would become ill or die alone. The "hurt heart" also functioned as a metaphor for previous unresolved losses, including the deaths of his father and his brother. Continuing medical follow-up gave him realistic reassurance about his heart condition and a forum in which he felt it was permissible to ask sexual questions. He was able to master his separation anxiety, to begin dating, and to ease the pressure on his ex-wife for a reunion.

Case 7 A 33-year-old Spanish-American man had been cast in the role of family rescuer by his wife and stepdaughters. Even after the revelation of the incest led to divorce, his ex-wife and the stepdaughters made many financial and emotional demands on him. He presented himself as a competent, manly man, and rationalized the incest as having satisfied the sexual needs of his daughters. He agreed to volunteer for a physical examination as part of a health survey of parents. On review of systems, he had multiple physical complaints and a long history of severe alcoholism. He was overweight, and had an early retinopathy indicative of vascular problems. His blood sugar and triglycerides were elevated. A glucose tolerance test confirmed a prediabetic condition. He began a weight reduction program. The doctor-patient relationship became one in which he could admit to feelings of physical vulnerability. Later, he described intermittent impotence which was probably a result of his alcoholism (there was, as yet, no diabetic neuropathy). His increased capacity to admit to normal human limitations became apparent in his psychotherapy group. He became less driven to rescue his wife and stepdaughters and more realistically concerned about his own problems, in particular, about his alcoholism.

CONCLUSIONS

Long-term medical follow-up is often necessary for incest victims and for their families. The medical setting may be the most accessible and acceptable setting for treatment in some situations. The male victim, the crisis-ridden teenage victim, the battered incest mother living in a chaotic household, and the alcoholic father-perpetrator may choose to see a physician rather than a more psychologically oriented therapist. Empathic care during the initial examination of an incest victim can provide a foundation for helpful long-term family care.

REFERENCES

1. Tilelli J, Turek D, Jaffe AC: Sexual abuse of children: Clinical findings and implications for management. *N Engl J Med.* 302:319-323.
2. Zumwalt RE, Petty CC: Community investigation of rape, in Curran WJ, McGarry AL, Petty CS (eds.): *Modern Legal Medicine: Psychiatry and Forensic Science.* New York, F.A. Davis, 1980.
3. Queen's Bench Foundation, San Francisco General Hospital. Medical management of sexually abused children and adolescents, in Jones B, Jenstrom L, MacFarlane K (eds): *Sexual Abuse of Children: Selected Readings.* Washington, D.C., U.S. Department of Health and Human Services, 1980.
4. Herjanic B, Wilbois RP: Sexual abuse of children, detection and management. *JAMA* 239:331-333, 1978.
5. Breen JL, Greenwald E, Gregori CA: The molested young female: Evaluation and therapy of alleged rape. *Ped Clin N Am* 19:717-725, 1973.
6. Huffman J: Examination of the pre-menarchal child, in *The Gynecology of Childhood and Adolescence.* New York, W.B. Saunders, 1968.
7. Paul DM: The medical examination in sexual offences against children. *Med Sci Law* 17:251-258, 1977.
8. Dahlke MB, Cooke C, Cunnane M, et al: Identification of semen in 500 patients seen because of rape. *Am J Clin Pathol* 68:740-746, 1977.
9. Fenz WZ, Medeiros AA, Murray ES: Diagnosis of gonorrhea in male patients by culture of first-voided urine. *JAMA* 237:896-897, 1977.
10. Kaufman A, DiVasto P, Jackson R, et al: Male rape victims: Non-institutionalized assault. *Am J Psychiatry* 137:221-223, 1980.
11. Finkelhor D: *Sexually Victimized Children.* New York, Free Press, 1979.

12. Jaffe AC, Dynneson L, ten Bensel RW: Sexual abuse of children: An epidemiologic study. *Am J Dis Child* 129:689–692, 1975.

13. Ellerstein NS, Canavan JW: Sexual abuse of boys. *Am J Dis Child* 134:255–257, 1980.

14. Dixon KN, Eugene AL, Calestro K: Father-son incest: Under-reported psychiatric problem? *Am J Psychiatry* 135:835–838, 1978.

15. Blumberg ML: Child sexual abuse: Ultimate in maltreatment syndrome. *NY State J Med.* 78:612–616, 1978.

16. Kempe CH: Sexual abuse. Another hidden pediatric problem. The 1977 C. Anderson Aldrich Lecture. *Pediatrics* 62:382–389, 1978.

17. Koranyi EK: Morbidity and rate of undiagnosed physical illness in a psychiatric clinic population. *Arch Gen Psychiatry* 36:414–419, 1979.

18. Selzer M: The Michigan alcoholism screening test: The quest for a new diagnostic instrument. *Am J Psychiatry* 127:1653–1658, 1971.

19. Kellner R, Sheffield BF: A self-rating scale for distress. *Psychol Med* 3:88–100, 1973.

5 The Use of Drawings in Incest Cases

Jean Goodwin

Psychiatrists, pediatricians, and gynecologists tend to find the task of evaluating an alleged incest victim troubling and perplexing. The physician who evaluates such a child will often be asked to testify in court about whether the child's complaint about incest is true. Physicians are uncomfortable in this role of truthfinder, especially when the child involved seems to need rest from the trauma of family upset rather than more lengthy interrogation about the sexual allegations. In addition, preschool children may not have the abstracting skills, the ability to assess duration, or the ability to sequence events, that are necessary to describe in words what has happened to them. However, a detailed understanding of the child's sexual complaint may be necessary in order to protect the child and to plan necessary medical treatment. This chapter describes how drawings can be used with the child victim, both to obtain more information about what happened to the child sexually, and to respond to the child's need to escape from the traumatic situation into fantasy and play.

This chapter is based on 19 consecutive interviews with girls aged 5 to 16 who were suspected incest victims. Drawing were collected in each interview and analyzed together with other diagnostic information about the child and her family. The child's drawing of the alleged perpetrator was particularly helpful in understanding the allegation of incest. The use of drawing was introduced in the evaluation of each victim, but a particular drawing task often became an important metaphor that regularly recurred throughout the child's treatment.[1]

STUDY POPULATION AND METHODS

The author is psychiatric consultant to a protective service agency which treats approximately 50 incest cases a year. Cases in which substantiation is difficult are referred for psychiatric consultation. This series of 19 consecutive cases represents the author's experience over an 18-month period. All 19 children were girls; father-daughter incest was suspected in ten cases and stepfather-daughter incest in nine cases. Fourteen of the girls were eventually judged to have been victimized by the suspected father figure. This judgment was reached as a consensus by the treatment team after studying other medical and family evaluations as well as results of the psychiatric interview with the victim. Five children were judged by the same procedure to be nonvictims. Three of these girls were younger siblings of actual victims and had not themselves alleged incest. Two girls, one 5 and one 13, were judged to have made false accusations. Both were seriously emotionally disturbed and the 5-year-old had been a victim of actual incest before making the false accusation against an innocent family member. This preschooler was also mildly retarded and had difficulty differentiating the many different father figures in her life, and also in differentiating present from past experiences. The 13-year-old was being physically and emotionally abused by her father and was later diagnosed as schizophrenic. This adolescent was extremely hostile toward the father and intermittently delusional. Schizophrenics often have delusions about incest which may be related to the core schizophrenic experience that one's thoughts, words, and actions are being forcibly controlled by someone else[2] (see also Chapter 1). The frequency of false accusation is higher in this referred population than the frequency (less than 5%) in the program's total incest caseload.[2]

All children were asked during a playroom session to draw whatever they wanted. The children were then asked to draw a picture of the whole family doing something together and then to draw a picture of the perpetrator. Depending on problems expressed in the interview, some children were asked to draw a picture of their house, of the inside of their bodies, or of a dream. For example, a child with a possibly psychosomatic symptom might be asked to draw her body, or a child whose mother reported the child's frequent nightmares would be asked to draw the frightening dream. In three cases, male siblings of actual victims were seen and asked to do a similar set of drawings. The draw-a-person task is given during the routine psychological testing which is also done with these children,[3] and so was omitted from this battery.

RESULTS

All nine children under 12 drew freely and completed at least three drawings. However, of the ten children aged 12 and older, only two would draw at all. Except as indicated, the following results apply only to children under 12.

Draw-the-Perpetrator

This drawing task was developed by the author after it became apparent that children refused to draw the incest event as frequently as they refused to talk about the event. Figure 5-1 shows with its many false attempts that even the more neutral task of drawing the perpetrator was often painfully difficult for these girls. Of the seven actual victims under 12, three could not draw the father at all, "x"ing out repeated attempts and finally giving up. Three others were able to draw the father but drew the figure with an obvious phallus as shown in Figures 5-1 and 5-2.

Figure 5-1 A 10-year-old girl's drawing of her sexually abusive father. Reprinted by permission from *Child Youth Services Review*.

Figure 5-2 A 5-year-old girl's drawing of her sexually abusive father. Reprinted by permission from *Child Youth Services Review.*

Children who drew such figures identified the apparent phallus as a "decoration" or said it was "nothing." Only one of the seven actual victims was able to easily produce a nonphallic drawing of the perpetrator. Both of the nonvictims under 12 did this easily. Alcoholic perpetrators were often drawn without hands or without feet.

One girl was referred for evaluation of possible incest when she drew a picture of her father for her therapist. The father was drawn after many unsuccessful attempts without legs or feet, in a dress, and with an obvious phallus. Investigation revealed that the father had become an alcoholic after his wife abandoned him and this small daughter. He and the girl had been involved in an incest relationship for five years. Further evaluation of the father indicated that he had initiated the incest relationship in part to defend against the masculine shame and the homosexual anxiety he felt in assuming the maternal role. The daughter's perception of her father's dilemma about sexual identity could not be verbalized, but emerged in her drawing.

Another incest victim drew her father holding a baseball bat; the bat was touching the obvious phallus in the drawing. This father had engaged in mutual masturbation with his daughter before and during severe physical beatings.

In two cases the child's drawing was the first clue to psychosis in the father. The father was drawn surrounded by small, disembodied heads which represented his "voices."

Kinetic Family Drawing

In this drawing task the child is asked to draw a picture of the whole family doing something together. This allows the child to represent overall family relationships and her view of her own role in the family.[4] Johnson[5] has found evidence of isolation (manifested by drawing the family members in separate compartments), and evidence of role reversal (seen by drawing the child larger than the mother) in the drawings of incest victims and in the drawings of children raped by strangers.

Two of the kinetic family drawings in this series were particularly eloquent depictions of the child's situation. One 10-year-old girl had been expelled from her family because of an incest accusation (judged to be true) which both parents angrily rejected as a lie. Her kinetic family drawing depicted a vast barren mountain with only a few thornbushes and no people. In another case, an 8-year-old girl drew her family with an extra person standing between herself and her father. "That's the watcher," she said. Her alcoholic father was still drinking heavily and she was afraid that without the monitoring of the protective services caseworker incest would recur.

In an earlier report describing drawings in incest hoaxes, we explained how the kinetic family drawing of a 10-year-old helped to reveal her motivation for falsely accusing her new stepfather of incest.[2,3] She depicted her parents standing together holding dagger-like pens and staring accusingly at her. The stepfather shared the mother's work as well as social and sexual parts of the marital relationship. The child's false accusation expressed both her anger at feeling excluded from their relationship and her wish to be included.

52

Draw-Your-House

Incest victims are often frightened of bedrooms and of houses in general. They may express this by drawing themselves carefully outside of a house they have drawn or, in play, by removing all the child-dolls from the dollhouse. The house in Figure 5-3, with front and back doors wide open, was drawn by a 5-year-old who was afraid to sleep in her own bed. Other children compulsively draw walls in their house picture, as if in an effort to keep family members in their assigned places.[3]

Reluctant-to-draw older girls will often become interested in helping the therapist to draw a floor plan of their house. Rene Spitz recommended this technique for adult analytic patients who denied exposure to the primal scene. Confronted with their own sketched floor plan of the house in which they were reared, patients realized that they must have been exposed to the sights and sounds of parental intercourse (D. Metcalf, personal communication).

Such a floor plan is very helpful in understanding the lack of privacy and the bizarre sleeping arrangements that make the incest situation possible. In one family the father had built the home himself and had placed the bedrooms of the four daughters in a long wing extending between the parents' bedroom and the only bathroom. Each daughter had

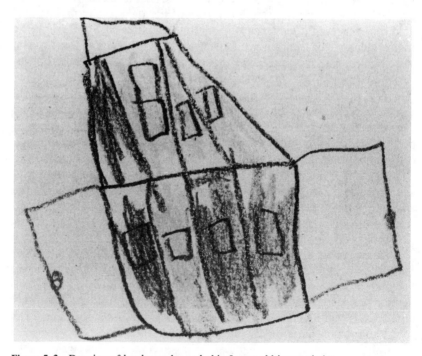

Figure 5-3 Drawing of her house by a phobic 5-year-old incest victim.

to pass through the parents' bedroom to get in or out of her room, and the father had to go through each daughter's room in turn to get to or from the bathroom.

Draw-the-Inside-of-Your-Body

About 20% of child incest victims complain of somatic symptoms such as stomachache or headache.[6] Some child victims asked if they had been "ruined" by the experience or assumed that they could never have children because of what had happened. Children with these problems were asked to draw their body as though the skin were transparent and one could see through to the inside. A girl who had presented with pharyngeal gonorrhea drew a recognizable vagina where the pharynx should have been. She was experiencing recurrent nausea and vomiting, and expressed great relief when the therapist explained that one could not be impregnated through oral intercourse.

The physician or therapist can often proceed from this drawing to using drawings to help clarify the child's questions about her own and the perpetrator's genitals.

Draw-a-Dream

About 15% of child incest victims suffer nightmares or other sleep disorders.[5] Some of these children will draw a dream as their free drawing. A 9-year-old drew a dream picture which showed herself in a wedding dress standing outside a house in a field of flowers. As she discussed the dream and her drawing, the child revealed her own longing for a new father and a new wedding for her mother, and her fears that her mother might be unable to divorce the incestuous father. Flowers like those depicted in this dream are often seen in the drawings of these children who feel "deflowered." One depressed 7-year-old victim drew page after page of drooping flowers without petals. Another 7-year-old drew a weeping tree surrounded by black flowers.

In another case, an 8-year-old girl's drawing of a dream about camping showed a zipped-up tent. She was inside the tent, but in the drawing, a phallic-appearing tree intrusively overlapped the tent despite the careful zipping. As she described her drawing of the dream, this girl told about an earlier attempt to escape the incestuous relationship. Several years before, she had told a boy in her class about her incest relationship with her father. The two had decided that she must leave home and had gathered together a tent and camping equipment in a vacant lot near their school. Their runaway was discovered after a few hours, but the motive for running away to the tent did not emerge until the incest was revealed[3] (see also Chapter 7).

Drawings by Brothers

Families are often determined to keep an incest problem secret from uninvolved siblings. Yet a recent study shows that a year after the incest accusation it is the uninvolved siblings who are the most distressed family members.[7] Recently, I have begun asking brothers to do the same set of drawings that victims are asked to do and, in addition, to draw the victim. Brothers are often less stressed by the task of drawing the father or the family than is the actual victim. Playroom evaluations of these boys show they have much sensitivity to the family's problems despite parental attempts to shield them from information about the incest accusation.

Figure 5-4 is a free drawing of a 9-year-old boy who had moved out of the family home with his mother and sister after an incest accusation was made. His drawing shows a large phallic tree splitting his house in two. At the time of this interview, he was desperately homesick for the old house; he drew this fractured house repetitively until his mother found an apartment of her own. This fractured house is reminiscent of a previously published drawing by a 13-year-old victim who depicted her house as being lifted up into a phallic tornado.[8]

Figure 5-4 Drawing of his house by the 9-year-old brother of an incest victim.

A brother in another family drew as his free drawing a picture of the older sister who had been the father's incest partner. The drawing shows the sister battered and bruised like a prize fighter, but dressed and with the proportions of a young toddler. This was a very accurate portrait of the sister's feelings after the father was acquitted in a criminal incest trial that had been, for her, a humiliating battle. Bringing the brother into joint sessions between mother and daughter helped the family to integrate the court's verdict with their experience that actual incest had occurred.

DISCUSSION

The use of drawings is usually helpful in evaluating incest victims under the age of 12. The majority of teenage victims will not draw at all, and those who did so in a compliant way revealed little in the drawings. However, teenage victims can become interested in sketching house plans or anatomic diagrams.

With the younger child, drawings can be used in pediatric settings and in the gynecologic examination as well as in the psychiatric interview. During the forensic pelvic examination, the pediatrician and the child victim can use the paper sheet that covers the examining table to draw pictures of what part of the body was touched, of the person who did the touching, of the place where all this happened, and of the parts of the body that hurt now or that might be damaged (see Chapter 1).

Diagnostically, the drawings are helpful in understanding the child's fears and anxieties, her view of the family, and her self-image. Fear and anxiety emerge in the repeated, unsuccessful attempts by incest victims to draw the fathers and also in their drawings of phallic objects intruding into homes. Children who drew their alcoholic incestuous fathers without hands or feet and with an obvious phallus convey elements of both their conscious and unconscious images of the father. Drawings of the victim as a defeated prizefighter or a flower without petals convey in a singularly rich way the child's self-image.

Such drawings, by themselves, are not sufficient to make a diagnostic decision. It is the child's increasing sense of being able to communicate and her experience of being understood that are helpful to the clinician in reconstructing what is happening in the family. The discovery of a workable avenue of communication is also helpful in reducing the anxiety of a child whose enmeshment in family secrets has often blocked verbal means of asking for help.

Children usually show relief when asked to draw. Asking a child to draw conveys many messages: that the child needs to be treated as a child, that the child in play can create something the physician values, and that the child can defend herself from traumatic experience through

56

play and drawing without having to resort prematurely to the defensive strategies of the adult world.

Often, the next step in therapy is to help the child to draw with other people[8] such as with the therapist, with other children in a victims' group, with her siblings, or with her mother. In a group for incest victims aged 9 to 12, it has become a standard procedure to drape one wall of the group room with white drawing paper. Group members are encouraged to use that space to write, draw or paint anything they feel like expressing during, before, or after the group. The mural is removed after group members leave in order to maintain confidentiality. Children who are reluctant to draw often scribble affirming comments under the drawings of other group members. Poems are added to the mural as well as critical comments about the group experience. For victims who have been burdened for years with prohibitions against revealing their incest secret the mural is a challenging and liberating exercise.

Drawings can be helpful in court settings because they convey the power of conflicts and the presence of unconscious perceptions in a more direct way than can the explanations of expert witnesses. When the subjective plight of a child is being ignored or misunderstood in a court proceeding, the discussion of the child's drawings can be useful.[9]

REFERENCES

1. Goodwin J: Use of drawings in evaluating children who may be incest victims. *Child Youth Services Rev* (in press).
2. Goodwin J, Sahd D, Rada R: Incest hoax: False accusations, false denials. *Bull Am Acad Psychiatry Law* 6 (3): 269-276, 1979.
3. Sahd D: Psychological assessment of sexually abusing families and treatment implications, in Holder W (ed): *Sexual Abuse of Children*. Englewood, Colorado, The American Humane Association, 1980, pp. 71-86.
4. Burns RC, Kaufman SH: *Action, Styles and Symbols in Kinetic Family Drawings*. New York, Brunner/Mazel, 1972.
5. Johnson MSK: Dynamic themes in the psychosocial diagnosis of sexually mistreated children. Presented at the Second International Congress of Child Abuse and Neglect, London, England, September 1978.
6. Maisch H: *Incest*. New York, Stein & Day, 1973.
7. Kroth JA: Family therapy impact on intrafamilial child sexual abuse. Presented at the Second International Congress of Child Abuse and Neglect, London, England, September 1978.
8. Stember CJ: Art therapy: A new use in the diagnosis and treatment of sexually abused children, in Jones B, MacFarlane K (eds): *Sexual Abuse and Neglect: Selected Readings*. Washington, DC, U.S. Department of Health and Human Services, 1980, pp. 59-63.
9. Uhlen DM: The use of drawings for psychiatric evaluation of a defendant in a case of homicide. *Ment Health Soc* 4:61-73, 1978.

6 What Families Say: The Dialogue of Incest

Julie Ortiz y Pino
Jean Goodwin

Myths and legends about incest often describe riddles and their solutions. A medieval legend tells about a king who demanded that each of his daughter's suitors answer a riddle. None of them could solve the riddle, so suitor after suitor was sent away. Finally, one of the suitors realized that the answer to the riddle was that the king wanted his daughter for himself. The suitor who finally understood the riddle was also banished angrily by the king.[1]

Those of us who work with incest families often feel that the family members are speaking to us in riddles. If we misunderstand these messages, we lose our relationship with the family. Sometimes, even if we understand the messages correctly, the relationship is placed in jeopardy by this new understanding.

Several years ago we began collecting quotations from children and parents who were in treatment for problems related to incest. We knew that these statements, like the riddle in the story, were valuable keys to understanding the families. We also realized that such statements could be puzzling, shocking, or alienating, especially to inexperienced therapists. We looked in particular for statements that therapists at first dismissed as unreal, exaggerated, or deceptive, but that later came to be understood as a serious description of the family's reality.[2,3] The following is an example of the kind of statement that therapists brought to us.

A mother described how she had come home from work and had opened the door of her 7-year-old daughter's bedroom to find her husband and her daughter naked on the bed. Her husband ran for the closet. The mother opened the closet door and noticed her husband's full erection. "It's not what you think!" he said. The social worker at first thought that the mother was being derisive about this feeble attempt at explanation, but then went on to experience a sense of helpless incredulity as the mother explained that her husband had completely reassured her that nothing was wrong.

We began to suspect that therapists who rejected as fabrications children's statements about incest were experiencing similar feelings of incredulity related to difficulties in understanding the family's dialogue about incest.

Orienting therapists and social workers to the communications they could expect to hear from family members became a useful way to introduce the values, needs, fears, and conflicts that characterize incestuous families. We also found that careful attention to statements made by family members could be helpful even to experienced therapists in resolving certain impasses that developed in treatment.

In this chapter direct quotations are presented in the order in which the therapist is likely to hear them as she interviews an incest family: First, quotations from child victims, then from the mother, then from the father. Except as specified in the text, father- or stepfather-daughter incest was the problem in all families. Quotations from victims have been arranged in a developmental sequence from toddler and preschool victims, to latency age victims, to early and late adolescent victims. We have found it helpful to catalogue quotations in this way in order to gain a more precise sense of the kinds of statements about sexual worries that children are able and inclined to make at various ages (see also Chapter 7).

This "dialogue" of incest is presented as a series of individual quotations, in part to clarify the concerns of each family member, but also because the communications often occur as isolated statements made into a relative vacuum. Family members seem not to hear fully many of these statements and are often unable to respond to them. It is not surprising that the taboo against talking about incest has rendered families—and therapists as well—inexperienced and incompetent in communicating in this area[4] (see also Chapter 15). Family therapy, group therapy, and bibliotherapy with materials like *Kiss Daddy Goodnight*[5] may all rely for effectiveness on providing families with words about incest, and with practice in using those words so that the painful and recondite dialogue of incest can be transformed into normally empathic conversation.

WHAT VICTIMS SAY

Typically, incest is revealed when the victim gives some clue about her distress to a neighbor, a relative, a babysitter, a teacher, or a physician. In most cases similar clues have previously been given to the mother, but they have not been deciphered by her.

Victims Aged 2 and 3

A child under four years of age cannot be expected to make a definitive statement alleging incest; therefore, it is necessary to take seriously any possibly sexual complaint expressed by a very young child. The following statements were made by 2-year-olds experiencing digital penetration from the father.

— "Daddy hurt my pee pee."
— "My ya ya hurts."
— "My heiney hurts."

Another 2-year-old said simply, "I hurt" as the first clue.

Victims Aged 4, 5 and 6

Language development enables a child, aged 4 to 6, to say considerably more about a sexual contact, but one still needs to listen for simple statements. A 4-year-old girl who had been violently raped by her mother's boyfriend said, before surgery, "That man hurt my bottom!" A 4-year-old boy who was being abused by his 13-year-old female cousin told his mother, "That girl says we're fucking." Another 4-year-old girl said, "This is the third time it happened, only this time I started to bleed and Daddy wiped it away." Fortunately, someone asked what "it" was.

Sometimes the child's entry into the complaint sounds deceptively innocent. "He gives me an ice cream cone," said a 4-year-old girl. The grandmother asked, "What for?" "If I let him touch me," the 4-year-old replied. The mother's boyfriend had been fondling the child.

It is common for these preschoolers to slip in a clue about the secret of incest into other complaints or conversation. One 5-year-old who was being violently abused by her 14-year-old stepbrother told a neighbor, "My brother does naughty things. He eats in his room when he's not supposed to, and he does naughty things to me." "Did you tell your parents?" asked the neighbor. "Yes, but my stepfather sent me to my room." "What naughty things?" "He hits me, that's all . . . no, he does something else, but I don't know what it is." The 5-year-old then hid her face in a cushion, turned red, and pointed to her vagina and said, "He hurts me with his dick sometimes when he babysits me. My sister told last summer and Daddy spanked her." Another victim of brother incest said, "My brother does things he's not supposed to." When asked what, she said, "Oh, he plays piggyback in the house and looks in my sister's purse and he puts his tail in my butt. My brother stuck his tail in my bottom, and he asked me to suck on it. It's supposed to be a secret. I don't like how it tastes, but I didn't want my brother mad at me. I don't want to get him in trouble. He'll be mad at me for telling." The child's drawings identified the tail as the brother's penis.

Once a 5-year-old trusts the interviewer, the child can make surprisingly descriptive statements:

— "He put his thing in my mouth. It's yucky. It tastes like food, like milk going down the back of my throat. He told me not to tell."
— "Dad tickles me. He starts on the inside of my leg and then rubs between my legs. I tickle him on the outside of his underwear."

Accepting, but sad, comments about the mother's inadequacy are heard again and again in children of this age. One articulate 5-year-old with gonorrhea of the throat and vagina had a mother who had repeatedly refused to get medical treatment for the child. The daughter said, "I can't sleep at night. When I take my bath my bottom hurts. It keeps hurting all night. I felt sick last night. I asked Mama to take me to the doctor. She promised she would. This morning she went out of town. I don't know how long she'll be gone. I guess she forgot." The babysitter with whom the child had been left did not know either how long the mother would be gone.

Quotations from other children describe this sense of abandonment by the mother:

— "There are no grown-ups here."
— "Mom brought me in here so I'll straighten up. I drive her up the wall."
— "Will you be my mommy? My mommy is too busy."
— "Dad gets on top of me when Mother is gone."
— "I like to sleep with Papa. He doesn't get mad at me the way Mom does. He takes care of me. He gets me up for school and makes my breakfast."

When these children are placed in foster care, one of their major worries is, "Who's going to take care of Mom when I'm gone?" One 5-year-old living in a foster home told her mother reassuringly, "I have my own home now."

Worry about the mother acts together with fear and respect for the father to make many of these children hesitate to talk about the incest:

— "I told my mom. Mom told me it was a lie. But just because someone says it's a lie doesn't mean it is a lie."
— "Will you help me to tell my mom?"
— "He'd spank me if he knew I didn't like it."
— "Ain't no way I'm going home. They'll be too mad."

Victims Aged 7 to 10

Fears of losing their families or hurting the parents are the major obstacles that prevent latency age children from describing secret sexual events in the family. Some children simply refuse to admit the sexual event, even if an adult has witnessed it. However, if the therapist can break through the child's fear of telling the secret, a child in this age range can make explicit and direct statements about what happened. For an inexperienced interviewer, this directness can be disconcerting. An interviewer who has not talked about sex with many latency age children may misinterpret these flat, graphic, bald statements as clues that the child is fabricating the complaint.

— "My brother's been screwing me."
— "Dad uses us in bed."
— "He's been doing it to me."
— "He sticks his finger in my vagina."
— "He made me take off my panties. Then he would lay on top of me and rub his thing on me. He tried to get it in but couldn't. He tried front and back but never got it in."
— "He takes us to the bedroom and jumps on us, one at a time."
— "He put his weiner in my thing this morning while it was still dark and blood came out. He made me throw my panties away. My dad tells me I have to do it with him because my mom doesn't like to do it with him any more."
— "He took my panties off and laid me on my back. He had a stick on his body. He put it inside me right between my legs."
— "He took me into his room and told me we would play a game. He got out the game, but then he locked the door and he did something to me. He put his thing in me all the way inside. Down below. We were both undressed."
— "You know what Mom and Dad do in bed together? That's what Dad was doing to me."
— "He takes his weiner out and makes me touch it, but when Mom comes in he covers himself quickly."

— "He got on top of me and hurt me. He hurt me two or three times."
— "Dad wanted me to go to bed with him. He came to my bed when Mom was asleep and lay on top of me. He said, 'Give me some.' I'm afraid of him. I hate him. He would rub me up and down. Sometimes he hurt me. He'd stick his weiner inside me."

One hears many statements from children that reflect the parents' inability to protect the child and the child's inappropriate overprotectiveness about the parents.

— "I told my mother. She whipped me and told me to talk to my dad about it, not to bother her."
— "Maybe it was a dream. Mom says it was a dream."
— "I don't believe Mom any more. I told her he put his hand in my pants and she didn't believe me."
— "Is Mom going to jail? She told me she might and it would be because I told the police officer what he did to me."
— "Once I told my dad I didn't like him; he went up to his room and cried all night."
— "I told my mom that I needed to move out and get a house of my own."
— "I can't count on Mom. She sends my sisters to sleep with Grandpa, (the abuser) but I won't go. I scream when he touches me. I get nervous and run away. I'm just a little girl. I run home to my dog. He protects me."

Victims Aged 11 to 13

Children of this age are more aware of and curious about the dangers and the implications of the incestuous event. The following quotation from a retarded 13-year-old has the matter-of-fact concrete quality that is more characteristic of early latency than of preadolescence. Asked by her teacher what she had done over the weekend, this girl said, "I've been screwing my brothers. They take off their clothes and I take off mine. He gets his thing hard and spreads my legs and puts his thing in mine. It's ucky and it hurts. He wants to make me a baby." A 13-year-old who was functioning cognitively at her age level described her incest experience in a more complex way, "I still dream about it. My uncle took me to the movie. He took my clothes off and had intercourse with me. He told me he'd kill my family if I told. I decided he couldn't hurt me any more than he already had, so I told my mother. She said she had suspected . . . Why did she let me go with him? I guess she didn't realize." This more characteristically preadolescent account describes the event in the context of the motivations that led up to it and the consequences that may follow. There is more fear, dread, and anger about the relationship. It is no longer seen as something to be blindly accepted.

Fears about pregnancy and about damage to the pubertal body, a body that already seems frighteningly unpredictable, are connected with the increased sense of danger and the focus on consequences. The following comments illustrate these fears:

— "I feel sick today. Do you think I am pregnant?"
— "I'm sure I'm pregnant."
— "I want to be checked out by a doctor so I can get on with the rest of my life."

In the face of these dangers preadolescent children now require some explanation or quid pro quo from the perpetrator if they are to continue to comply with his sexual demands. They describe their fathers as offering simple threats, excuses, rationalizations as sex education, or protestations of romantic love.

— "I was afraid to tell. He said he'd kill my brother if I told."
— "He comes into my room and climbs into bed with me and tries to talk me into intercourse. He told me not to tell or he'd be mad."
— "He tried to unzip my pants on the way home from bowling. I told him to stop or I'd tell. He said no one would believe me."
— "He did it, but, if I tell, it might make Mama get a divorce."
— "I asked my stepfather what rape meant because my friends at school were talking about it. I didn't know he would show me."
— "Dad read me the *Joy of Sex* and then he did cunnilingus. I cried. Later he told me if I didn't want it next time I should just say so."
— "He said he thinks about me all the time. He promised to stop, but he did it again."

These older girls still describe the mother as unavailable to help them control their fears and worries.

— "Mom told me not to worry about it."
— "Why did she marry him?"
— "Why did she go back with him?"
— "Why didn't she listen to me?"
— "Mom would walk right by us and Dad would be lying on top of me on the couch and she never noticed."
— "Mom says I'm a bad influence because I talk about how I feel."
— "Mom gets so mad at me. She blames me now that Dad is gone. I can handle the kids better than she can."

The protective feeling toward the mother that characterized the younger child is now being replaced by criticism, recrimination and hostility.

Preadolescents who appear asymptomatic on the surface often

reveal in treatment burdensome, pent-up anxieties, violent fantasies, and feelings that they are about to lose control. The following communications occurred after trust had been established in a victims' group for preadolescents.

— "I'm going to run away. I don't want to be at home. I don't want to go to school."
— "I feel out of control. I might kill myself."
— "I'm a teenager on the surface and a 3-year-old underneath."
— "Maybe I'll just cut my wrists; no, I was just kidding."
— "I'm afraid there might be bloodshed."
— "I'll fix him. I'll get a gun."
— "The only person I can talk to is my teddy bear."
— "Who would I have told?"

Victims Aged 14 to 18

Teenage victims understand more fully that the intrafamilial relationship is not only dangerous but illicitly sexual. They often refer to the incest contact as "rape" and are sometimes strong and motivated enough to resist, so the contacts more literally resemble a rape. Their adolescent developmental interest in mastering sexuality, in competing sexually, and the increased capacity to enjoy genital stimulation tend to make these adolescents feel even more guilty about continuing the relationship. The following statements illustrate how adolescents assume more responsibility and blame for the sexual events they describe.

— "I know it was my fault. He'd give me money and buy me something and I'd let him do it."
— "The problem with my younger sister is that she likes it."
— "I'm more developed than my younger sister. I just don't know why he went for her instead of me."
— "I got in trouble and Dad said I could have 14 swats with the paddle or intercourse with him. I chose intercourse because I was not a virgin and it would be a one-time thing. But then he did it twice a week. He played tapes of him and my stepmother having intercourse to excite me and sometimes taped our intercourse too. I told my stepmother. I was crying. She said I was lying. She said he never could have intercourse with her so how could he have it with me."
— "He's been touching me sexually and tried to get in bed with me. He asks me to have sex with him and when I get angry and say no, he says, 'You wouldn't reject a boyfriend's request; why do you refuse me?' He kisses my ear and tries to get to me."

Revealing the situation is difficult for these adolescents and can be associated with pervasive feelings of disloyalty and guilt about the whole range of steps toward individuation that they are beginning to take. Accusations of incest tend to be carefully justified by the adolescent victim. Teenagers who finally decide to ask for help often feel an additional burden of guilt because they have not told earlier in the relationship.

— "He did it to me for four years but, when I walked in and saw him doing it to my little sister, I had to tell. My older sister had his baby."
— "I can't forgive him the way Mother asks me to. Too much has happened. My mother says my sister forgave him so why can't I."
— "I never wanted to hurt him. I didn't think he could take it. I never told anyone. I was afraid he couldn't take a confrontation."
— "After five years I finally said no and he said to me, 'Why didn't you say no in the first place if you didn't like it?' "

Necessary adolescent exercises in individuation are at times directly distorted by the incestuous relationship. For example dating or evening rehearsals or jobs may be prohibited. The following statements describe additional examples.

— "Dad would get out of the shower with a hard-on and make me ejaculate him. I couldn't have friends spend the night because he'd come into my bedroom and talk about sex. He'd point between our legs and say, 'You know your thing there, guys are always after it.' "
— "He comes into the bathroom when I'm taking a shower."
— "He bumps into me in the living room, and he has the whole living room to walk in."

Despite their deliberately rebellious actions and critical statements, adolescents often have a significant nostalgia for the families they must shortly leave. Their fears of prematurely losing precious ties can make them vulnerable to discounting the seriousness of their complaints or to aborting efforts to stop the incest.

— "I don't know what you're planning to do with my father, but I don't want to hate him always."
— "I'm confused about why Mother won't do anything. It's hard to run away to my sister's."
— "I tried to refuse him but I was raised never to say no to an adult and he was my father. I was raised to respect adults."
— "It took me a long time to become aware that I had a right to say no. The greatest fear is to lose Dad's love and acceptance. I needed someone to go to."

— "I know it is true. It happened to me too, but I can't say, because I'll lose Mom." (Her younger sister had alleged intercourse with the father.)
— "My head says he thought I was Mom. Like Mom and Dad said, he had a concussion and didn't know what he was doing. In my heart I know he did it on purpose."
— "When I was small, a man looked just like my dad and got in bed with me. My parents say that's what must have happened."
— "It's okay as long as Mom is happy."
— "I don't know why I ran away. I have everything I want at home."
— "I do crazy things. I threatened to cut my wrists when they told me I would have to go home."

Adolescents are already expressing worries about how the incestuous relationship will affect their success as a wife and mother.

— "I think I am gay because I have no feeling around guys."
— "I never told him I couldn't be around guys because of him."
— "I always thought I was gay. My uncle raped me to show me I wasn't gay and how much I could enjoy sex with a man."
— "I knew it was wrong, so I learned how to turn my sexual feelings off. How do I turn them back on?"
— "I hope I never have a girl child. I could never trust my husband with her. I could never trust any man."

WHAT MOTHERS SAY

Mothers in incest families resist recognizing and putting a stop to the incest and are often described as passive. However, close attention to their words shows that this passivity is a paradoxically active process. It is not that the mother has been unable to perceive what was happening; in many cases, she has become aware enough to actively flee from her own perceptions.

— "I blacked out when I heard. It happened right there in front of me and I didn't notice. My neighbor said, 'he's fondling your daughter.' Things had gotten so bad I wasn't even seeing it."
— "When my daughter started to tell me I just ran out the door. I didn't want to hear it."
— "When I first saw it, I wanted to kill myself. I prayed for God to help me."
— "When she told me last night, I just left. I didn't want to confront him."

Some of the mother's motivations for avoiding a confrontation may be stated by her quite explicitly. Fear of the perpetrator's violence and fear of losing her family are common.

— "He'd wake me up in the middle of the night, jealous. I've been like a prisoner."

— "I had another dream that he killed me. He came at me with a knife. I decided to press charges. I refuse to be threatened by him anymore."

— "He couldn't have done it. He is the best man I've ever had. He is so good to both of us. . . . I don't know his last name; I just met him Tuesday." The 6-year-old daughter had been violently raped by this boyfriend.

"I can't confront him on this, we haven't been married long enough." This mother had just married her second sexually abusing husband.

— "He's the best man I've ever been involved with. He helps support the family and is very good to the kids."

— "My new husband (the abuser) fills me up. I have this vision of how things can be. We're friends as well as lovers."

— "We have always been a close knit family. I talked to my husband. I feel it wasn't all his fault. She's to blame too. I told him I'd stand beside him."

— "I can't press charges. I feel sorry for him. He is an old man."

— "I know he is molesting her but he promised me inheritance benefits." The victimized daughter was four.

— "I feel powerless about finding a new house and making it on my own . . ."

— "I could never go through dating again. I'd feel too guilty."

Other mothers describe being sexually rejected by the husband for an enviable younger rival.

— "My husband doesn't find me attractive anymore. He wants a younger girl."

— "He told me he liked her better because she is tighter . . ."

— "Sometimes I feel like everyone is against me."

These mothers seem to be avoiding the reality of the incest in order to avoid being possessed, like the wicked queen in *Snow White*, by feelings of envy and envious rage.

Defensive techniques of denial, repression, and minimization help these mothers to disavow the necessity of confronting the incest situation.

— "I believe it was only one incident and no penetration occurred."

— "There was no intercourse." (Oral and rectal penetration had taken place.)

— "I know he wouldn't abuse his own children."

— "Yes, he abused his stepchildren, but he wouldn't do it to his own kids. He was just trying to get back at me."

— "I don't know what to believe. I don't believe it ever happened."

— "I always knew he went into our daughter's bedroom, but I thought they just stayed up all night talking."

— "He couldn't have done it; if anything, he spoils her. I've seen him in bed with her, but I didn't think anything of it since he's her dad."

— "You don't have to hate him. Hate grows too thick. I used to think he was just close to the kids." This mother had refused to believe the first daughter who reported incest. The second daughter was impregnated by the abusive uncle.

— "I asked my new husband and he told me he had just explained the facts of life to her. He just stepped over the bounds. I asked her not to condemn him. He just made a mistake."

— "He is just oversexed. He fondles her in the bathtub or when she changes clothes. He seems to pick on her more than the other kids. I can't let my child keep me home all the time. I feel like a prisoner." This mother placed her 5-year-old outside of the home and remained with her husband.

Mothers often resent it terribly when a child goes to an outsider for help, and they can be very effective at keeping their daughters from complaining.

— "We could have worked it out if she hadn't told."

— (To the daughter) "If you bring that up again, I'll tell your father what you are saying about him."

— "If you tell anybody about what he does to you, I'll beat the hell out of you." The abuser was her boyfriend. Her daughters were 7 and 9.

— "So she misses me; she should have thought of that before she told."

However, the child is often driven to complain elsewhere because the mother's own protective maneuvers for the child have been so hopelessly feeble. The mother is not a good protector; in part, because her perception of the situation is so distorted by minimization; in part, because she is too afraid of her own anger to be tough; and in part, because she has so few resources.

— "He couldn't have. I never leave him alone with the kids. I couldn't trust him."

— "I told the girls to call for help if he tried to get in bed with them again. I told them to call for help. I'd wake up and he'd be out of bed. Later, I'd go look for him and he'd be in the girls' room."

— "I'm afraid of him. I try to stay late at work so I don't have to be around him. I just tell the girls to lock themselves in their bedroom." This mother's 6- and 8-year-old daughters were being sexually abused by her 16-year-old stepson.

— "I didn't want this to happen, but they just do what they want."

When complaints about sexual abuse can no longer be denied or suppressed, these mothers can still explain them away in various ways.

— "He attempted incest with my daughter (5 years old.) I came home and found him (the boyfriend) attempting to put his penis in her mouth. I have no intention of pressing charges because he's been in trouble ever since someone made him the subject of a voodoo plot."
— "That pest down the street told you. I think the girls mixed him up with someone else. It couldn't have been him. My daughter is sick. She needs an evaluation."
— "My sister is vicious. She put her (the daughter) up to this."
— "Her natural father sold her a bill of goods. He wants her to think I'm a bad mother." The 11-year-old daughter had complained to her natural father about ongoing sexual abuse by the stepfather.
— "Her father's new wife told her to say this so he could get her back."
— "I was worried about her (the daughter), but I found out all she needed was glasses. She does not need to see you now."
— "She got gonorrhea from the sheets, then she touched herself and put her fingers down her throat." The 5-year-old daughter had oral and vaginal gonorrhea.

One of the most effective ways for mothers to make these problems go away is to blame or disbelieve the complaining daughter. This maneuver maintains the mother's alliance with her husband, removes by displacement the mother's guilt about having chosen the husband or having failed to protect the daughter, and reduces the pressure on the mother to respond to the complaint with constructive change. The mother who focuses on the daughter's fatal seductiveness avoids fears that she is no longer attractive to her husband while, at the same time, allowing herself to vent in a disguised way her envy of the rival daughter's attractiveness.

— "What man could have resisted a 14-year-old throwing herself at him? I understand."
— "I'd die without him. The child is emotionally disturbed. She's sick. He is so gentle. I'll choose my husband over her (the daughter) any day. She's a psychopathic liar, a sociopath. My husband is a fastidious man. He couldn't possibly be attracted to her; she's so repulsive and unclean."
— "No way I could see her with this lie standing between us. I'm on the verge of a nervous breakdown; seeing her would push me over the edge."
— "My daughters are all whores. They're a bad influence."

Mothers can use almost these same words when they blame the social worker or the therapist for the family problems. The following statements to therapists could easily have been made to daughters.

— "It's all your fault; he is innocent."

— "You people picked out names out of the phone book. You just pick out names to call." The 6-year-old daughter had gonorrhea.

— "You social workers are just jealous of my job. That's the reason you are taking my daughter from me."

— "I can't see any point in talking to you since you think my husband did it. No one else in the world is in a situation like ours. Any contact from you serves to upset me terribly."

— "You've got to tell me the truth."

— "Please don't leave, I'd take it out on my daughter."

During these angry storms, it can be helpful for the therapist to remember that she is bearing the brunt of blame that would otherwise be heaped on the victimized daughter.

If the therapist can weather such storms and remain in empathic contact with the mother's feelings of guilt, jealousy, rejection, isolation and fear of her own rage, mothers can become insightful cotherapists for their families.

— "We take our anger at him out on each other."

— "The girls are spoiled. I try to discipline; then he tells me I'm a bad mother."

— "I'm the one who needs help. I don't know how to show my husband love."

WHAT FATHERS SAY

One clinical advantage of transcribing statements made by incestuous fathers is that their rationalizations seem much less plausible on paper than they do in person.

Sex education has a long history as a rationalization for incest.[6] Not only is the incest activity justified as sex education, but sexual misinformation is used to convince the child to participate. In the renaissance incest case described in Shelley's *Cenci*, the father tells his daughter that she must have intercourse with him because any child conceived between father and daughter will automatically become a saint.[7] The following statements made to victims are more recent efforts in this genre.

— "I do this because you are my second wife."

— "Let me put it in you so it won't hurt when a boyfriend puts it in you."

— "You are old enough to have a baby and I want you to do that."

— "When her baby brother was born, I wanted to keep her from hurting him so I tried to explain where babies came from."

Underlying the attempt to educate are the father's own lack of knowledge, inhibitions, and fears about sexuality.

— "After my wife had the tubal ligation, there was no point in having sex with her any more; she couldn't reproduce."
— "I know sex is wrong."
— "This is too crude for me to discuss with a woman."
— "It stopped for a while, but then she started developing. I wanted to see it. I couldn't let her develop without watching. I guess she wanted her privacy."

Achieving control of the sexual knowledge and actions of the child may compensate the father for his sense of being out of control of his own sexuality. One father said to his daughter, "I could mess with your mind and make you do anything I want you to do."

In addition to the didactic rationalizations for the incest, there are several other excuses and explanations that are heard repeatedly.

— "I must have been drinking. I don't remember."
— "I couldn't resist her because she looked so much like my wife."
— "My wife and I are sexually incompatible."
— "Penetration never took place."
— "I never knew she didn't want me to do it."
— "I never realized it hurt the kids."
— "I've been charged with this before but the child lied."
— "That kid will go to jail for perjury." (He was referring to his 9-year-old stepdaughter.)
— "We can do whatever we want to do in our own home and nobody can interfere."
— "If she wanted something—money, a bike—I'd get it for her and ask her what she'd give me for it."
— "The 11-year-old girl next door and her uncle do it every night. It's all right."

This last statement is reminiscent of the Marquis de Sade's rationalization for incest in *Eugenie de Franval*.[7] "Is not the world full of such weaknesses? Is not this how man had to begin populating the earth? . . . Let us crush these disgusting prejudices which are hostile to happiness."

Loss of control is an important aspect in the father's descriptions of the incestuous event. It is as though the fathers feel it is unfair to expect them to control their sexual impulses.

— "She came and got into bed with me naked. What could I do?"
— "She got into the bathtub with me. What could I do?"
— "She grabbed me by the balls. What could I do?"

— "If you put ten men in a room with my daughter, what do you think those ten men would do?"
— "When she started sucking on my penis, what could I do?"
— "I did what any man would have done."
— "I couldn't help it. I'm in love with her."

When fathers describe the incest event, they often seem to be describing an unfortunate but unavoidable accident.

— "I never ask her to come into the bedroom. I just leave the door open."
— "The only reason my daughter was in bed with me was because she came into the room and was feeling bad and asked me to pray for her. So I prayed for her and then asked if she'd rub my back. You see, she was already in the bed."
— "I was just trying to get her warm after her bath."
— "I wanted to save water and they couldn't get clean by themselves."
— "One of the girls was getting into the tub and she slipped on my hand." (The father was explaining digital penetration of daughters aged 6 and 9.)

Since it is so difficult for the fathers to feel any responsibility for what has happened, they often end by attributing excessive power to the child.

— "I know it is my fault, but how did a 14-year-old get so good at it?" He had begun abusing her when she was nine.
— "I never thought she would hurt me like this."
— "She is a little witch."

Many fathers are so isolated they have no one with whom to check out their assumptions and confusions about sexuality. The child is their closest companion, and she is too young to help.

— "The loneliness kills me."
— "If you want to talk about anything intimate, I think you'd better see my wife alone." The father was speaking to a marital therapist.
— "Loneliness is a weapon; it can destroy someone."
— "I'd sleep with any of the girls whenever there was room in the bed because I didn't want to sleep with my wife."
— "I just wanted to turn loose sexually and I did it with the wrong people."
— "I tried to forget about it but I couldn't. I wanted to talk to someone but I didn't know who to tell."

Fathers who are feeling helpless and confused can respond with indignation when others treat them as though they did something wrong or imply that someone else is the victim in the situation.

— "My wife has been cold and distant since this thing with my daughter. I don't know why."
— "My wife is jealous of me because I am close to the kids."
— "Stop picking on me."

DISCUSSION

Statements made by incest victims, by their mothers, and by their fathers make several points that are useful to the inexperienced therapist.

Children do not talk about sexuality in the same way adults do. Two-year-olds talk about hurting. Four-year-olds make cryptic, offhand comments which must be expanded with adult support. Eight-year-olds either refuse to talk or recount sexual details in a graphic, matter-of-fact way. Ten-year-olds describe dread of the sexual encounter but also feel entrapped by the father's threats and enticements. Fourteen-year-olds describe the relationship in a way that casts blame upon themselves. They feel guilty and disloyal about revealing the incest and doubly guilty because they feel they should have told earlier or resisted more effectively.

Mothers in incestuous families resist allying themselves with the complaining daughter even if she is telling the truth. The mother's fear of her husband, and her fears of losing her maternal role, her marriage, and her self-esteem act as powerful motivations for disbelieving the daughter, for minimizing what happened, and for blaming the daughter for the incest.

Fathers in incestuous families will resist acknowledging what they have done. They feel too isolated, confused, and out of control of their sexuality to take responsibility for their incestuous sexual activity.

More experienced therapists may find additional lessons in this material. As one examines these statements, one realizes that therapists often intervene in ways that cut off the expression of pressing anxieties.[2] It is an almost automatic response to tell a 5-year-old victim not to worry about her mother, while telling the mother not to blame the child for what happened. We tell adolescent victims that the incest was not their fault and tell fathers that they must accept responsibility for what they have done. If these simple interventions fail, it may be helpful to return to the individual's original statements and to try to explore why the 5-year-old worries more about her mother than the mother allows herself to worry about the child, or to talk more about the ways in which the teenager takes on more blame for the incest than the father is able to feel. As family members perceive the meanings and the relationships that support their communications, they may then be able to use reassurance or confrontation to change them.

Reviewing family members' statements also raises developmental questions. Will the child who has experienced incest at age 4 to 8 inevitably begin to feel fearful about what happened as she enters preadolescence? Will she inevitably become guilty about the experience in adolescence? In adult victims' groups there does not seem to be a reversed developmental unfolding of statements about the incest. Typically adults present with developmentally adult problems about how the incest experience is interfering with motherhood and marriage. They go on to struggle with adolescent issues of whether they were to blame for the incest and then with latency issues of whether they must continue to protect the father. Earlier memories about the incest often emerge at this point. Group members express more fear and confusion as they remember the sexual activity. Like preadolescents, they begin to criticize the mothers for being unavailable and then, like preschoolers, they begin to feel how intensely they needed the mother. Finally, like the 2-year-olds, some women reexperience a sense of desperate hurt and vulnerability, and a need for comfort, feelings that may have been disguised for many years.

CONCLUSIONS

Social workers and therapists who are familiar with the dialogue of incest are less likely to misinterpret statements made in incestuous families. If the mother says her daughters are psychopathic liars, if the 8-year-old "victim" refuses to talk, if the 14-year-old "victim" is seductive and promiscuous, if the father denies everything, an inexperienced therapist may assume it is safe to close the case, unless she recognizes this as the type of communication that occurs in families where actual incest is a factor (see Chapter 1). When the therapist begins to feel incredulous or alienated from the family, it can be helpful to attend more closely to the exact words family members are using, and to ask whether one is cutting off or discounting important communications before having fully understood them. The exact words used by family members can often be more effective in conveying their plight to a judge or to another therapist than can diagnostic paraphrases.

REFERENCES

1. Hesse-Fink E: *Etudes sur le theme de l'inceste dans la litterature française.* Berne, Herbert Long, 1971.
2. Watzlawick P, Beavin JH, Jackson DD: *Pragmatics of Human Communication.* New York, Norton, 1967.

3. Ekstein R: Borderline states and ego disturbances, in Sholevar, GP, Benson RM, Blinder BJ (eds): *Treatment of Emotional Disorders in Children and Adolescents*. New York, Spectrum, 1980, pp. 403–413.

4. Butler S: *Conspiracy of Silence: The Trauma of Incest*. San Francisco, New Glide, 1978.

5. Armstrong L: *Kiss Daddy Goodnight: A Speak-Out on Incest*. New York, Pocket Books, 1979.

6. Justice B, Justice R: *The Broken Taboo: Sex in the Family*. New York, Human Sciences Press, 1979.

7. Maisch H: *Incest*. New York, Stein & Day, 1972.

7 Incest from Infancy to Adulthood: A Developmental Approach to Victims and Families

Jean Goodwin
John Owen

Part of the difficulty in developing a unified approach to the treatment of incest is the wide variation in the needs of the victimized child and her family depending on her developmental age. This chapter will review for each developmental stage—infancy, preschool, latency, adolescence, and adulthood—the type of sexual abuse seen most commonly, the physical, emotional, and family symptoms seen most often, and the kinds of interventions which tend to be most helpful.

In our experience the developmental approach is important in the treatment of the parents and of the entire family, as well as in the individual treatment of the child victim. Development itself produces specific crises in parents, in the marriage, and in the family. In any family a daughter's entry into the oedipal stage will tax the father's ability to develop a warm relationship with his daughter and the mother's ability to cope with triangles, and with competition. However, if the mother feels that she lost her own mother irretrievably during her own oedipal conflict, her child's entry into the oedipal stage may become a more serious crisis.[1] Sensitive help to such parents can offer them the opportunity to rectify their own developmental failures as they allow the child to progress.[2]

When, as in the incest situation, family crisis is added to the child's and the parents' current developmental crises, there is potential for great disorganization but also for significant growth in the family.

The Incest Victim from Infancy to Age Four

In infants who have no language as yet, the substantiation of sexual abuse can be difficult indeed. It is an important diagnosis to make, however, because one death has been reported in an infant who was suffocated when the perpetrator attempted fellatio.[3] The following is a case example.

> **Case 1** A paranoid schizophrenic and alcoholic man and his passive dependent wife had had 10 of their 12 children removed from the home because of sexual and physical abuse. Protective services were asked to investigate what was happening to the couple's new infant daughter. The parents responded angrily to requests for a family interview and for physical examination of the infant. On interview the father hugged and kissed the infant passionately while displaying an obvious erection. On physical examination there was redness around the infant's vulva and anal area. The family's overwhelming concern was to protect the parents, and especially the father, from interference and harassment by "agencies." Neither the mother nor the two adult cousins living in the home had a commitment to protect this infant. An older daughter who had been adopted into another home because of sexual abuse said that her sexual experience with her father had begun before she could remember, and that she had observed her father sexually abusing younger siblings when they were infants and toddlers.

Although this kind of evidence would not have been adequate to substantiate sexual abuse in an older victim, it was felt that in a 6-month-old infant no more conclusive evidence could be expected.

Incest victims between 1 and 4 years of age often present with loss of toilet training, sleep disturbances, fear of men, or with excessive clinging to the mother. They have usually made a communication about having been "bothered" sexually; vulvar reddening may be the only physical evidence of what happened.

Renee Brant and co-workers[4] have described several cases in which toddlers from ages 1 to 3 have been able to communicate a sexual abuse incident. In one case the older sisters of a 2½-year-old boy described how he had been sexually abused by their mother's boyfriends. This boy was usually withdrawn, frightened, and watchful, but displayed outbursts of inappropriate sexual behavior such as jumping into the psychiatrist's lap and fondling his genitals. At one point, this 2-year-old startled a nurse on the pediatrics ward by asking her if she "wanted some cock." This child was able to return to superior functioning after living in a foster home for six months. A second 2-year-old was able to complain to her mother about sexual abuse, pointing to her perineal area and saying, "Joe stick bum-bum." When the mother examined the child, she found vulvar redness and irritation. For several weeks after her report, the child became anxious around male strangers. She also became more clinging than usual with her mother, slept restlessly, and had a poor appetite. Play with dolls in a therapeutic setting clarified the identity of Joe who turned out to be a male day care worker.

Brant and co-workers concluded that toddlers are able to complain about sexual abuse, that their complaints should be taken seriously, and that techniques of physical examination and of play therapy can be helpful in this age group. Our own experience confirms that children aged 2 and 3 can be fairly effective in complaining about sexual abuse. One 2-year-old on a routine visit to her pediatrician pointed to her genital area and then to her mouth, and said the words, "Ya ya . . . Daddy." The pediatrician took this cryptic statement seriously enough to examine the child, and found a severe perianal bruise consistent with attempted penetration. Another 2-year-old said, "Daddy hurts my pee pee." Three-year-olds are able to make complex and even poetic statements about what has happened. A 3-year-old boy said, "A man crawled on top of me and he had a big potato." A 3-year-old girl said, "Daddy gets on top of me and pulls my panties down."

Decisions about where the infant or toddler will be placed must be made swiftly. Institutional or temporary environments are not appropriate for the care of these young children. If the young child returns home, it must be in the context of intensive work with the parents. The mother is usually the involved parent, as in our experience fathers who abuse children at this young age are often seriously disturbed and will flee from the family rather than accept treatment. Gebhard's work also indicates that incest offenders who molest children under 12 are more likely to have alcoholism, sociopathy, and other psychiatric diagnoses.[5] So far, we have been unable to return a child of this age to live at home with the sexually abusing father. It has been necessary either to place the child in preadoptive foster care with a view to termination of paternal rights, or to work intensively with the mother to help her to sever her relationship with the disturbed perpetrator. Mothers of victims in this age group, despite showing some signs of the passivity characteristic of many mothers in incest families, have been uncharacteristically willing to separate from the abusive male and to actively participate in the treatment plan for their daughters.

Very brief (2 to 8 sessions) play therapy is often entirely successful in removing emotional symptoms in toddlers who have been sexually abused. Play therapy can take place at a therapeutic preschool which both mother and child attend. A typical set of goals for play therapy with a 3-year-old would be: 1) to help the child express her anger toward the perpetrator, 2) to help her say goodbye to him; he has usually left precipitously and dramatically, and 3) to resolve the child's anxiety enough so that symptoms resolve, eg, she can return to sleeping in her own bed. If problems recur in the family, the very young child is likely to signal this by developing a recurrence of symptoms or a developmental delay.[6]

The Preschool or Oedipal Age Child

Not surprisingly, to those who have read Freud some of the most difficult clinical situations arise when incest is revealed in a child aged 4, 5, or 6. Often, it is a physical complaint such as a pharyngeal gonorrheal infection or a vaginal discharge secondary to finger penetration that brings the family into treatment, not a spoken complaint from the child. Children in this age group usually require surgical repair if vaginal intercourse has been attempted.

When incest presents at this age, the child's warm attachment to the perpetrator, the child's alienation from her mother, and the serious marital difficulties between the parents are clear. The child feels terribly guilty and utterly cut off from her mother. She may act the wild child because she has given up hope of making anyone love her. Individual therapy for the child may give her a first opportunity to feel that she is important in her own right, not only as a pawn in the ongoing battles between her parents. Compulsive cleaning and repetitive symbolic destruction of both parents are important play sequences, as shown in the following case.

Case 2 Five-year-old Sandy was diagnosed by her pediatrician as having pharyngeal gonorrhea. Despite repeated telephone contacts from the physician and the Public Health Department her parents failed to bring her back for follow-up medical care. The case was referred to Child Protective Services because of medical neglect, and Sandy was placed temporarily with grandparents. On psychological evaluation, she drew pictures that showed her sucking on her father's penis. Sandy had been overactive in preschool, unable to concentrate well or to share or cooperate with the other children. These problems cleared after she was placed with her grandparents. Both parents vehemently denied that sexual contact had occurred and were outraged and indignant about the placement, but neither took any action to comply with the legal and medical appointments that were required. Sandy's placement with her grandparents became permanent. In therapy Sandy constantly repeated play sequences in which fathers and children undressed and, after that, the father was somehow killed.

Characteristically, the mothers in these families are terribly angry. They may be in a literal rage at the husband for having betrayed them, and divorce is a frequent outcome. The mothers may be openly rageful with the daughter as well. The mother will often react to the daughter's eager attachment to a woman therapist or to a foster mother with jealousy and increased withdrawal of affection, as if this were yet a further betrayal. The mother's rage at the child's attachments is defensive against her own guilty conviction that it is her own sexual sins that have precipitated the disastrous losses she is experiencing.

Marital therapy is important, even though this will often end as divorce therapy. In either case marital therapy should focus on the parents' responsibility to settle their battles without involving the child and to spare some of their energies for the care of the child. The child must often be removed from the home until this work can be completed.

The following cases illustrate some of the difficulties involved in working with these angry and rejecting mothers and with the more nurturing, but often absent fathers.

Case 3 Sherry, aged 5 years, had been in a sexual relationship with her natural father which included vulvar fondling and finger penetration of the vagina. Her father was genuinely attached to Sherry, upset by what had happened, and was very eager for treatment. However, Sherry's mother was absolutely unforgiving of the father and was determined "to put it all behind me." Marital therapy ended in divorce counseling, and Sherry's mother took the child to live in another state, refusing a recommendation that the child's play therapy continue.

Case 4 Six-year-old Maria was referred to Child Protective Services because of physical neglect. Maria's mother had become depressed after the death of her father and had ceased to care for the child. Further investigation showed that Maria's mother had been living in an incestuous relationship with her father for many years and that Maria was the child of this incestuous relationship. Maria described mutual oral-genital stimulation with her father/grandfather. Maria was having violent tantrums which her mother could not control. These cleared after the child was placed in a foster home, except when they occurred immediately after visits from her mother. Maria's mother was hostile to caseworkers and therapists and finally ceased visiting her daughter.

In both of these cases the daughter's attachment to her father was her major source of nurturance. Unfortunately, in our experience incest in the oedipal stage inevitably ruptures this father-daughter relationship. As with the victims under four, we have not been able to reunite families in which the victim is between 4 and 7. The mothers feel they must choose either the daughter or the father. In other jurisdictions where fathers are routinely prosecuted, the prognosis for family reunion may be better if the legal process provides more barriers to the parents' attempting to flee treatment and to flee their guilt about what has happened.

The Latency Age Victim

The majority of children who complain of sexual abuse are of latency age.[7] In our program the modal age of the reporting child is ten. Most are in late latency, the period from age 9 to 12, when the defense mechanisms of latency are fully elaborated.[8] The suppression of sexuality that is characteristic of latency accounts for much of the difficulty these girls have in talking about the sexual abuse. Cognitively, they have a good grasp of the reality and sequencing of events, but their embarrassment about sexual topics may lead them to describe events in a forcedly brazen way, in a dissociated or silly way, or to refuse to talk about it at all. Because of the importance of fantasy as a defense, the therapist must as soon as possible allow children of this age to speak metaphorically rather than directly about what happened. Dreams are important, as are drawings and play sequences. Successful therapy is characterized by the rapid transformation of the sexual trauma into fantasy play which can be translated into reality by the child when necessary. Well-defended children of this age will persistently and appropriately refuse therapeutic attempts to "let it all out." However, some of these children demonstrate a determined preoccupation with bringing the perpetrator to justice. They will tell their story patiently and repeatedly in the interests of "making things right" and of ensuring that the perpetrator is fairly punished.

Latency is the age of industry, and a detailed history of school activities and hobbies is critical in the evaluation. A recent decline in grades is a common finding, as is school refusal, or the abandonment of a sport or musical activity. One of the first priorities of therapy should be the restoration of normal performance at school. Therapy, whether group or individual, will be most successful when it can be described as "learning something" or "doing something." For example, sexuality can be broached by a physician as part of "sex education" with children who otherwise refuse to speak about the sexual abuse. Even if the family refuses treatment, much can be accomplished with the latency age girl through school-related activities and relationships. The school counselor, the Girl Scout leader, the special education teacher, can do much of the therapeutic work.

The latency age child, regardless of how bleak is the reality of family life, will idealize her home and family, and will be terrified of losing her place there. There often will be recurrent nightmares about death and separation, or phobias about either leaving the house or being trapped inside the house. She will inevitably see her parents as more powerful than they are, and putting the parents into realistic perspective will be one of the continuing tasks of therapy. The issue of confidentiality must always be clarified with the late latency child who is trying to differentiate herself from her family without losing her secure place there. The therapist should explain to the child that the details of the child's play sessions are confidential, but that the therapist will be available to answer parents' questions, and that the therapist will let the child know before speaking with the parents.

Children in late latency seek out role models of the same sex, and it usually makes sense for therapy to follow this line of least resistance. For example, older sisters, especially if they were victimized too, can be helpfully involved in the therapy. Volunteers who were incest victims in childhood can also be helpful. Groups of late latency incest victims have worked well under male-female co-leaders. This system allows the girls to explore, and to relate to a healthy reality, their fantasies about how a grown-up man and woman relate to each other.[9]

On physical examination, many of the children over 9 years old will have the absent hymen and widened vaginal canal characteristic of repeated intercourse. Somatic symptoms are common in this age group, and are often the first sign of a serious depression secondary to the separation from home that is sometimes necessary after incest is reported.

The following case illustrates the pattern:

Case 5 Jamie, aged 11 years, was removed from her large, chaotic family because she had been having sexual intercourse with her father since age eight. Her family left the state after she reported incest. Physical examination was consistent with regular and repeated intercourse. Jamie did not talk about the sexual abuse, and said she could not talk about it with anyone except the police. She thinks a lot about testifying against her father. She daydreams that she and her siblings will be reunited someday in a foster home in the country. She has a recurring nightmare that her parents' car goes over the edge of a cliff. Her youngest sister is killed, and Jamie is crying, but her father says, "There's no need to cry. We never loved her anyway." Jamie often complains of pain in her stomach, chest, and head. She has been enuretic at night and has refused school saying, "I'll go back to school when everything is settled." She had straight As in school until the previous semester when she got a D in physical education because she refused to dress out. After that, she became afraid that she would fail and began to be truant. Play therapy was begun; Jamie was given practice in testifying, and she was sent back to school with special tutoring in those subjects she was afraid of failing.

The next case shows how a less symptomatic latency age child still manifests preoccupations with school and with loss, fantasizes extensively as a defense, and may develop somatic symptoms when stressed.

Case 6 Connie is a 9-year-old referred by her pediatrician because of pharyngeal and anal gonorrhea. She described a three-year relationship with her natural father which began after her parents divorced; she visited her father on school holidays. Physical examination showed small tears around the anal sphincter characteristic of anal intercourse; the hymen was intact. Her father is an alcoholic who had been jailed for incest at the time of the interview. In the playroom Connie played with soldiers who kept getting eaten by a crocodile. She said she has dreams about green slimy animals who sneak up and try to eat her. She commented about the dollhouse, "There are not enough rooms," and put all the child-dolls outside of the house. She daydreams about camping trips.

A year before she had told a 7-year-old school classmate about the forced sexual activity with her father. She and her friend had made plans to run away. They collected a tent, cooking pans, and other camping equipment in a vacant lot near the school. The teacher found them doing homework in the tent, about two hours after school dismissal, when the mothers reported that they had not returned home. The children were planning to attend school during the day and do yardwork in the after-noons to pay for food. Her mother scolded Connie for running away say-ing, "You might have been raped." She has frequent sore throats, and is afraid she will never have children "because of the things that have hap-pened." Connie said she did not want to talk about the sexual things her father did because "I don't like to talk about things; I like to do things."

THE ADOLESCENT VICTIM

The adolescent incest victim typically presents with runaways, promiscuity, or suicide attempts.[10] The mood swings of adolescence make great demands on the therapist who may find the adolescent "fine" and uninterested in discussing anything during the treatment hour but attempting suicide later that evening. Some adolescents will have decided to leave the home but may still be struggling with guilt about leaving. This conflict may become manifest in multiple unsuc-cessful placements. One 15-year-old victim went through 13 different placements in the first year after she reported sexual abuse. Group therapy is helpful for victims who have weathered the "acting out" phase of their reaction. Unlike the latency age victims, the adolescent vic-tim will want to explore the sexual details of the incest and her feelings about the perpetrator. An understanding general practitioner can be in-valuable in helping such adolescents deal with dating, birth control, rape prevention, drug use and abuse, and somatic symptoms (see Chapter 4). The incest pregnancy is a particularly tragic complication in this age group (see Chapter 12).

When one sees two victims of different ages in the same family, the developmental differences become apparent. The following case was a clear example.

Case 7 Dorothy, aged 11 years, has had poor school attendance since her mother was diagnosed as having a potentially fatal collagen disease. "I wouldn't mind the school work if I could do it at home. One reason I ditch school is to take care of my mother. Is there any way to treat that disease she has?'' Her school performance has improved since she revealed the ongoing sexual abuse with her stepfather. ''In court I'll say he's mean, a drunk, and powerful with hits. He thought I was asleep the whole time he had his finger in me. My mom doesn't want me to testify, but he didn't do anything to her. I want everyone there when I testify.'' Dorothy fantasizes that a ghost lives in her room and watches over her. She is having nightmares which she described and about which she drew detailed pictures. She is extensively involved in church activities.

Dorothy's sister Joan is 14. She is on probation for curfew violation and is sexually active with many boyfriends. ''My mom really does try to be a mother. She doesn't have close friends, and her temper gets out of hand. She's overworried by this court thing.'' About the sexual abuse: ''He said, 'lie down on the couch' and, like a fool, I did. I guess he was just horny. My mom wasn't enough for him. He was cruel to Mom. I could hear her scream in bed. I don't want to marry or have children. Married people fight. I don't really like sex but I do it anyway. It's confusing. I'm really a shy person and I get embarrassed easily.'' Joan complains of insomnia. She has a best friend.

Wheras the preadolescent sister was oriented toward school, church, and the idealized relationship with her mother, the adolescent sister is oriented toward peers and sees her parents in a deflatingly realistic light. The preadolescent is symptomatic at school; the adolescent violates rules and sexually misbehaves. The preadolescent communicates through fantasy and dreams. The adolescent talks directly about feelings and about sexuality.

The teenage victim has usually found some strategies for resisting the sexual abuse, and parents can often be overwhelmed even by a token resistance. The parent's distress can make it easier for the therapist to empathize with the abusive father of an adolescent. The father, who for years has been quietly getting away with the sexual relationship and who has not had to contribute much to the actual parenting of the child, now finds many chickens coming home to roost. The following are quotes from a 14-year-old who had been sexually abused since age nine but who had only recently begun to resist. ''A couple of months ago is when I started turning him down all the time. I was used to it when I was young. It didn't bother me. Then lately I thought maybe I was going crazy. I would get mad and cuss and hit the pillows and cry. I told him I hated him for what he's been doing to me. I feel like he owes me everything to make it up. After I told my grandmother, he promised me he would never do it again. Then he did it again, so I called the police. My father said, 'It was her fault, too.' That was when I told everyone in the family that I had called the police because I couldn't trust him. My dad can't keep his word. He's an alcoholic; he is not successful at working and he's not successful as a father.'' This adolescent described her mother in similarly unflattering terms, "Mother has to get her way, so she makes up fake headaches. I have learned not to be like her." In this case the parents could not tolerate the strengths emerging in their child and asked the grandmother to take custody.

The following case illustrates how one family was able to adapt to sexual abuse when it occurred in late latency but how that adjustment crumbled as the children became adolescents. This family also illustrates the chaos that can result when two adolescent incest victims attempt to live in the same household. The two victimized daughters can seem almost to be competing to see which can exact the worst punishment and extract the most attention from the no longer idealized parents; in another such family this competition culminated when one of the daughters burned down the family home.

Case 8 Mrs. Connor has been married four times and her two daughters are now 15 and 14. The 14-year-old, Linda, reported a six-year sexual relationship with her stepfather when Mrs. Connor returned to him after a marital separation. Three years earlier the older girl, Carol, then 12, had reported sexual abuse. Carol had said that her stepfather told her to take off her clothes, and that he then made her lie on top of him while he sang *Rock-a-Bye Baby* and put his finger into her vagina. On that occasion the younger sister, then 11, denied that anything sexual had happened to her. Mrs. Connor said that Carol was lying and should be put into a foster home to teach her a lesson. Mr. Connor said that perhaps his hand had slipped and he had touched Carol "where I shouldn't" but that everything was innocent. Carol retracted her accusation at that time.

Three years later, at the time of Linda's adolescent accusation, both girls had been expelled from school because of truancy. Carol experienced episodes when she spoke only in baby talk and hit herself compulsively. Linda had run away from home several times and had attempted suicide. Fighting had become constant between Linda, Carol, and their mother. Mrs. Connor's denial of the incest broke down when she joined a group of other mothers from sexual abuse families. After an episode of amnesia in the group, she revealed a system of five different personalities that she had used since adolescence "to keep myself together." She also revealed that she had herself been an incest victim. Mr. Connor gained enough support from a fathers' group to admit what he had done sexually with his stepdaughters. Physical and psychological examination showed that frontal lobe problems and impaired liver function had developed secondary to his chronic alcoholism. Both adolescents had to be placed in separate therapeutic group homes; the parents decided to divorce. It seemed that even with support this family no longer had the energy to resolve the many problems that had developed.

It is possible that, had this family come into treatment at the time of the first referral when the girls were still preadolescent, the mutual investment in family that characterizes the latency stage would have made it possible to work toward keeping the family together. Three years later the additional years of trauma, disillusion and symptom formation, and the development of an adolescent focus on identity had acted to transform the feasible treatment goal into helping family members to terminate their relationships with each other in order to seek individual fulfillment.

The Adult Victim

Most therapists have treated women who report prior incest experiences; such women comprise 5% to 20% of psychiatric outpatients.[11] However, many therapists forget to ask if the sexual relationship is continuing. If asked, some adult patients will describe being fondled by the father, being undressed by father, or even continuing to have intercourse with the father during family visits. We have even seen one case where it was the adult daughter who had become the tyrant of the relationship, threatening her father with exposure or with physical abuse if he tried to avoid her sexual advances.

Like adolescent victims, adult victims will present with suicidal depression or with sexual problems, usually at a time when these symptoms are threatening an important relationship such as the marital bond. About one third of women who have been raped multiple times are prior incest victims.[12] The realization that they are not able to protect themselves sexually may bring some women to treatment. Parenting is the major additional stress in the developmental lives of these adults. New presenting complaints are fears that they might harm their own child, fears that the father might sexually abuse his grandchild, fears that the extended family will never be a normal one because of all the secrets still present. The therapist needs to recognize the validity of these fears and to help the victim to take responsible self-protective action. It is therapeutic as well as legally sound for the therapist to insist on making a protective service referral if the perpetrator is living with minor children. The therapist may be found liable for damages if a child is sexually abused by the identified perpetrator after the therapist decides not to report.[13]

Group therapy is helpful and should focus on 1) abreacting aspects of the traumatic experience, 2) dispelling guilt by reviewing the experience from a shared adult point of view, and 3) clarifying moments in current situations when the woman responds as she did in the incest situation. Many women use these groups to design action plans to resolve their incest experience: confronting the perpetrator, confronting the mother, telling a spouse or a sibling about what happened.[14] Women seem relieved when they can bring to bear on the childhood trauma the tools of their maturity—autonomous rational thinking, decision-making, and responsibility-taking.

The following case illustrates some of the developmental issues which are important in adulthood.

Case 9 Roxanne is a 23-year-old housewife, three months' pregnant with her second child. She was referred to a psychiatrist by her obstetrician because "things from my past are bothering me to the point where I don't want the baby."

Roxanne's father began fondling her when she was 3 years old. Intercourse began when she was seven. When she was 15, she and her older sister went to the police with their complaint of sexual abuse. Their mother who has a chronic physical problem refused to believe them and testified in court against them. Roxanne's father was acquitted. The father reacted with anger when Roxanne married at 17. One year later he and his wife divorced. At that point, the father began visiting Roxanne while her husband was at work. "He helped me with my first baby a lot. My father puts me on a pedestal in a way." Intercourse resumed. Roxanne says she is certain that it is her husband who fathered this pregnancy, but she is deeply ambivalent about having the baby. She has now told her husband about the incest. Although she now finds sex with her father intolerable, she is not certain she can stop it.

In the history of this adult victim one finds echoes of all the earlier developmental problems: 1) Toddler—"I was a mean baby. I wet my bed, walked in my sleep, and had temper tantrums;" 2) Preschool—"Now mother blames me for what happened with my dad. I resented her not being there for us, but I wanted to protect her from being hurt too. Maybe the divorce was my fault;" 3) Latency—"I was not a good student; I was only interested in arts and crafts;" 4) Adolescence—"I didn't have too many female friends. I had boyfriends my dad didn't know about. I slept around a lot until finally I got gonorrhea." Coming after all these unresolved conflicts, the possibly incestuous pregnancy presented conflicts around generativity that could not be untangled without psychotherapy.

CONCLUSIONS

Depending on her developmental stage, the incest victim will present with different constellations of medical and psychological symptoms, and the physician's concerns and interventions will be different. The child under four will present with clinging and fears, and a communicated complaint about the assailant. The physician should examine the perineal area for redness and irritation due to penile rubbing. The assailant will often be absent, severely disturbed, or otherwise unavailable for treatment. However, the mothers are usually very willing to become involved in a therapeutic play school or in play therapy with the child.

The oedipal age child will present with severe medical complications of incest such as gonorrhea or perineal injury, with tantrums, or with parental neglect. The physician needs to focus on decreasing the child's guilt and on helping the parents to sort out their marital difficulties so they can respond to their child's needs for care. The fathers feel so guilty they often literally flee the situation, and the mothers may flee the child by rejecting her. Long-term play therapy and long-term placement of the child with a nonhostile relative should be considered.

The latency age child presents with school problems, somatic complaints, phobias, and fears of losing her comfortable place in the family. These children have the cognitive skills necessary to describe the sexual abuse, but are resistant to doing so except in fantasy play. With the exception of very disturbed families, parents and children are committed to each other and are willing to do therapeutic work to stay together.

Adolescent incest victims present with runaways, suicide attempts, sexual acting-out, and other behavioral problems. They use therapy to talk in a very direct way about sexuality and feelings. They are actively involved in the process of leaving home, and parents may need to work on their own individuation skills in order to allow the adolescent to become strong enough to leave them. The physician needs to ask about fears of incest pregnancy and to provide sex education and sex counseling in many areas. The therapist should be prepared for crises, especially if there are two or more adolescent incest victims in a single family. In family therapy it is often helpful to break the family into subunits or to ask individual family members to work in separate therapy groups in order to sharpen the focus on individuation and differentiation.

In the adult incest victims, problems around parenting and other aspects of generativity are important. The therapist should take seriously a victim's concern that the former perpetrator will find new victims in a new generation of granddaughters or nieces. It is prudent to ask if an adult complaining of prior incest continues to be unable to say no to the incestuous partner.

Arguments continue about whether victims under 12 are more or less harmed by incest than are older victims.[15,17] Bender[15] felt that the younger victim was less likely to be harmed by the experience. Recent studies have supported this view, but link it to the longer duration of incest in children who report later.[16] From a developmental point of view, this question may be so complex that it has no helpful answer. "Children under 12" include the oedipal child who is rejected by her mother, loses a loving father, and suffers a frightening medical complication; this category also includes the late latency victim who is able to stop the relationship early and to repress memories of the experience. Although both children are under 12, they may have very different outcomes to incest

90

situations that have developmental impacts and meanings which are quite different.

In a group of incest victims who later presented as psychiatric patients, 33% (2 of 6) had been victimized between ages 4 and 7.[11] In a group of incest victims who presented as child abusive mothers, 21% (4 of 24) were in that age group. Only 6% of incest victims (1 of 15) in a "normal" control group described the prior incest as having occurred during the oedipal stage.[17] These data would support the simple hypothesis that the developmental and family pressures on the preschool victim increase her risk for later sequelae. It may be that similar analyses of other outcome data will make more precise the developmental pathways that lead to the late sequelae of incest.

REFERENCES

1. Berlin I: Parents' developmental crises: Treatment of the child. Presented at the Annual Meeting of the American Psychiatric Association, Toronto, May 1978.

2. Berlin I: Opportunities in adolescence to rectify developmental failures, in Feinstein SC, Giovacchini PL, Looney JG et al (eds): *Adolescent Psychiatry, Developmental and Clinical Studies, Volume VIII*. Chicago, University of Chicago Press, 1981, pp. 225-240.

3. Sgroi S: Molestation of children: The last frontier. *Child Today* 4:18-21, 1975.

4. Brant RST, Herzog JM: Sexual abuse of children under three years of age. Presented at the Annual Meeting of the American Academy of Child Psychiatry, Atlanta, 1980.

5. Gebhard PH, Gagnon JH, Pomeroy WB, et al: *Sex Offenders: An Analysis of Types*. New York, Hoeber Medical Books, Harper & Row, 1965.

6. Kempe RS: Individual treatment planning for the abused and neglected child. Presented at the Third International Congress on Child Abuse and Neglect, Amsterdam, April 21-25, 1981.

7. Greenberg NH: The epidemiology of childhood sexual abuse. *Pediatr Ann* 8:289-299, 1979.

8. Sarnoff C: *Latency*. New York, Jason Aronson, 1976.

9. Gottlieb B, Dean J: The co-therapy relationship in group treatment of the sexually mistreated adolescent. Presented at the Second International Congress on Child Abuse and Neglect. London, September 12-15, 1978.

10. Goodwin J, Zouhar M, Bergman R: Hysterical Seizures: A sequel to incest. *Am J Orthopsychiatry* 49:698-703, 1979.

11. Rosenfeld A: Incidence of a history of incest among 18 female psychiatric patients. *Am J Psychiatry* 136:791-795, 1979.

12. Miller J, Moeller D, Kaufman A, et al: Recidivism among sex assault victims. *Am J Psychiatry* 135:1103-1104, 1978.

13. Forward S, Buck C: *Betrayal of Innocence*. Los Angeles, J.P. Tarcher, 1978.

14. Tsai M, Wagner NN: Therapy groups for women sexually molested as children. *Arch Sex Behav* 7:417–427, 1978.

15. Bender L, Blau A: The reaction of children to sexual relations with adults. *Am J Orthopsychiatry* 7:500–518, 1937.

16. Tsai M, Feldman-Summers S, Edgar M: Childhood molestation: Variables related to differential impacts on psychosexual functioning in adult women. *J Abnorm Psychol* 88:407–417, 1979.

17. Goodwin J, McCarty T, DiVasto P: Prior incest in abusive mothers. *Child Abuse Neglect* 5:1–9, 1981.

8

Simulated Neglect as a Sequel to Physical and Sexual Abuse: The Cinderella Syndrome

Jean Goodwin
Catherine G. Cauthorne
Richard T. Rada

In this chapter we will describe three adopted girls, aged 9 and 10, who falsely alleged that their adoptive mothers dressed them in rags, made them do all the chores, and favored their stepsiblings. Underlying these false accusations of abuse was a history that included: 1) actual abuse of the child in a previous placement; two of the three had been sexually abused, 2) early loss of a mothering figure, and 3) emotional abuse in the adoptive home. Professionals involved in child protection need to recognize this syndrome because intensive family therapy and temporary placement of the child outside the home are required in all cases. The child's false accusation of abuse is a cry for help and should not be dismissed as a manipulative fabrication.

When professionals responsible for child protection discover that a child has exaggerated, fabricated, or simulated abuse, they tend to respond by simply closing the case. However, we have previously shown that false accusations of sexual abuse are often a child's way of calling for help in a family situation that has become desperate for other reasons.[1] This chapter describes a similar pattern in false accusations of child neglect. In the three cases we report, the child's false accusation of neglect called attention to underlying family dysfunction that did require the intervention of a child protection agency.

The adopted girls in these three cases of simulated neglect had complaints remarkably like those of the fairy-tale heroine Cinderella. Each falsely alleged that her stepmother dressed her in rags, made her do all the chores, and showed preference for her stepsiblings. All three girls had been adopted by relatives after suffering the traumatic death of an early mothering figure.

The children's Cinderella-like accusations functioned at several levels as a cry for help: 1) they were being emotionally abused and probably would have been physically abused had their false accusations not led to the involvement of a child protection agency and their temporary removal from the home, 2) they had never resolved experiences of abuse and abandonment that occurred before adoption, and 3) all three stepmothers had been abused as children and needed to integrate those past experiences before they could fully accept their stepdaughters. In addition, the Cinderella tale mapped inner conflicts that these children needed to explore in treatment. All of the families were hostile to psychotherapy. It was only under pressure of the legally mandated investigation triggered by the child's false accusation of neglect that these families allowed the troubled child to receive needed treatment.

Case Reports

Case 1   Adele, a 9-year-old girl, was referred to a child protection agency when a policeman found her wandering outside school clad only in an undershirt and panties. She explained that because she had been unable to finish her chores at home, her adoptive mother had locked her out of the house. She said her adoptive parents often took her stepsiblings on outings, leaving her at home to do all the chores. A family interview established that Adele had taken off her own clothes and hidden them.

Adele's biological mother died when Adele was 1 year old. Adele was then placed with another relative, an alcoholic woman who neglected and physically and sexually abused her. This woman died when Adele was six; she was then adopted by her current parents. Her adoptive father was also her uncle.

Adele's adoptive father who held two jobs tended to be distant and aloof. His wife, herself sexually abused and brutally beaten as a child, was an anxious woman with many compulsive rituals who bitterly resented Adele's uncontrollable behavior. The stepsiblings became angry with Adele for upsetting their mother. Adele said she wanted to be a member of the family and to get all her chores done.

The adoptive parents decided to voluntarily place Adele in foster care while she received therapy. They refused family therapy, but the mother agreed to participate in joint sessions with Adele's therapist. After four months, Adele was reintegrated into the adoptive family.

Case 2 Betty, a 9-year-old girl, was referred by the school because she came to class in shabby clothes and without shoes. Betty said her adoptive mother had thrown away her shoes as punishment for not cleaning under the bed. A family interview established that Betty had changed into shabby clothes on her way to school.

Betty had been adopted into this family at age six. Her adoptive mother was her biological mother. Because Betty's mother was an unmarried schoolgirl when Betty was born, Betty was raised from birth by a friend of her mother who was killed in an auto accident when Betty was six. This foster mother had been overprotective and indulgent, keeping Betty on a bottle until age four. After the foster mother's death, the girl's biological mother forcibly removed her from the foster home, not telling the child until a year later that she was her biological mother. Betty had many questions about her biological father, but her mother refused to speak of him.

The mother's present husband was a volatile man who refused to become involved with Betty. The mother felt frustrated about disciplining Betty, saying that the child responded to reprimands by tearing up clothes and toys. Betty's adoptive/natural mother had been the victim of sadistic abuse as a child. The stepsiblings resented Betty and physically abused her by locking her in the doghouse and feeding her dog food. Betty had frequent stomachaches, had one episode of hysterical paralysis, and daydreamed that a race car driver would come and rescue her. After a year of play therapy, Betty was able to be in the home only on weekends. Her adoptive parents still refused to become involved in her treatment and finally agreed to place Betty permanently with other relatives.

Case 3 Carol, a 10-year-old girl, was referred to a child protective agency by a passerby. Carol had run up to this man and told him that her adoptive mother had kicked her and was keeping her home from school to do all the household chores. Carol used terms such as "child sexual abuse" in describing her problems. A family interview revealed that the bruise Carol offered as evidence of being kicked had been sustained in a baseball accident and that she had refused to go to school because she had not been given the part of the princess in a school play. At age nine, Carol had claimed that her adoptive mother was trying to drown her in the bathtub. That complaint had been dismissed as fiction, and therapy was not offered.

Before her adoption, Carol had been an abused child raised in a psychotic family situation. Carol's psychotic mother had abused her by tying her hands and forcing her head into the toilet. Carol first lived with her adoptive parents at ages five and six while her mother, a relative of the adoptive father, was psychiatrically hospitalized. At age seven, Carol returned to live with her mother who had remarried. The new stepfather began a sexual relationship with Carol. Within a year, Carol's mother committed suicide.

When Carol was nine, her current parents adopted her; their only biological child, a blind and severely retarded son, had been institutionalized shortly before. Soon after her adoption, Carol had one episode of hysterical blindness. The adoptive father held two jobs. He was ashamed of the mental illness of his relative, Carol's natural mother, and refused to allow Carol to speak of her. The adoptive mother had been sadistically beaten as a child by her mother and had been sexually abused by her father, but never complained about these incidents because she feared that she would not be believed. She felt defeated by Carol, something she denied having felt with her severely handicapped son, and she spanked Carol hard enough at times to leave bruises. Carol was not certain that her natural mother was dead and daydreamed about returning to her.

Carol was placed in a foster home. The foster mother complained that Carol refused to go to school or to do chores and that she made false accusations against her foster siblings. After three months of family therapy, Carol was able to be with her adoptive parents on weekends. However, the family ultimately decided that Carol should be placed permanently with other relatives.

DISCUSSION

These three cases were the only documented instances of simulated neglect seen over a three-year period in a child protection agency that screens 150 complaints of neglect each month. Since the children were treated by different therapists, their remarkable similarities were not recognized until a systematic review of the agency's cases.

Child protection workers are understandably reluctant to make the judgment that a child is lying about parental abuse. One case report[2] described a 3-year-old whose allegation that his mother beat and burned him was dismissed as a false accusation planted by his father who was estranged from the mother. Four months later this child was beaten to death by his mother. The cases reported here make the additional point that even if the worker is correct in judging a child's accusation to be a lie, other kinds of abuse may still be occurring in the home.

These three cases are remarkably similar and appear to represent a specific syndrome. All three children were 9- or 10-year-old girls who had entered their adoptive homes at about age six. Each had experienced the traumatic death of an earlier mothering figure before adoption. Two of the girls had been sexually abused in their earlier homes; two had developed hysterical symptoms after adoption (one paralysis and the other blindness). The adoptive fathers were emotionally distant and unavailable to the children. The adoptive mothers had been severely abused as children and were appalled at being regarded as "bad" mothers, in part because that was how they viewed their own mothers. There was intense rivalry with stepsiblings in all cases. Betty was physically abused by her stepsiblings, and Carol developed the symptom of blindness, which mimicked the handicap of her stepbrother.[3]

The false accusations made by these girls closely resemble the complaints of the fairy-tale heroine Cinderella. There is one report[4] of a 5-year-old girl who briefly took on the role of Cinderella, complaining that her mother made her do the hardest chores, made her sleep in the ashes, and favored her younger sister. The three girls reported here had similar complaints, but they were unable to deal with their grievances in fantasy or in play; instead, they presented them as realities. There is a disillusion that any girl of this age experiences as her mother becomes a taskmaster, a rival, and a person with many loves, rather than the always indulgent child-centered mother of infancy. For the girls described here, that disillusion was made unworkable by the circumstances that forced them to actually switch to a new mother just as this developmental change in their perception of the mothering figure was emerging.

In the original fairy tale, Cinderella's grief for her dead mother is a central issue. *Cinderella* is one of a series of fairy tales which includes *Cap o' Rushes* (the source for Shakespeare's *King Lear*), and several tales like *Thousandfurs* and *Manekine* in which the father's incestuous desire for his daughter is explicitly described as the cause of the child's wandering and loss of her birthright (see Chapter 15). The normal rivalry of the oedipal-age girl with her mother is intensified by actual incest with the father and, should the mother die at the height of this intense competitive conflict, the child may experience the unconscious fear that she caused the mother's death.[5] The girl must blot out all negative feelings about the mother in order to avoid intolerable guilt about her mother's death. In the Cinderella story these negative feelings were displaced and projected onto the stepmother, and the dead mother was idealized.

Sibling rivalry is particularly intense for the Cinderella child, partly because she feels that her parents prefer her siblings to someone guilty of incest and murder, and partly because she may provoke victimization by her siblings to punish herself and assuage her guilt. The therapeutic solution prescribed in the fairy tale was for Cinderella to complete the grief work for her mother—in the story she watered a tree on her mother's grave with her tears daily—and to accept the tasks requested both by the "bad" stepmother and the "good" fairy godmother. This acceptance of chores is a nucleus for the identification with the mother that must supplant rivalry.

Treatment of these cases is complex. Strategies include family therapy, individual therapy for the adoptive parents, and play therapy for the children. Family therapy defines the situation as a family problem and resists the family's effort to find a scapegoat. In our cases individual play therapy focused on helping the child to mourn the idealized dead mother and to give up fantasies of reunion with her. It was critical for the therapist to visit the child in her home—as did the prince in the fairy tale. These children tended to shamefully conceal from the therapist the rejecting and lacerating family battles that constituted the actual abuse;

the false accusation was a face-saving version of the actual situation revealed in the home visit.

The therapist had to monitor the family situation carefully throughout treatment because premature therapeutic interventions tended to trigger new cycles of simulated abuse. When the child felt rejected or blamed because of a therapeutic confrontation, she would provoke or invent a situation in which she felt unfairly abused by the family. This process assuaged the child's guilt and renewed her hopes that she might be rescued by a perfect, fantasized family, perhaps with the therapist. However, this acting out also provoked actual rejection and abuse by the outraged adoptive family. Ultimately, the "wicked stepmother" had to be brought into the child's treatment in order to break this cycle.

Therapy with the adoptive parents focused on their unresolved feelings about the child's lost parent and about their own parents. Two of the adoptive fathers—Carol's and Adele's—felt intense rage and shame about their psychotic female relatives who had abused these girls and thus would not allow the girls to speak of these mother-figures. Similarly, the adoptive mothers needed help in resolving their anger and guilt about their own abusive mothers and childhood experiences of sexual abuse. The adoptive mothers' guilt about childhood incest fostered their identification with the girls' guilt-ridden attempts to degrade themselves as well as their mothers. They seemed unconsciously gratified that the adoptive daughters were voicing complaints that they themselves had never dared to make; at the same time, the false accusations freed these mothers from the dangers of surpassing their own mothers by being "good," nonabusing mothers.[6] As the adoptive mothers' fear and rage lessened, they were better able to consistently enforce the performance of chores and to allow the girls to identify with them in more positive ways.

Although they are rare, cases involving simulated child abuse should be actively evaluated by professionals. In each of these three cases of simulated abuse, actual physical abuse or neglect was subsequently uncovered.[7] It is possible that more severe abuse would have occurred had the child's simulated abuse not brought her family to professional attention.

REFERENCES

1. Goodwin J, Sahd D, Rada R: Incest hoax: False accusations, false denials. *Bull Am Acad Psychiatry Law* 6:269–276, 1978.
2. Kaplun D, Reich R: The murdered child and his killers. *Am J Psychiatry* 133:809–813, 1976.

3. Rada RT, Meyer GG, Kellner R: Visual conversion reaction in children and adults. *J Nerv Ment Dis* 166:580–587, 1978.

4. Rubenstein B: The meaning of the Cinderella story in the development of a little girl. *Am Imago* 12:197–205, 1955.

5. Bettelheim B: *The Uses of Enchantment.* New York, Alfred A. Knopf, 1976, pp 236–277.

6. Shainess N: The structure of the mother encounter. *J Nerv Ment Dis* 126:146–161, 1963.

7. Goodwin J, Cauthorne C, Rada R: Cinderella syndrome: Children who simulate neglect. *Am J Psychiatry* 137:1223–1225, 1980.

9 Hysterical Seizures in Adolescent Incest Victims

Jean Goodwin
Mary Simms Zouhar
Robert Bergman

This chapter describes six cases of hysterical or conversion seizures occurring in adolescents who had previously experienced incest. Eight similar cases have been reported in the psychiatric literature. The simultaneous occurrence of these two uncommon conditions suggests a causal connection. In addition, the cases described have other characteristics in common and appear to define a specific syndrome.

Galen, the second century Greek physician, believed that seizures were the result of premature intercourse in childhood.[1] This is not too distant from Freud's perception that the hysterical seizure repeats a traumatic event.[2] The Navajo Indians have recognized for centuries a syndrome that includes incest, seizures, suicide attempts, and witchcraft. When a Navajo has a seizure, it is often assumed that she has experienced incest and may be a witch.[3] The Navajo phrase for epilepsy includes the word for incest. It is said also that the act of incest plants a moth embryo in the brain. As this moth matures, it will draw the incest offender into the fire. A case has been reported of a Navajo incest victim who fell into a fire during a seizure and was seriously burned.[4]

Our first two cases were drawn from the experience of two of the authors. After noting the similarities between these two cases, we reviewed the records of 12 psychiatric admissions for hysterical epilepsy.

Four of these 12 patients had reported prior incest. This finding and data from 25 previously reported cases of hysterical seizures[5] suggest that at least 10% of such seizures are associated with prior incest. Better recognition of this syndrome would be of diagnostic and therapeutic importance.

Case Reports

Case 1 *A* was an Anglo teenager hospitalized at age 14 following convulsions in the detention center in which she was placed after running away from home for the second time. Two weeks previously, her natural father had had intercourse with her. He was an alcoholic who had been separated from the family since this child was four. She said that her father had been seductive with her before this episode, as had a maternal uncle. The father admitted having had intercourse with her. *A* was sexually active with peers and had threatened suicide. She said that she was conscious during the seizures and that they usually occurred when she was alone. She said that she had had them as a child but no one had ever seen them before. Seizure activity included fine, rapid trembling of all extremities, and mouth movements that resembled a silent scream. She recalled having "shaken all over" whenever her mother whipped her. Electroencephalogram was normal. Conversion disorder with hysterical seizures was diagnosed. Psychotherapy was begun and the seizures disappeared, but promiscuity and runaways continued as problems.

Case 2 *B* was an Anglo girl who was first seen psychiatrically in mid-adolescence because of runaways and self-mutilating behavior. Psychomotor epilepsy had been diagnosed when she was five, despite repeatedly negative electroencephalograms. Seizures consisted of "automatic behavior"—usually lying down and taking off her panties—followed by violent thrashing movements that left her severely bruised. Despite the violence of her seizures, she experienced a feeling of control during convulsions. Phenytoin and phenobarbitol were begun and continued until she entered intensive psychotherapy in her mid-20s. In therapy she disclosed a history of genital fondling by her mother, which extended from infancy to age six. At that time, she refused further contact from her mother but entered a relationship with a cleric, which included undressing and mutual masturbation. She became promiscuous as a teenager, but seizures were often triggered by sexual contact. Seizures decreased in psychotherapy and her antiepileptics were discontinued. It was determined that her 20-year history of seizures had been hysterical rather than organic in origin.

Case 3 *C* was an Anglo who presented at age 17 with seizures characterized by dizziness, stiffness, and jerking. She said she had had seizures as a child but had not complained of them. These episodes were precipitated by anger, and *C* could be roused from seizures. Electroencephalogram and brain scan were normal. In hospital she disclosed a brief incestuous relationship with her stepfather at age ten. This was explored in conjoint sessions with C and her mother, and the seizures disappeared. C had attempted suicide and had run away from home earlier in adolescence. She had been a practicing homosexual since a two-week marriage, which she left because she found the experience of intercourse "horrible." The marriage immediately preceded the onset of seizures. She was diagnosed as having hysterical seizures and an intermittent depressive disorder.

Case 4 D was an Anglo woman who presented at age 18 with seizures that she said had started at age five "but nobody ever noticed them." The seizures began with an aura of flashing colored lights; D would then fall to the ground and thrash from side to side while groaning. She described being raped by a teenage neighbor at age five; she remembered having been left by him lying on the ground crying and rocking from side to side. After this, she began a sexual relationship with her brother, which ended a few months prior to her complaining about seizures. Electroencephalogram was negative and seizures disappeared in hospital. The seizures were diagnosed as hysterical. D said she had never had orgasm and had been "on the road" for two years since running away from her home and from the incestuous relationship. She had attempted suicide twice. Psychological testing showed a schizotypal personality.

Case 5 E was a 17-year-old Spanish American woman whose left temporal lobe epilepsy had been diagnosed at the age of eight. The diagnosis had been confirmed electroencephalographically. She was psychiatrically hospitalized after overdosing with her seizure medication. In hospital she disclosed incestuous relationships with a younger brother, a paternal uncle, and a first cousin, which had taken place between ages 8 and 12. Her mother confirmed this. Over the two years preceding hospitalization, E had developed a new type of seizure in which she would scream and strike out at people; her usual seizures were brief absence attacks with urinary incontinence. The violent seizures cleared in hospital. She had run away from out-of-home placements as well as from her own home. She was promiscuous, but very naive about menstruation and pregnancy. She was diagnosed as having a mixed personality disorder with hysterical seizures, in addition to temporal lobe epilepsy.

Case 6 F was a Navajo girl evaluated at age 15 because of promiscuity, multiple runaways, and suicide attempts. She had been diagnosed as having temporal lobe epilepsy at age five. At ten, she entered an incestuous relationship with her stepfather which ended when she became pregnant by him. After this, her seizures became uncontrolled on medication. The seizures changed in character, becoming longer, and involving more violent limb movements. She felt she could partially control these seizures. Electroencephalography showed abnormalities in the right temporal lobe, but the seizures were not accompanied by electroencephalographic change. These violent seizures disappeared after psychotherapy was initiated. Psychological testing showed a mixed character disorder with depression. This girl was probably uniquely at risk for incest because of the cultural belief that her epilepsy was a sign of incest. It was felt that hysterical seizures had been superimposed on the temporal lobe attacks after her incestuous experience.

DISCUSSION

These six cases share characteristics in addition to the history of prior incest. All six patients experienced relief from their hysterical seizures when psychotherapy began to explore the incest experience. All six had histories of running away from home; all had either threatened or attempted suicide. Four were promiscuous, one was nonorgasmic, and the sixth was homosexual. All presented psychiatrically in their teenage years. Prior incest should be suspected in cases of hysterical epilepsy which present in this way, since psychotherapy is rapidly effective in such cases.

Review of the psychiatric literature revealed four additional cases. Schechter and Roberge[6] described a 14-year-old American Indian boy who convulsed on his way home from church after hearing a sermon about incest. He was involved in incest with his sister. This boy was not Navajo but had been influenced by other American Indian folk-beliefs that associate incest with epilepsy and witchcraft. McAnarney[7] reported the case of a 15-year-old Anglo girl who presented with hysterical seizures and subsequently revealed ongoing incest with both father and brother.

Standage[5] collected 25 cases of hysterical seizures. No systematic effort had been made to obtain complete sexual histories of these patients, and many were interviewed by neurologists rather than by psychiatrists. Despite this, 2 (9%) of the 21 women in the sample reported prior incest experiences. One of these patients had been diagnosed as having petit mal epilepsy at age three. However, in adolescence she developed more violent attacks in which she would fall to the ground and injure herself. During an amobarbital interview, she revealed a long history of incest with her father. The other patient experienced her first seizure at age 15, shortly after her alcoholic father attempted intercourse with her. Seizures consisted of her spitting; screaming, "Don't touch me"; throwing her limbs about widely; and assuming the position of arc de cercle. Seizures stopped when she was allowed to live apart from her father. In another case report[8] an adolescent girl with hysterical seizures described, under amobarbital, a sexual attack. However, because there was no physical evidence of intercourse, her account was assumed to be fantasy.

Recently, Meir Gross[9] reported four cases of incest victims aged 13 to 15 who presented with hysterical absence attacks or convulsions. All four had either threatened or attempted suicide. All four perpetrators were alcoholic fathers and the girls' "ictal" amnesias seemed to mimic their fathers' "alcoholic blackouts" as a defense against taking responsibility for the sexual involvement.

Early in his career, Freud postulated that many hysterical symptoms resulted from early sexual traumata. However, he did not publish any cases of hysterical seizures resulting from incest. Freud later modified this trauma theory, taking the position that most hysterical symptoms result not from actual incest, but from anxiety caused by incestuous wishes and fantasies.

We obtained independent confirmation of prior incest in all six cases reported here. Four of the six women reported sexual assaults by more than one perpetrator, and one of the four cases in the literature involved multiple incestuous relationships. In our cases this multiplicity results not from the child's tendency to fantasize such relationships, but from a powerful compulsion to repeat an early overwhelming experience. We had expected that some Navajo epileptics would present with fantasized accounts of childhood incest because of the cultural belief that this must have occurred. Temporal lobe seizures that include an orgasmic aura might also produce such fantasies.[10] However, we have not been able to confirm any such case of incest fantasy in a Navajo epileptic. It did seem, however, that in Case 6 the Navajo child was uniquely at risk for incestuous acting out because she was epileptic. Levy[3] has found that among female Navajos with grand mal epilepsy 30% have experienced incest. In true epileptics the incest experience usually develops after the onset of seizures as relatives realize that this child is not protected by the incest taboo. These epileptic children are at risk for rape, illegitimate pregnancies, and murder, as a result of the family and community scapegoating engendered by the disease. Psychoses, hysterical reactions and suicide attempts are also frequent in these epileptic Navajo women. In Navajos with hysterical epilepsy the incest precedes the seizure.

It is possible that epileptic children other than Navajos (as Case 5) are also at higher risk for incest. A "special" or "different" epileptic child may be less clearly protected by the incest taboo.[6] A similar and familiar situation is the incest victimization of retarded children in Anglo-American culture. There is often a feeling that such children are "fair game." One pediatrician belatedly and reluctantly reported to authorities a family in which all three sons were having intercourse with their retarded sister. The pediatrician asked, "Isn't it better to save three normal boys rather than one retarded girl?"

We could not document suggestion or contagion as explanations for the concurrence of childhood incest and hysterical seizures. Navajo beliefs about epilepsy and incest are known only to a few anthropologists and physicians; the Navajo are so reluctant to talk about epilepsy that the condition is not even mentioned in most Navajo ethnographies. It is very unlikely that any of the Anglo patients reported on here knew of these Navajo beliefs. None of the patients were hospitalized simultaneously or treated by the same therapist.

The similarities among these cases led us to question whether hysteroepilepsy might be a particularly natural symptom choice in incest victims. The incest victim experiences guilt, conflict between pleasure and shame, and fears of being controlled or of being damaged or punished.[11] The hysterical seizure repeats movements related to sexual stimulation, as well as those related to resisting sexual assault. Weiss[12] pointed out that the position of arc de cercle is highly unsuitable for intercourse; however, this position is also an exaggeration of the back-arching that occurs in orgasm and childbirth. The sense of control described by many victims may refer to the power of the convulsions to control their own tensions, as well as the power to influence and frighten observers. Instead of being terrified herself as she was in the sexual attack, the patient who repeats the attack in a pseudoepileptic mode is able to terrify others. Through her unconscious control of the hysterical attack, the victim identifies with the aggressor in the original sexual attack. The seizure disorder often helps the child attain realistic control, acting to reconcile the girl's mother and to reinvolve her in a parental relationship with the child.

Hysterical seizures serve other defensive functions. The victim magically substitutes the conversion symptoms for the more fearful punishment that might come from an outside source. In three of these six cases, seizures were described as "violent." Freud observed that bodily damage during convulsions was not necessarily diagnostic of "true" seizures in patients who have unconscious needs for self-mutilation. The amnesia that the victim experiences during her hysterical "attack" strengthens the defenses of repression, denial, and dissociation, which are often used to forget the original sexual attack. Also, by having "epileptic attacks" in public, the child can release some of the tension associated with keeping the sexual attack secret. A symbolic identification of the epileptic attack with the prior sexual attack is seen not only in the sexual characteristics of the observed seizures, but also in the child's description of the present illness. Three of the four women without coexisting "true" epilepsy dated the onset of their seizures to the time of the first seduction, but said that "seizures" had occurred secretly at that time. For girls who have dealt with the incestuous activity by pretending to be asleep during the act, the questions from physicians about whether they are "really" unconscious during or after seizures mirror their own questions about how conscious they are allowed to be. They may violently resist the suggestion that they were "really" awake during the seizure because this would mean they were "really" awake during the incest and must therefore assume the blame for what happened.

It is often assumed that folk-beliefs act as self-fulfilling prophesies to create hysterical symptoms. Observation of the six cases reported here has led us to an alternative hypothesis. Navajo and European beliefs that incest and epilepsy are connected may be based on valid psychological connections between the experience of childhood incest and the symptom of hysterical seizures. These folk-beliefs may result from observation of these symptoms in incest victims in the community.

These psychodynamic underpinnings of Navajo and Greek beliefs about incest and epilepsy led us to question whether other folk-beliefs about incest may rest on similar observations of a fairly uniform pattern of traumatic neurosis in incest victims. Weinberg[13] described beliefs about incest in 11 cultures. Banishment was the most common punishment for incest, occurring in 7 of the 11 cultures. Suicide was enforced on incest participants in five cultures. Two of the cultures predicted sterility for incest participants and two believed that incest led to magical power.

This tetrad of banishment, forced suicide, sterility, and magical power is similar to the clinical picture of runaways, suicide attempts, sexual dysfunction, and narcissistic difficulties that were present in the six patients discussed in this paper. Devereaux,[4] in his description of shamanism as a sequel to incest among the Mojave Indians, demonstrated how this particular cultural prescription channels the isolation and guilt of incest participants, allowing them a special role in which their dissociative symptoms can be used as a way to help others. Banishment may have functioned to resolve the deep ambivalence about separation that occurs in incest situations. Many of the founders in creation myths are incest participants. This may parallel the clinical observation that creativity and complete ego functioning can occur only after the incest participant has achieved a meaningful separation from his family (see also Chapter 15).

The Navajo belief that epilepsy results from incest is based on underlying psychological realities valid in many cultures. It may be better understood as a valid psychological insight than as a culturally determined pathogenic influence.[14]

CONCLUSION

The physician should always take a complete sexual history when pseudoseizures are in the differential diagnosis. In a teenager with atypical seizures and a history of incest, suicide attempts, and runaways, it may be possible to diagnose hysterical seizures by history alone. If the seizures recapitulate movements and vocalizations that occurred during the sexual event, if the onset of seizures coincides with a major change in the incest ritual, if seizures disappear once the incest is discussed with the family, the seizures are probably psychogenic. However, since two of our

108

six patients with pseudoseizures had organically based seizures as well,[15] a complete neurological examination including electroencephalography is also important.

REFERENCES

1. Temkin O: *The Falling Sickness*. Baltimore, Johns Hopkins Press, 1971.
2. Freud S: Some general remarks on hysterical attacks (1909), in *Standard Edition* 9:229–234, 1959.
3. Neutra R, Levy J, Parker D: Cultural expectations versus reality in Navajo seizure patterns and sick roles. *Cult Med Psychiatry* 1:255–275, 1977.
4. Devereaux G: The social and cultural implications of incest among the Mohave Indians. *Psychoanal Rev* 8:510–533, 1939.
5. Standage K: The etiology of hysterical seizures. *Can Psychiatr Assoc J* 20:67–73, 1975.
6. Schechter M, Roberge L: Sexual exploitation, in Helfer R, Kempe CH (eds): *Child Abuse and Neglect: The Family and the Community*. Philadelphia, Balinger, 1976.
7. McAnarney E: The older abused child. *Pediatrics* 55:298–299, 1975.
8. Glenn T, Simonds J: Hypnotherapy of a psychogenic seizure disorder in an adolescent. *Am J Clin Hypnos* 19:245–249, 1977.
9. Gross M: Incestuous rape: A cause for hysterical seizures in four adolescent girls. *Am J Orthopsychiatry* 49:704–708, 1979.
10. Warneke L: A case of temporal lobe epilepsy with an orgasmic component. *Can Psychiatr Assoc J* 21:319–324, 1976.
11. Lewis M, Sarrel P: Some psychological aspects of seduction, incest and rape in childhood. *J Am Acad Child Psychiatry* 8:606–619, 1969.
12. Weiss E: A contribution to the psychological explanation of the Arc de Cercle. *Int J Psychoanal* 6:323, 1925.
13. Weinberg S: *Incest Behavior*. New York, Citadel, 1955.
14. Goodwin J, Simms M, Bergman R: Hysterical seizures in adolescent incest victims. *Am J Orthopsychiatry* 49:704–708, 1979.
15. Liske E, Forster F: Pseudoseizures: A problem in the diagnosis and management of epileptic patients. *Neurology* 14:41–49, 1964.

10 Suicide Attempts: A Preventable Complication of Incest

Jean Goodwin

Suicides and suicide attempts are among the many complications that accrue in the wake of an incest event. In *Oedipus Rex,* that foremost of incest stories, the "victim" mutilates himself by plucking out his eyes, the "perpetrator" Jocasta commits suicide, and a nonparticipant in the incest, their child Antigone, ultimately hangs herself. In a series of German cases where fathers were convicted of incest in court, Maisch[1] reported that 2 of the 63 fathers (3%) committed suicide after conviction. Roberts and Hawton report that in 20% of 114 families where physical abuse had occurred, a parent made a suicide attempt after the report.[2] We have previously described a triad of runaways, suicide attempts, and sexual misbehavior in teenagers whose seizures are determined to be conversion responses to prior incest.[3] It is not known what percentage of all suicide attemptors belong to incestuous families. It has been estimated that 3% to 5% of suicide attemptors abuse their children.[2]

This chapter presents a study which reports on the frequency of suicide attempts in families where sexual abuse had been substantiated. The aim is to define how often and under what circumstances suicide attempts occur in incestuous families so that involved professionals can be better prepared to cope with this complication.

109

METHODS

In a busy protective service agency that provides treatment to families where intrafamilial sexual abuse has been substantiated, records were reviewed for suicide attempts that occurred during a 2½-year study period. Intrafamilial sexual abuse was defined as exploitative sexual behavior toward a child by a socially defined family member (this includes stepfathers and stepbrothers). Two hundred and one cases were substantiated during the study period; fathers, stepfathers or common-law fathers were the perpetrators in over 80% of cases. The 201 study families were followed from 3 months to 33 months after the substantiation of sexual abuse, and all suicide attempts recorded in the casework charts were tabulated. Suicide attempts were defined as self-destructive behaviors taking place in the context of a suicidal plan. Suicidal threats were excluded.

RESULTS

Thirteen suicide attempts occurred in 11 families; that is, attempts occurred in 5.4% of the 201 treated families. Five suicide attempts occurred in mothers and eight attempts occurred in daughter-victims during the 2½ years. Six attempters were Anglo (English-speaking Caucasians), five were Spanish-American, one was Black, and one American Indian. None of the suicide attempts was life-threatening, and no completed suicides occurred. No attempts occurred in perpetrators or in uninvolved fathers or siblings. It may be relevant for understanding this absence of suicidal behaviors in perpetrators that only five perpetrators were successfully prosecuted during this time.

Suicide Attempts in Mothers

Three of the five suicidal mothers were diagnosed as having borderline personalities and drug abuse problems, and had made prior suicide attempts. All three took overdoses in the first week after the revelation of an atypical sexual abuse situation; for example, in one case a teenage stepson forced oral sex on the mother, and he was sexually abusing his 6-year-old brother as well. As might be expected given the poor reality testing of these mothers, a prolonged period of confusion about what was actually happening sexually in the family characterized the investigations in all three cases. These three mothers had themselves been incest victims in childhood, and were so panicked by the repetition of the sexual trauma that they were unable to cope with the immediate realities of their children's needs. Two mothers had to be psychiatrically hospitalized. Professionals who interviewed these mothers at the time of the suicide attempts were amazed at how rapidly the mothers reintegrated their lives and their maternal functioning. These mothers readily misinterpreted agency decisions as harsh criticism. One suicide attempt was aborted when the mother telephoned her therapist while taking pills and discovered that there was no plan to remove her child from her custody. Another mother interpreted the placement of her child with her mother (the grandmother) as a rejection and condemnation of her mothering abilities as she became more suicidal.

The two mothers who made suicide attempts later than the first week of accusation and crisis came from families where more usual patterns of father- or stepfather-daughter incest had occurred. One mother overdosed a month after the incest disclosure, on the night before a legal decision had to be made about whether her daughter would be placed. The mother had decided to leave her husband and keep her daughter, but after the overdose, she reversed her decision, and placement of the daughter was arranged. The second mother overdosed five months after the incest disclosure when she learned, on the same day, that her daughter could not be psychiatrically hospitalized and that her husband was leaving her. Both these mothers felt torn between the husband and the daughter. The suicide attempt communicated a protest at feeling forced to choose the daughter. Both these women were depressed with dependent personalities. One of the two responded well to tricyclic antidepressants; the other did not respond. However, neither was able to reestablish a mothering relationship with her daughter despite extensive treatment. Both daughters went on to attempt suicide themselves as they struggled with their side of the guilt about losing the mother-daughter relationship.

All five mothers were young women (aged 24 to 32) involved in ambivalent struggles with their own mothers as well as with their daughters. All described feeling unable to forgive their mothers for prior abandonments, and feeling that their mothers in turn would never forgive them if they abandoned their daughters. One woman had been abandoned at age two by her mother; another had been scapegoated by the family since "turning mother in for child abuse" at age 14; another had never forgiven her mother for keeping her from her father's deathbed. Another said, "I hate my mother. She made me marry at 14. If I kill myself, my daughter will have a good home." Still another said, "My mother will never forgive me now." It was impossible for these mothers to imagine mobilizing the resources necessary to adequately mother their children, but it was equally impossible for them to face the blame from their mothers and the self-blame for failing at that task. In addition, four had been surgically sterilized and the fifth had been told she was sterile secondary to multiple bouts of gonorrhea. The knowledge that they could not bear substitute children must have increased their panic at the possibility of losing the victimized daughter.

Suicide Attempts in Victim-Daughters

In this retrospective review, all eight suicide attempts in daughters occurred in victims aged 14 to 16. This is the peak age for adolescent suicides;[4] however, the median age for sexual abuse victims referred to this agency is ten years. Three attempts occurred more than one year after the child disclosed incest. It is almost as though the 14 to 16 age range developmentally produces a vulnerability to suicide regardless of the age at which the incest occurred or was revealed. It may be that the combination of adolescent sexual experimentation and adolescent exploration of values rekindles feelings of moral repugnance about the incest, which may be directed toward the self as well as toward parents. Three of the suicide attempts occurred immediately after a sexual crisis with a boyfriend, such as a first experience with breast petting.

None of the eight had been diagnosed as depressed; however, the behavior problems seen in seven of the girls may have been signs of masked depression. Five had been runaways, four were truant, three were promiscuous, and two were abusing drugs. These kinds of behavior can mask depression in teenagers.[5] None of the teenagers was treated with antidepressants.

The suicide attempt was only one of many severe complications in these cases. None of the eight families managed to remain intact after the reporting of the incest. Either the father or the victimized daughter had moved out of the home. Such an outcome will occur in less than one half of the families treated by our agency which has, as a priority, keeping families together. In all cases the mothers actively blamed the daughters for the breakup of the family and, at times, refused to believe that incest had occurred. One mother physically abused the daughter for disclosing the incest; another voluntarily relinquished custody of her daughter "for telling." Two of the mothers had previously attempted suicide in response to the incest accusation.

Like the mothers who attempted suicide, these suicidal victims directed most of their anger at their mothers. Their comments about their mothers were bitter: "Mother will want my sister back, but not me." "If I have to go back to my mother, I'll just give up."

In three cases the victim's suicide attempt occurred at a point when the victim interpreted the agency's actions as siding with the mother in condemning the girl for having made the accusation. In one instance the daughter had left therapy and returned to live with her incestuous stepfather; despite this, the therapist had neither remonstrated with the family nor reported the situation to the authorities. In a second case the agency had threatened to drop custody of the child because of the victim's misbehavior. And in a third situation the agency had just placed the youngest and only unmolested daughter with the abusing father. (He was in treatment and was the most stable family member, but the sister experienced the decision as one more occasion when her complaints were minimized and her father was the one chosen to be trusted.)

In six cases precipitants of the suicide attempts were incidents which intensified the daughter's grief and guilt about having made the family disintegrate: a visit from an accused and now accusing father, a visit from a depressed and lonely sister, assaultive behavior by the now estranged father, and in three cases the dissolution of a foster placement.

The two attempts that occurred about one year after disclosure of the incest may have signalled anniversary reactions. In both cases the teenagers were able, after the suicide attempt, to cease ruminating about the incest situation and to become more productively involved with work and peers.

Seven of the eight daughters overdosed, using a variety of drugs ranging in lethality from antibiotics to heroin. The other attempter pushed her hand through a window. Only one of these children was hospitalized after the attempt, and three were able to keep the attempt secret from their families and their therapists, and did not discuss what they had done until months afterward.

SUMMARY

Suicide attempts occurred in 5.4% of 201 families where sexual abuse was substantiated and families were followed from 3 to 33 months. It is likely that this percentage will rise as the duration of follow-up lengthens. No attempts were seen in perpetrators or in uninvolved siblings. The absence of suicide in perpetrators may be secondary to the rarity of prosecution in our jurisdiction. Mothers who made attempts within the first week after disclosure of the incest had severe personality disorders with histories of prior incest in childhood and of prior suicide attempts. They swiftly returned to successful mothering. Mothers who made suicide attempts later in treatment were depressed and did not reestablish a mothering relationship with the victim. Victims who made suicide attempts were between 14 and 16 years of age, and tended to have behavior problems. Their families were not able to remain intact through the incest crisis and their mothers blamed the victims for this. Attempts were triggered by incidents which made the victim feel that mother was right to blame them, or by incidents which rekindled their grief at the dismantling of their families.

IMPLICATIONS

Despite the retrospective nature of the study, the data suggest several preventive interventions which are simple and consistent with good case management.[6]

1. Mothers who become panicked and lose touch with reality when sexual abuse is revealed deserve a thorough psychiatric evaluation and reassurance that they will not lose their children if hospitalization is necessary.

2. All mothers facing a sexual abuse accusation should be asked about prior sexual abuse in their own childhoods and about prior suicidal thoughts and behaviors.

3. Mothers and victims over 14 should be screened for depression, and depressions should be actively treated. Two studies, which have screened consecutively-identified incest mothers for depression, report that over one-half are found to be significantly depressed[7] (see also Chapter 4). In surveying consecutive psychiatric evaluations in my own practice, I found that 7 of 20 incest mothers were prescribed psychotropic medication as compared to only 1 in 20 physically abusive mothers. Four women in each group had made prior suicide attempts. Tricyclic antidepressants were the drugs most commonly prescribed to incest mothers. In prescribing such potentially lethal drugs for these women, one must be concerned not only about their own potential to use medication suicidally, but also about suicidal misuse by their husbands or daughters.

4. Incest victims with behavior problems and disintegrating families who are between 14 and 16 should be asked about suicidal thoughts and plans. Such children should be followed at least until the first anniversary of the incest accusation.

5. Case management decisions in cases where suicidal behavior is a risk should be examined from the point of view of the suicidal family member. Is this decision saying, "You are a bad mother"? Is it saying to the victim, "Your mother is right, you did this on purpose"? Such decisions should be discussed at length with the family in a way that leaves the door open for further clarification and for calling the therapist rather than taking an overdose. When a mother or daughter becomes suicidal, her relationship with her own mother should be explored. It may be necessary to bring the maternal grandmother or another grandmother-figure into the family's treatment to provide support and to dispel shame and guilt.

REFERENCES

1. Maisch H: *Incest*. New York, Stein and Day, 1972.

2. Roberts JC, Hawton K: Child abuse and attempted suicide. *Br J Psychiatry* 137:319–323, 1980.

3. Goodwin J, Simms M, and Bergman R: Hysterical seizures: A sequel to incest. *Am J Orthopsychiatry* 49:698–703, 1979.

4. Teicher JD: Suicide and suicide attempts, in Noshpitz JD (ed): *Basic Handbook of Child Psychiatry*. New York, Basic Books, 1979.

5. Anthony EJ: Two contrasting types of adolescent depression and their treatment. *J Am Psychoanal Assoc* 18:841–859, 1970.

6. Goodwin J: Suicide attempts in sexual abuse victims and their mothers. *Child Abuse Neglect* (in press).

7. Browning DH, Boatman B: Incest: Children at risk. *Am J Psychiatry* 134:69–72, 1977.

11 Female Homosexuality: A Sequel To Mother-Daughter Incest

Jean Goodwin
Peter DiVasto

With increasing attention to the problem of incest, better understanding of the complexity and variability of such relationships has emerged. Reports describing homosexual incest between males[1] have appeared only in the past 20 years. Awad, in his review,[2] found only five reported cases of father-son incest and one reported case of mother-daughter incest. However, data from retrospective surveys indicate that the incidence of homosexual incest may be higher than suggested by these few case reports. A retrospective review of the histories of 1500 male child psychiatric patients showed that six (0.4%) had experienced father-son incest.[3] A German survey found that 4 of 78 incest cases involved father-son relationships and that one involved mother-daughter incest.[4]

This chapter reviews five cases of mother-daughter incest and elaborates on one further case. Two cases of grandmother-granddaughter incest will be reviewed and some patterns seen in homosexual incest between females will be described.

Previous Reports

The two previously reported cases of grandmother-granddaughter incest are similar in that both grandmothers were ill when they initiated

117

the children into sexual relationships. Barry and Johnson[5] describe a nurse who came into psychotherapy because of anxiety about her dislike of elderly female patients. As a teenager, this woman had engaged in mutual masturbation with a terminally ill grandmother. The child was simultaneously involved in an incestuous relationship with her father. The latter she experienced as guilt-free, but she felt ashamed about the relationship with the grandmother and ended the sexual activity at age 15. A case report from Germany[6] describes a 74-year-old woman who made her 8-year-old granddaughter manipulate the grandmother's genitals "to strengthen the abdomen." The grandmother was found to be abusing barbiturates and to have hypochondria with depression and dementia.

The five cases of sexual contact between mother and daughter deviate in some ways from the usual definition of sexual abuse as the sexual exploitation of a child by a caretaking adult.

Weiner[7] describes a sexual relationship between a mother and her 26-year-old daughter. The daughter had been in foster homes since infancy and first met the natural mother at the onset of their four-month-long sexual relationship. The daughter subsequently married and had five children before being hospitalized with depression at age 39, at which time she disclosed the relationship. Since this case involves consenting adults and a natural mother who was not her caretaking figure, it does not qualify as sexual abuse even though the relationship was biologically incestuous.

Two cases reported from Germany involve multiple familial perversions and are also dissimilar from most cases of incest. In one case[6] the mother physically abused her 6-year-old son and 5-year-old daughter while smearing them with excrement. While beating the daughter, the mother would masturbate the girl with her hand or with a shoehorn. The father was involved as a spectator. Both parents were alcoholic. Maisch[4] describes a case in which the stepfather's perverse sexual needs led to mother-daughter as well as father-daughter incest. This man came to depend, for sexual arousal, on watching his wife masturbate while she described fictitious lesbian experiences. When he began a clandestine relationship with his pubertal stepdaughter, he insisted on the same preintercourse performance. Eventually, he persuaded his wife and daughter to stage lesbian dramas for him. After watching them engaged in mutual masturbation, he became sexually excited and had intercourse with both mother and daughter.

The reported mother-daughter relationships which most resemble the more common father-daughter patterns of sexual abuse are those reported by schizophrenic women who describe childhood sexual relationships with mothers.[8] In one case a woman who became psychotic in college described a ritual which began at puberty. Her mother would frequently have the child strip while the mother commented on the ugliness of the child's body and made the child do special exercises to correct these defects. A few years later when the mother became terminally ill, she frequently had the child massage her. Sexual aspects of this idiosyncratic relationship are so mixed with other material, it is unclear that it can be defined as incest. A more clearcut case involves a 30-year-old married woman who came into treatment after a psychotic episode. Early in treatment she complained of her father's seductiveness. Later, she revealed that she had always slept with her mother and that at night the mother would lie behind her and fondle her breasts. This woman was unable, even as an adult, to refuse her mother this favor until she had been in treatment for many months.

The following case describes a mother-daughter relationship which shares many characteristics with father-daughter incest. The sexual contact began in early puberty and was ended by the daughter several years later. The mother initiated the sexual contact in the context of a deteriorating marital relationship. The secret remained shrouded in amnesia, confusion, and shame, and was not revealed by the daughter until her second year of psychotherapy. This is a unique case of mother-daughter sexual contact in that the mother was a practicing homosexual outside the home and the daughter later engaged in overt homosexuality.

Case History

J was a 28-year-old Anglo graduate student, who entered psychotherapy on the recommendation of her physician. Her presenting problem was migraine headaches of several years duration. J presented herself as a bright, verbal, somewhat hostile woman. She related a five-year history of severe migraine-like headaches which began when she returned to her parents' home after an unsuccessful attempt to emancipate herself by attending a distant university.

J was the only child of a highly religious, energetic woman and her quiet, withdrawn husband. The family lived in a small town where her father was employed as an engineer. The family interactions were controlled by the mother who made excessive demands upon both her daughter and her husband. The father would respond by withdrawing emotionally and taking as many business trips as possible. When J was approximately 6 years old she began sleeping in her mother's bed. The parents had had separate bedrooms for approximately a year prior to this. The mother's explanation for the new sleeping arrangement was that she "got lonely." They continued to sleep in the same room for eight years. At the same time J had a room of her own, which her mother fanatically insisted she keep neat; she even refused to let the child play in this room.

When J was prepubertal, she awoke on several occasions to find her mother leaning over her after having kissed her. After she reached puberty, there were two incidents in which she awoke to find her mother fondling her breasts. At age 14, J awoke after feeling a hand on her genitalia. Like the previous experiences, this had a dream-like, unreal quality. Soon after this, *J* demanded that she return to sleeping in a bed of her own. Her mother reluctantly agreed. Her mother then occasionally shared her bed with a female friend. *J* was convinced this was a sexual relationship and wished her father would demand that the relationship cease.

When *J* was 18, her father died and she attempted to leave home to attend college. Her mother soon fell ill and demanded that *J* return home to care for her. *J* did this and soon found a job. She then entered into a series of homosexual relationships, which characteristically ended with *J* rejecting her partner. *J* eventually convinced her mother to move to a town with a university and there she completed school.

J entered psychotherapy to gain relief from her headaches. She was hesitant to discuss her family history and was guarded in general. The process of psychotherapy focused on her ambivalent strivings to emancipate herself from her mother. Early in treatment she slashed herself in a mutilating suicidal gesture after a disagreement with her mother. After a year of therapy, which included chemotherapy for depression, she was able to move out of her mother's home.

She embarked on a short courtship which ended in marriage to a young man with whom she shared many mutual interests. She had hopes that mother would no longer intrude into her life after the marriage, but these have proven untrue. She remains in therapy, although at less frequent intervals.

DISCUSSION

This case of mother-daughter incest more closely fits the definition of sexual abuse than do the five prior cases. Nevertheless, both therapist and patient were uncertain at times as to whether these incidents were indeed sexual abuse or simply part of the normal closeness that exists between mothers and daughters. Had these same incidents occurred with the father rather than the mother, it would have been clear that these incidents were sexual and exploitative in nature.

Examination of the anthropological and psychiatric literature reveals that physical closeness between mothers and daughters is much less subject to taboo than are father and daughter contacts. In some cultures mothers commonly fondle the genitals of their nursing infants. This occurs among the Hopi in North America, the Siriono in South America and the Alorese in Indonesia.[9] In Western culture mothers tend to show more emotional and physical closeness toward their daughters than toward their sons.[10] This closeness has been shown to have positive effects[11] and may be biologically necessary in preparing girls to nurture their own children.

This greater toleration of physical intimacy between mothers and daughters makes it more difficult for the child, the parent, and eventually the therapist to recognize when these contacts become incestuous.

The ambiguity of the taboo makes it more difficult for the child to set limits upon the mother. Children in other cultures may face similar ambiguity. Among Anatolian peasants, genital stimulation of nuising infants is prescribed; however, some individuals, as adults, recall the experience as disturbing, and wonder if the mother crossed some undefined line (Michael Meeker, personal communication). We have found that a useful guideline in defining mother-daughter incest is to ask oneself, "Would I consider this to be incest if the father were the initiator?"

Since the reports of mother-daughter incest are both few and brief, we can only make tentative statements in regard to this form of incest. These mothers seem to be similar in some ways to those mothers who initiate mother-son incest.[12,13] Most notably, they are aggressive women who have abandoned their maternal role for an exploitative relationship with their children. The mother's need for nurturance, especially while she is physically ill, often precipitates a sexual relationship with the child. In both of the grandmother-granddaughter cases and in one of the mother-daughter cases, illness in the perpetrator precipitated the sexual contacts. In *J*'s case the mother used her own illnesses to maintain her long-time hold on her daughter.

The sexual contact in the reported cases varies greatly. It ranges from voyeurism through kissing and fondling to mutual masturbation. In both cases of grandmother-granddaughter contact and in two of the cases of mother-daughter incest, sleeping in the same bed was the precursor to more explicit sexual contact. Kaplan and Poznanski[14] found that daughters who sleep with mothers constitute a distinctive sub-group of child psychiatric patients. The five mothers they studied were involved in deteriorating marriages. The fathers were passive but very angry with their wives because of the sleeping arrangements. The mothers were seen as using the sleeping arrangement as a means of avoiding sex with the husband.

The victims of mother-daughter incest presented with a variety of serious symptoms. These included encopresis, depression, psychosis, and migraine headache with homosexual acting out. One of the granddaughter victims presented with mixed phobic and neurotic complaints. This picture of varying psychotic, depressive, and psychosomatic complaints is similar to the sequelae of father-son incest. The presenting symptoms in the child victims of father-son incest have included: 1) sex play with sister,[15] 2) effeminate behavior and suicidal gestures,[16] 3) drug-induced psychosis and homosexual fears,[17] 4) acute psychosis and homosexual encounters,[18] and 5) eczema and delinquent behavior.[2]

In one of the mother-daughter cases and in one of the grandmother-granddaughter cases, the victim's presenting complaint was sexual abuse by the father. Careful therapeutic work was required before the victim could reveal the homosexual incest as well. In two of the other cases, the father was an active participant in sexual activity between mother and daughter. These observations lead to a concern that mothers may be more actively involved in cases of father-daughter incest than previously thought.

The case of *J* described homosexual behavior in the daughter as a sequel to mother-daughter incest. It also involved a mother who was a practicing homosexual outside of the family. This pattern has been described in father-son incest. In 2 of the 5 reported father-son cases, the father had been a victim of homosexual incest as a child.[17,18] One had been a practicing homosexual for many years. Two of the victims of father-son incest developed homosexual behaviors. This raises the question of whether homosexual incest may be less rare in families of homosexuals. However, there is as yet no evidence that the children of homosexuals are at any special risk.[19]

Previous studies have discussed female homosexuality as a consequence of heterosexual incest. A survey, which compared homosexual and heterosexual women in a non-patient population, found a significantly higher incidence of prior incest among homosexual women (7% *vs* < 1%).[20] In this case of mother-daughter incest the homosexual experimentation seemed to be part of the girl's attempt to find a resolution to the incest by repeating it. This may be similar to the heterosexual promiscuity that is a symptomatic solution chosen by some victims of heterosexual incest. Recently, two additional cases have been published,[21] in both of which the victim of mother-daughter incest subsequently developed homosexual fantasies or relationships. One of these women identified with the mother to the extent of sexually abusing her younger sister in an even more brutal way than her mother, who was abusing both daughters, had done. Victims of heterosexual incest may resort to homosexuality as a way out of the anxiety and the sexual dysfunction that heterosexual contact would precipitate.

CONCLUSION

Mother-daughter incest is probably more common than the rare case reports would indicate. To facilitate the identification of such cases, the following is suggested:[22]

1. Examine reports of mother-daughter physical contacts with the question in mind, "Would this contact be judged incestuous if the initiator had been father rather than mother?"
2. Explore in detail those family situations in which mother and daughter share a bed.
3. Consider the possibility of active involvement by mother in father-daughter incest cases.

"Softer" clues which should also prompt the therapist to consider homosexual incest include:

A. The reliance of a physically ill mother on a particular daughter for nurturance.

B. The presence of overt homosexuality in either mother or daughter.

REFERENCES

1. Cory W: Homosexual incest, in Masters REL (ed): *Patterns of Incest.* New York, Basic Books, 1963.
2. Awad GA: Father-son incest: A case report. *J Nerv Ment Dis* 162:135–139, 1976.
3. Dixon KN, Arnold LE, Calestro K: Father-son incest: Underreported psychiatric problem? *Am J Psychiatry* 135:835–838, 1978.
4. Maisch HS: *Incest.* New York, Stein and Day, 1973.
5. Barry MJ, Johnson A: The incest barrier, *Psychoanal Q* 27:485–500, 1958.
6. Cabanis D, Phillip E: The paedophile homosexual incest in court. *Dtsch Z Gesamte Gerichtl Med* 66:46–74, 1969.
7. Weiner IB: On incest: A survey. *Excerpt Criminol* 4:135–155, 1964.
8. Lidz RW, Lidz T: Homosexual tendencies in mothers of schizophrenic women. *J Nerv Ment Dis* 149:229–235, 1969.
9. Ford CS, Beach FA: *Patterns of Sexual Behavior.* New York, Harper & Row, 1951.
10. Diamond M: Biological foundations for social development, in Beach FA (ed): *Human Sexuality in Four Perspectives.* Baltimore: Johns Hopkins Press, 1977.
11. Miller TW: The effects of core facilitative conditions in mother on adolescent self-esteem, *J Soc Psychol* 100:147–148, 1976.
12. Weinberg SK: *Incest Behavior.* New York, Citadel Press, 1955.
13. Wahl CW: The psychodynamics of consummated maternal incest. *Arch Gen Psychiatry* 3:188–193, 1960.
14. Kaplan SL, Poznanski E: Child psychiatric patients who share a bed with a parent. *J Am Acad Child Psychiatry* 13:344–356, 1974.
15. Bender L: *A Dynamic Psychopathology of Childhood.* Springfield, Charles Thomas, 1954.
16. Rhinehart JW: Genesis of overt incest, *Compr Psychiatry* 2:338–349, 1961.
17. Langsley DG, Schwartz MN, Fairbairn RH: Father-son incest. *Compr Psychiatry* 9:218–226, 1968.
18. Raybin JB: Homosexual incest: Report of a case involving three generations of a family. *J Nerv Ment Dis* 148:105–110, 1969.
19. Green R: Sexual identity of 37 children raised by homosexual or transsexual parents. *Am J Psychiatry* 135:692–697, 1978.
20. Gundlach RH: Sexual molestation and rape reported by homosexual and heterosexual women. *J Homosexuality* 2:367–384, 1977.
21. Forward S, Buck C: *Betrayal of Innocence.* Los Angeles, J.P. Tarcher, 1978.
22. Goodwin J, Divasto P: Mother-daughter incest, *Child Abuse Neglect* 3:953–957, 1979.

12 The Incest Pregnancy

Lydia Roybal
Jean Goodwin

This chapter will review the theoretical importance of the incest pregnancy and the studies which have documented the genetic hazards of incest. It will also describe the clinical problems that develop when the accident of pregnancy intervenes in a family already enmeshed in an incest situation.

The Incest Taboo and the Incest Pregnancy

The incest taboo appears in all times and all cultures, and students of human beings have stressed the importance of understanding it as a universal taboo. In some of the most widely accepted theoretical explanations for the incest taboo, it is the incest pregnancy which is singled out as the intolerable eventuality against which the taboo is guarding. The sexual relationship itself threatens social and familial priorities, but it is the potential for progeny that creates a disequilibrium serious enough to warrant proscription.

The biological explanation for the origin of the incest taboo hinges on the increased risk of damaged offspring when close relatives mate. Long before modern genetics had precisely defined these risks, there was a popular impression that incestuous offspring were somehow degenerate, both mentally and morally.[1] Such genetic fears led to laws forbidding sexual intercourse among consanguineous relations; these are the "incest" laws which survive in many states. The genetic hazards of incest are now understood to include both 1) an increased risk of homozygosity which may lead to mortality, malformation, or decreased ability to adapt and to procreate, and 2) other genetic and extragenetic effects that decrease fertility in the offspring.[2]

Anthropological explanations of the incest taboo[3,4] focus on its efficacy in extending social contacts and promoting interdependency among human groups. In some cultures the belief is stated quite matter-of-factly that human beings would never leave the security of the family home unless driven by the desire to mate and by the taboo against mating within the family unit. The incest taboo, together with the biological drives toward mating and procreation, forces families to create the network of cooperative and economic bonds that is necessary for human survival.

Explanations which depend more on intrapsychic realities point out how disruptive is the incest situation to family functioning. Incest violates generational boundaries, and superimposes rules for behavior between lovers on the contradictory rules about how father and child interrelate. Jealous rivalry between mother and daughter is dissonant with the behaviors prescribed in their parent-child roles. The incongruity between behaving as a daughter to the father and behaving as mother to the father's child strains even our culture's streamlined kinship terminology. The incestuous father would be both father and grandfather to such a child; the incest victim's brothers are uncles to the child and also half-brothers; the infant's mother is also its half-sibling. Anthropologists argue that the incest taboo is designed to prevent such conflicting and incongruous situations which are psychologically intolerable.

The "Typical" Incest Situation

In 70% to 80% of incest cases, it is a father or father-figure who is involved with a daughter in the sexual relationship.[5,6] There are probably many reasons for this. The taboo on mother-son incest is so powerful as to prevent the occurrence or at least the confession of this type of incest, except in very disturbed families. In most cultures not only the mother, but all maternal relatives are more stringently interdicted as sexual partners than are paternal relatives.[7] Sexual relations between siblings seem often to be experienced as sexual play rather than as incest; the current Anglo-American focus on the nuclear family provides few opportunities for incest to occur between extended family members. In about one half of the cases of father-daughter incest, it is the natural father who is involved. The balance of cases involve stepfathers.[2]

The incestuous father is often a man who was emotionally deprived as a child. He seeks the nurturance denied him as a child through his new family. He is therefore overinvested in his family. As well as being a social introvert, he is unable to develop any outlets outside the family. Weinberg[8] has called these fathers "endogamic." The father is usually of average intelligence and without major psychiatric disorder (such as psychosis or pedophilia) or criminal tendencies (sociopathic personality). He limits his social and sexual contacts to his family. He is usually the dominant figure in the family; this dominance may become paranoid in nature if any family member (especially his sexual partner) begins to form social relations outside the home.

Mothers are as needy and dependent as the fathers, if not more so.[9] The mother's own mother was often unavailable and hostile. Since the mother is unable to fulfill her role as "mother," she relinquishes her duties as mother and wife to her daughter. She withdraws sexually from her husband, and subtly encourages her daughter to take on sexual aspects of the wifely role. Mother's desperate dependence emotionally and economically on father perpetuates the incest situation. She cannot assert herself against her husband to protect the daughter, and, indeed, silently sanctions the incestuous arrangement.

Daughters are usually eldest daughters (64%, according to Weinberg) and are locked into a role-reversal situation with the mother. The daughter's relationship with her mother is usually poor. She may inadvertently seek affection from father, even sexual affection, for she is often socially isolated and in need of human contact. Secondary gain plays a role in sustaining the incestuous relationship, since this incest victim is often showered with special presents and privileges. Daughters may also see themselves as the only person who can hold the family together through pacifying the father.

Pregnancy as an Exit from the Incest Situation

As can be seen, incest is a triangular situation perpetuated by many emotional and social factors. The incest relationships last several years[2] and terminate in a number of ways. Some possible exits are: 1) the daughter refuses to continue the relationship, 2) the daughter leaves home, 3) the mother, the daughter, or another family member argues with father and reports the incest, or 4) the daughter becomes pregnant (venereal disease rarely provides a similar exit into a medical discovery of the incest).

The frequency of incest pregnancy has been quoted in several studies. It ranges from 1.7% in Meiselman's study[2] in California in the 1970s, to 50% in Kubo's study[10] in Japan in the 1950s. Weinberg[8] found a 20% frequency of pregnancy; Maisch[11] found the same frequency when studying a similar group of forensically-identified cases in Germany.

Merland et al from France[12] reported that 14% of incest victims were pregnant. De Francis,[5] in a 1965 study of 269 incest victims in New York City, found that 29 (11%) were pregnant. Meiselman's low figure for pregnancy frequency fits into a pattern of declining frequencies in this country since the 1960s; Gligor,[9] in 1966, found that only 7% of victims were pregnant. In New Mexico in 1977, a survey showed that 10% of victims were pregnant.[13] In 1980 in a New Mexico county with an active treatment program for incest, less than 1% of victims were pregnant. The increases in use of the birth control pill and in sex education in the schools have probably influenced this observed decline in frequency. Forensic series of cases always seem to include more pregnancies than do series identified by therapists, perhaps because cases involving pregnancy are more likely to be prosecuted.

The figures would also support a hypothesis that exit from the incest situation via pregnancy occurs less often when other exits become more available, such as reporting and treatment.

Genetic Risks in Incest

The child of a biologically incestuous union is at higher risk for malformation, both because of the increased risk of autosomal recessive disease and because of an increase in the risk of polygenic malformation. For mates who are unrelated, the probability of their having a child with an autosomal recessive malformation depends on the carrier frequency of the deleterious gene in the general population. For mates who are genetically related, the probability of recessive disorder in the offspring varies with the percentage of shared genes in the parents. The following hypothetical case is an expanded version of an example used by Sarah Bundey:[14]

> The carrier frequency of Hurler's disease in the general population is 1/150. The probability that a carrier for Hurler's will mate with another carrier in the general population and have an affected child is 1/600 (1/150 × 1/4). On the other hand, if that carrier were to marry her first cousin the probability increases to 1/32: the proportion of their shared genes (1/8) times the risk that both recessive genes of the carriers would sort into a homozygous affected child (1/4). If the carrier for Hurler's mates with her father, the probability of having an affected child goes even higher: 1/2 (the proportion of shared genes in father and daughter) × 1/4 = 1/8; that is, there is one chance in eight that the child will be affected, as opposed to the 1 in 600 risk that would have prevailed had the woman chosen an unrelated mate.

As can be seen, the probability of having a homozygous child with a major single-gene defect increases with increasing shared genes. It is estimated that every individual carries 3 to 8 detrimental genes.[15]

In addition, children of an incestuous mating also have an increased possibility of having a polygenic malformation. These abnormalities are caused by many genes in combination. Since related parents have more shared genes, their risk of having offspring with polygenic malformations is also increased.

The translation of theory into actual data has been studied by several authors. Most studies of consanguinity have been evaluations of third-degree relatives, (matings between first cousins). Unfortunately very few studies have looked at offspring of the first-degree relatives usually involved in clinical cases of incest. The following is a review of existing studies on children of consanguineous matings.

Third-Degree Relatives: Matings Between First Cousins

Spontaneous Abortion Fraser and Biddle[16] measured the percentage of spontaneous abortion in first-cousin marriages. They found that 15.5% of pregnancies in the first-cousin group ended in fetal loss, compared to 13% for the control group. They concluded "There is no appreciable increase of recognizable fetal loss attributable to rare recessive genes." These percentages are in concordance with those found in Chicago by Slatis and co-workers.[15] They reported a rate of spontaneous abortion of 14.5% in first-cousin matings vs 13% in the control group. A study of consanguinity in Japan showed that inbreeding had no significant effect on the rate of fetal loss.[17] However, one study done in Iran[18] does report that the rate of spontaneous abortion as well as later mortality and morbidity are significantly higher in first-cousin matings. In the Iranian study, the rate of spontaneous abortions in controls was 9.5%, and the rate in related offspring was 14.5%. It is unknown whether this difference is due to environmental factors, such as available prenatal care, or is a pure result of inbreeding.

Mortality Many studies report a higher mortality rate for offspring of consanguineous matings. In these genetic studies, mortality is usually defined as neonatal or infant mortality plus later deaths resulting from congenital conditions. Naderi[18] found a 3.9% mortality in offspring of first-cousin matings vs a 2.6% mortality in controls. Fraser et al[16] reported an 8.8% mortality in the consanguineous offspring vs 4.1% in controls. In their Chicago study, Slatis and co-workers[15] found mortality figures of 8% in related couples and 2% in control couples. In the consanguineous group two children died of cystic fibrosis, one of von Gierke's disease, and one of muscular dystrophy. All these disorders are thought to be transmitted by autosomal recessive genes, creating a "nonrandomness" in the increased mortality among the consanguineous offspring. All 17 deaths in the Slatis study occurred in 12 of their 209 families.

Malformations As with mortality, anomalies in offspring of related partners are higher than in controls. Slatis et al[15] examined abnormalities which "seriously interfered with the processes of a normal life." Disabilities secondary to infection were included, since resistance to infections is genetically mediated. Using those criteria, major disabilities were found in 15% of consanguineous offspring and 10% of the control offspring. Naderi[18] found that the frequency of congenital abnormalities was 4% in consanguineous matings *vs* 1.6% in nonconsanguineous matings.

Second-Degree Relatives: Uncle-Niece Matings

Mortality In a study of Moroccan Jews by Fried and Davies,[19] the mortality rate in the consanguineous offspring (N = 131) was 16.8%. The control group's mortality rate was 6.7%.

Malformations Congenital abnormalities were found in 7.6% of incest offspring but in only 2.2% of the control children. In three of the consanguineous sibships a particular anomaly was manifested in more than one child.

First-Degree Relatives: Father-Daughter and Brother-Sister Matings

The more closely related two partners are, the more genes they share. This increases the probability that autosomal recessive disease and polygenic malformations will be expressed. Since first-degree relatives share one half of their genes, they run the highest risk for expression of deleterious genes.

Mortality Carter[20] reviewed the outcome for 13 offspring resulting from incestuous matings between first-degree relatives. Their mortality rate was 3 in 13, or 23%. All children who died had genetic diseases. The diseases and deaths were directly attributed to the incest. Seemanova's study[21] of 161 incest offspring also reported a higher mortality rate than has been reported for offspring of second- or third-degree relatives. Of the incest cases, 13% died (21 of 161) compared to 5.3% in the control group (5 of 95). Death again could be attributed to genetic problems resulting from the first-degree mating. Examples of abnormalities causing death in this study were cystic fibrosis, tetralogy of Fallot, cerebral degeneration, and lymphosarcoma in a child with cerebral palsy. None of the control children who died had congenital abnormalities. Adams and Neel[22] found a mortality rate of 16.7% in their study of 18 incest offspring. One of the deaths was attributed to glycogen storage disease, one to prematurity, and the third to respiratory distress syndrome. None of the control children in this study died.

Prematurity Prematurity was also more prevalent among the incest group in Seemanova's study.[21] Twelve percent of the incest pregnancies ended in premature deliveries *vs* 6% in the controls. On the other hand, Adams and Neel[22] found no difference in prematurity rates.

Malformations In the offspring of first-degree relatives, the frequency of congenital abnormalities is higher and the malformations are more detrimental. In Carter's study,[20] only 5 of the 13 children (38.5%) were normal at age 4 to 6 years. Of the ten surviving children, four had IQs in the range of 59 to 76, and one child was more severely mentally retarded.

Seemanova's study[21] confirms the above findings. Among the 130 living incest offspring whose mothers had no apparent defect, 53, or 41% had congenital abnormalities, compared to 4 of 86, or 4.7% of the control group. These differences are highly significant. Multiple congenital anomalies were found only in the incest group. Congenital abnormalities also tended to be severe (meningocele, heart malformations, cystic kidney disease, homocystinuria). In contrast, the polydactyly and luxation of the hip found in the control group were not as severely limiting to healthy functioning. Only 78 of the 161 children (48.4%) were normal at follow-up. In the incest offspring studied by Adams and Neel,[22] 3 of the 15 children who survived (20%) had major congenital abnormalities, two with severe cerebral palsy, and one with bilateral cleft lip. Of the control children, three had minor abnormalities and only one had a major abnormality. Two of the incest children had minor abnormalities (acetabular dysplasia). Three others (20%) had mental retardation without other abnormalities. Only 7 of the 18 children of first degree unions (38.9%) were normal at six months of age.

Summary of the Genetic Risks

The detrimental genetic effects of incest increase with the increasing genetic relatedness of the parents. Early death can be expected in 4% to 8% of the offspring of third-degree matings, in 17% of the offspring of second-degree matings and in 13% to 23% of offspring of first-degree matings. Among surviving offspring, serious malformations will occur in 4% of the products of third-degree matings, 8% of the products of second-degree matings, and in 21% to 41% of the products of first-degree matings. Bundey[14] estimates that 14% of these children will have autosomal recessive diseases, 12% will have polygenic malformations, and the balance of the affected children will have retardation only. When biological father and daughter mate, the likelihood that they will produce a healthy, surviving child is less than 50%. These data powerfully support the biological theory of the origin of the incest taboo.

Clinically, these genetic data suggest: 1) that the incest victim, pregnant by a first- or second-degree relative, deserves every opportunity to choose abortion, and 2) that when the children of such matings are relinquished for adoption, they need a thorough preadoptive medical evaluation. It has been suggested that children born as the result of incest have a strict program of audiometric, developmental, and ophthalmologic tests during the first year of life so that adoptive parents can be prepared for any handicap which will be a problem.[14]

Extragenetic Risks of Incest Pregnancy

In addition to the genetic effects, there may be extragenetic sequelae of father-daughter incest that would ultimately decrease the likelihood that the father's (and mother's) genes remain in the gene pool. The victimized daughter cannot reproduce if she dies, either from perineal damage secondary to premature intercourse, from complications of premature pregnancy, or from suicide. Her fertility might be decreased less drastically because of an increased risk of venereal disease secondary to promiscuity, or because frigidity, homosexuality, or psychosomatic disorder secondary to the incest decrease the likelihood of successful mating. If the victim has a child, and then batters it or cannot nurture it because of psychological sequelae of the incest, this is another type of reproductive failure. However, other forces may counterbalance such effects. For example, several studies have shown that incestuous fathers have more children than do control fathers of girls raped by non-family members.[23] Other data indicate that incest victims who reach a therapist actually have more children than do controls,[2] perhaps because they have been challenging their own fears of sterility.

The decreased fertility associated with incestuous matings may be advantageous in certain situations, as in royal families.[11] Social stability may actually increase if the monarch's fertility declines, producing fewer heirs to contend for the throne. This may explain the frequent exceptions to the incest taboo granted to royalty. In other royal incest situations, as in the Ganda and the Nyoro tribes of West Africa, the polygamous king's sister-wives are forbidden to have children, and abortifacients are used to maintain their sterility. It is believed that any children would be born deformed or dead.[7]

Clinical Realities of Incest Pregnancy

The incest pregnancy constitutes a clinical crisis even in situations where consanguinity is not a problem. In our small sample of eight cases, we find that incest pregnancies occur in families which are 1) intensely patriarchal, 2) extremely chaotic, or 3) unlucky.

In the intensely patriarchal family the father is a tyrannical and sometimes grandiose despot. The mission of the whole family is to obey him. Tormes[23] has described some of the bizarre demands that such fathers make. He may lock the mother in a closet while having intercourse with the children, brand the children, or lock family members out of the house. Paternity of the pregnancy is a well-guarded but proud secret. The father's desire is to keep and to raise the offspring within his family unit. Members of the family obey these wishes. The following case describes such a family:

Case 1 Mathilde is the eldest of four children. She had been in an incestuous relationship with her stepfather for three years (from age 12 to 15) before becoming pregnant. Her stepfather was also sexually involved with another sister and a brother. Mathilde concealed the pregnancy for the first five months. The stepfather accompanied Mathilde to all her prenatal visits and was present at the child's birth. Mathilde's mother knew of the paternity and was chided by the father for not joyfully accepting the pregnancy. When Mathilde's mother decided to file for divorce, Mathilde became hysterical and said she could not live without her stepfather. He returned to the home, tied the wife and children to chairs and held them at gunpoint. He wanted the family to go away with him, saying that all would return to normal if they did. After this episode, he was hospitalized and diagnosed a schizophrenic. Mathilde felt this "explained things" when she learned that her father was "crazy." The baby was a healthy premature female. She thrived and developed normally under the care of her grandmother, while Mathilde returned to high school.

The patriarchal system in these families diminishes the victim's chances to exit from the incest situation. The victim may feel "in love" with the father, feel "hypnotized" by him, or be diagnosable as suffering from a folie a deux.[24]

Incest pregnancy also occurs in the totally chaotic family where incest pregnancy is just one more in a series of problems. In such families the chaos can preclude other exits from the incest situation and can prolong the incest until pregnancy supervenes.

Case 2 Elena was a Navajo woman, the eldest of seven children. Her natural father was killed shortly after Elena was conceived. The mother never accepted Elena and sent her to live with missionaries. The mother remarried and, after her second husband died, she reclaimed Elena from the mission. When her mother married for the third time, Elena ran back to the mission but she was returned to her mother. When Elena was 15, her mother had a nervous breakdown. During her mother's illness, Elena and her stepfather began an incestuous relationship. Both the mother and the stepfather were alcoholics. At age 17, Elena gave birth to a daughter, Mary. Elena told doctors that her stepfather was the father, but her parents denied this and said she often lied. Elena's life continued to be filled with chaos; she became an alcoholic and began a series of involvements with men who abused her. After a younger child was killed by one of her boyfriends, Elena decided to relinquish her daughter, Mary, for adoption "and start a new life."

Elena's life had been riddled with chaos (loss of parents, foster care, alcoholic parents, psychotic mother, incest, and violence). The incest pregnancy was one element in a full spectrum of disorganization.

The following family combines elements of the excessively patriarchal and the chaotic families, and gives an example of the additional problems that consanguinity creates.

Case 3 Betty was the eldest of nine children living at home, and had been in an incestuous relationship with her natural father since age nine. The father had also had incest with two other daughters. In addition, two sons in the family were being physically abused. At 15, Betty became pregnant. She and the rest of the family failed to notice the pregnancy throughout the nine months. Betty delivered the baby into the toilet bowl at home. Betty's mother had wondered if Betty was pregnant but had not wanted to discuss it. Betty did not admit the paternity until she told her mother during a family argument, and the mother upon learning the truth, beat Betty so severely that hospitalization was required. The child suffered recurrent pneumonias secondary to an esophageal malformation. The infant was removed from the family at seven months of age because of failure to thrive, and Betty agreed to relinquish the child for adoption. She continued to live with her parents and to comply with their demands, including the patriarchal father's sexual demands.

All three of these victims were placed in unbearable conflict by the incest pregnancy. Mathilde defended against what happened by adaptively disassociating herself from her incestuous past ("that was crazy"); Elena and Betty ultimately dissociated themselves from their incestuous offspring. Elena fled into alcohol and Betty had to deny the very fact of her pregnancy. All of these victims were inhibited by the incest and by the pregnancy in making the normal adolescent transition from loyalty to parents to peer affiliation.

In our experience prognosis for the family is somewhat better when the pregnancy happens more literally as an "accident" and not as part of the family's patriarchal or chaotic coping system.

Case 4 Fifteen-year-old Natalia was raped by her alcoholic stepfather while her mother was in the hospital. This was the only sexual advance he had ever made toward her. She realized almost at once that she was pregnant, but was ashamed to tell her mother. After four months, Natalia's mother filed for divorce because of other problems, and Natalia told her mother about the rape and about her pregnancy. With the support of their priest, Natalia obtained an abortion. She returned to superior school performance and an active social life.

Abortion is almost never sought when incest pregnancy occurs in a patriarchal family (the pregnancy is wanted) or in a chaotic family (the pregnancy is unlikely to be noticed or to generate any adaptive response). It is in the better-integrated family that abortion can be helpful in resolving the crisis and in minimizing interference with the child's development.[25]

Pseudopregnancy in Incest Victims

Teenagers who have grown up in skewed and chaotic families where sex education is done via incest have difficulty in recognizing with confidence either the presence or absence of pregnancy. Some children confess the sexual experience because they fear they are pregnant. Such fears may not be banished by a simple negative physical examination.

Case 5 Cynthia is a bright 13-year-old who had not yet menstruated when her mother remarried for the fourth time. Cynthia's natural father had been physically abusive. A stepfather had sexually abused her older sister. Cynthia had lived with relatives and in foster care. The new stepfather was an alcoholic who teased Cynthia by telling her he would make her pregnant since her mother had been surgically sterilized and could no longer have his babies. Cynthia was terrified to be around him, and when he came into her bedroom and fondled her one night, she was certain he had made her pregnant. She did not confess this fear until after two months of foster care, when constant abdominal complaints, and a ten-pound weight gain drove her to consult a woman physician, who won her confidence. Arrangements were made for Cynthia to see the physician weekly for two months for counseling and sex education. The pseudopregnancy resolved.

In another case, where treatment was not so thorough, the incestuous pseudopregnancy was not resolved completely, and left as its residue a phantom child.

Case 6 Phyllis, a mildly retarded 13-year-old, told her mother that she thought she was having a miscarriage. She confessed that five months previously her alcoholic stepfather had raped her. When confronted, the stepfather fled the country. The physical examination was consistent with prior intercourse, and a general practitioner concurred with Phyllis's diagnosis of pregnancy. A gynecologist, however, said that Phyllis had not been pregnant, and diagnosed dysfunctional uterine bleeding of adolescence. Three years later, when Phyllis was hospitalized for multiple drug abuse, she told her counselor that she had a 3-year-old child in another country.

SUMMARY OF THE CLINICAL EXPERIENCE

Adolescents who become pregnant by a father or stepfather tend to conceal or deny the pregnancy itself and also the fact that it is an incestuous pregnancy. Abortion is rarely sought, especially not if the family is intensely patriarchal or excessively chaotic. In the majority of cases, someone other than the incest victim ultimately provides mothering to the baby. The incest pregnancy creates conflicts that seem even more destructive to family and individual stability than the incestuous relationship itself. Children who experience or even fantasize an incest pregnancy need support in understanding what has happened and in returning to age-appropriate developmental tasks.

In summary, the incest pregnancy is an untenable situation both genetically and psychologically. These extreme difficulties must have been noticeable throughout human history and may account for the universality of the taboo against first-degree matings. Treatment programs for incest families should aim at reducing the 10% to 20% incidence of pregnancy found in victims by encouraging early reporting, so that victims can exit from the situation before they become pregnant. Once pregnancy has occurred, the therapeutic interventions needed may include: abortion counseling, careful examination of the child for congenital defects, sensory deficits, and retardation, and arrangements for care of the baby so the young mother can return to normal adolescent activities.

REFERENCES

1. Morgan LH: *Ancient Society*. Chicago, Kerr, 1877.
2. Meiselman K: *Incest*. San Francisco, Jossey-Bass, 1978.
3. White LA: Definition and prohibition of incest. *Am Anthropol* 50:416–435, 1948.
4. Reimer S: A research note on incest. *Am J Sociology* 45:566–575, 1940.
5. DeFrancis V: *Protecting The Child Sex Victim*. Denver, American Humane Association, 1965.
6. Brant RST, Tisza VB: Sexually misused child. *Am J Orthopsychiatry* 47:80–90, 1977.
7. Heusch L: *de Essai sur le Symbolisme de L'inceste Royal en Afrique*. Brussels, Institut de Sociologie Solvay, 1958.
8. Weinberg SK: *Incest Behavior*. New York, Citadel, 1955.
9. Gligor AM: *Incest and Sexual Delinquency: A Comparative Analysis of Two Forms of Sexual Behavior in Minor Females*. Unpublished doctoral dissertation, Case Western Reserve University, 1966.
10. Kubo S: Researches and Studies on Incest in Japan. *Hiroshima J Med Sci* 8:99–159, 1959.
11. Maisch H: *Incest*. New York, Stein and Day, 1972.

12. Merland A, Fiorentini H, Orsini J: Concerning 34 psychiatric cases in which acts of father-daughter were reported. *Ann Med Legale* 42:353–359. 1962.

13. Goodwin J, Fried JM: Rape. *N Engl J Med* 298:167, 1978.

14. Bundey S: The child of an incestuous union, in Wolkind S (ed): *Clinics in Developmental Medicine No. 74.* London, Spastics International Medical Publications, 1979.

15. Slatis HM, Reis RH, Hoene RE: Consanguineous marriages in the Chicago region. *Am J Hum Genetics* 10:446–464, 1958.

16. Fraser FC, Biddle CJ: Estimating the risks for offspring of first-cousin matings. *Am J Hum Genetics* 28:522–526, 1976.

17. Schull MJ, Nagano H, Yamamoto M, et al: The effects of parental consanguinity and inbreeding in Hirado, Japan I. Stillbirth and pre-reproductive mortality. *Am J Hum Genetics* 22:239–262, 1970.

18. Naderi S: Congenital abnormalities in newborns of consanguineous parents. *Obstet Gynecol* 53:195–199, 1979.

19. Fried K, Davies AM: Some effects on the offspring of uncle-niece marriage in the Moroccan Jewish Community in Jerusalem. *Am J Hum Genetics* 26:65–72, 1974.

20. Carter CO: Risk to offspring of incest. *Lancet* 1:436, 1967.

21. Seemanova E: A study of children of incestuous matings. *Hum Heredity* 21:108–128, 1971.

22. Adams MS, Neel JV: Children of incest. *Pediatrics* 40:1:55–62, 1967.

23. Tormes Y: *Child Victims of Incest.* Englewood, Colorado, The American Humane Association, 1968.

24. Simonds JF, Glenn T: Folie a deux in a child. *J Autism Childhood Schiz* 6:61–73, 1976.

25. Sholevar G: A family therapist looks at incest. *Bull Am Acad Psychiatr Law* 2:25–31, 1975.

13 Physical and Sexual Abuse of the Children of Adult Incest Victims

Jean Goodwin
Teresita McCarty
Peter DiVasto

Previous studies have shown that most abusing parents have a history of physical abuse or neglect in their own childhoods. There is little data on the frequency of prior sexual abuse among parents who physically or sexually abuse their children. Many case reports describe the uncovering of a prior incest experience in a parent during the investigation of the child's current incest accusation, but it is unclear how frequently this occurs. One hundred mothers of abused children were asked about sexual incidents that occurred before age 18; the control group were 500 normal women from the same community who were surveyed during meetings of various voluntary organizations. Age and ethnicity did not differ in the two groups. Of the mothers of abused children, 24% reported a prior incest experience, whereas only 3% of the control women reported prior incest. This eightfold difference was highly significant. The 34 mothers from families where sexual abuse was occurring were no more likely to report prior incest than were the 66 mothers from families where physical abuse occurred. The one case of genital mutilation of a child occurred in a family where both parents had been incest victims. Case studies indicate that the parent who has been an incest victim has inhibitions and fears about tenderness, traceable to the childhood incest experience, which are important in the development of either physical or sexual abuse in the family.

PREVIOUS STUDIES

Steele and co-workers[1,2] have established that almost all abusing parents have a personal history of deprivation, neglect, or physical abuse in childhood. Such a history is found more commonly in abusing parents than is any other single demographic or diagnostic factor.

In working with abusing parents we have been impressed that many mothers have been victims of sexual abuse in childhood, as well as of other forms of abuse. This chapter reports a series of clinical observations which define the frequency of prior sexual abuse in mothers in incest families, in mothers in physical abuse or neglect families, and in women in the general population. Cases will also be described in which deficits in mothering can be traced to defensive reactions to the prior incest.

Many anecdotal accounts describe incestuous families in which one or both parents had been incest victims in childhood.[3-8] Some investigators have postulated a multigenerational victim-to-victim relationship underlying incest.[4,5,9,10]

However, there is little statistical data to support this hypothesis. Gebhard and associates[11] found that only 12% of imprisoned incestuous fathers had experienced sexual contact with an adult before puberty; (one half of those contacts were with women and one half with men). This was higher than found in general population controls (5%), but lower than found in the general prison population (28%). Brant[10] cites an unpublished study by Kent, reporting that 31% of the mothers in incestuous families were themselves victims of childhood incest.

Even fewer data are available about prior incest in parents involved in physical abuse. One report estimates that as many as 90% of Parents Anonymous participants have been victims of sexual abuse in childhood.[5] There are no published comparisons of the frequency of prior incest in abusing parents with the frequency in the general population.

METHODS

Information about childhood sexual experience was obtained through psychiatric interview or administration of the Sexual Stress Questionnaire (P. DiVasto, unpublished data, 1979) (See Appendix). Data was obtained from the following populations:

A. Five hundred normal women in the community: The sexual stress questionnaire was distributed to women in community, voluntary, and church groups. The questionnaire asks if subjects have experienced any upsetting sexual events in childhood, gives examples of such events, and then asks respondents to describe their experiences on the anonymous questionnaire. Nursing and medical students went to meetings of these groups, explained the nature of the questionnaire and the need for 100% return, and collected the questionnaires. The method is similar to that developed by Kinsey.[11] Five hundred sixteen questionnaires were collected, but 16 had to be discarded because of incomplete responses.

B. One hundred mothers of abused children, including:

1. Twenty mothers from families where physical abuse or neglect was occurring.
2. Twenty mothers from incestuous families; mothers in these first two groups were referred for psychiatric evaluation after child abuse was substantiated. Psychiatric evaluations were reviewed for reports of incest experiences or childhood rape.
3. Twenty-seven unselected mothers from families in which physical child abuse or neglect had been substantiated by a child protective agency. These women were given the Sexual Stress Questionnaire anonymously during required psychological group testing at intake. About one half of all mothers admitted for treatment actually came for this required testing. All mothers who presented for testing during the study period returned the questionnaire; 5 of the 27 failed to check either yes or no when asked about childhood sexual stress. These nonresponses were counted as negative responses.
4. Fourteen unselected mothers were from families where incest had been substantiated. These women were given the Sexual Stress Questionnaire with several other self-tests at the time of intake. During the time of data collection, three mothers refused all questionnaires.
5. Ten mothers with a child who died from maltreatment. After child abuse was substantiated, these women had psychiatric evaluations which were reviewed. Mothers were also mailed the Sexual Stress Questionnaire and asked to complete and return it; 4 of the 10 returned the mailed questionnaire. Two revealed incest experiences that had not been mentioned at the time of psychiatric evaluation.
6. Nine mothers attending a Parents Anonymous group. The Sexual Stress Questionnaire was distributed by the group coordinator and completed anonymously by the members as had been the procedure in other community groups.

All 100 mothers in these six groups will be referred to as mothers from abusive families or as abusive mothers. Many reports describe the difficulty in defining a single perpetrator in families where incest or physical abuse has occurred.[7,12] The mother in an incest family is often described as a nonperpetrator. However, three of the incest mothers in this sample had married more than one husband who sexually abused the daughters. As used in this chapter, "abusive mothers" are mothers who have contributed in some way to the development of a family situation where child abuse or neglect is substantiated.

RESULTS

Of the 500 normal women surveyed, 15 (3%) had experienced some form of incest before age 18 (Table 13-1). Five (1%) were involved with father or stepfather, four with uncles, three with brothers, and three with other relatives. Eight of the 15 had told a parent at the time of the incident, although three reported their mothers did not believe them. Of these 500 normal women, 122 (24%) had experienced some kind of sexually stressful incident prior to age 18. One of the five women who reported a father-daughter incest experience wrote on the questionnaire that she had never told anyone about the incest until she sought psychotherapy after the birth of her son because she was afraid that she might harm the child.

The 500 women in the general population sample had an average age of 27.6 years, almost the same as the average for the 100 mothers in the child abuse group (29.9 years). In the general population group 61% were Anglo and 31% Spanish-American. This too, was similar to the proportion in the abusing mothers (62% Anglo and 30% Spanish-American). Women in the general population sample had more years of schooling (13.5 years) than did mothers in abusive families (11.6 years). This difference of 1.9 years is statistically significant ($p < .01$). However, in the general population sample, women who had been incest victims tended to have even more schooling (14.4 years) than the group as a whole. The incest victims were also more likely to be English-speaking whites; 12 of the 15 incest victims were Anglo (80%), a higher percentage than found in the general population sample as a whole.

Among the 100 mothers from families involved in child abuse, 24 (24%) described incest experiences in childhood (see Table 13-1 and 13-2), about eight times the rate found in the general population sample ($X^2 = 60.5, p < .01$). An additional 14 women described other types of sexual stress in childhood; thus 38% of the women in this sample described some type of sexual stress in childhood.

Rates of prior incest in six subgroups were as follows: 1) physical abuse mothers referred for psychiatric evaluation, 15%; 2) incest mothers referred for psychiatric evaluation, 20%; 3) unselected physical abuse mothers, 19%; 4) unselected incest mothers, 29%; 5) mothers of children who died as a consequence of child maltreatment, 40%; and 6)

Table 13-1*
Incest Victims in the General Population.†

No.	Age at Interview	Ethnicity‡	Age at Incident	Incident	Told Someone
1.	47	SA	"young"	molested by uncle—ongoing	No
2.	25	A	13	incest with family member for 3 months	Mother
3.	24	A	11	uncle exposed himself	Never
4.	26	SA	4 or 5	relative exposed himself and fondled	Mother
5.	31	A	13	fondled by father	Never
6.	38	A	7 or 8	oral sex with uncle	Mother
7.	29	A	12–16	incest with father	Therapist at age 28
8.	33	A	8–11	paternal grandfather exposed himself Stepfather raped	Neighbor and mother
9.	30	A	gradeschool	oral sex with brother for 2 years	Parents "found out"
10.	30	A	until adolescence	incest with 2 older brothers	"Mother called me tattletale"
11.	52	A	10	foster uncle fondled	Father
12.	42	A	14–17	stepfather fondling and exposure	No
13.	30	A	14	stepfather fondling and attempted rape	Mother "did not believe"
14.	32	SA	15–16	older cousin exposed himself	Never
15.	32	A	17–18	intercourse with older brother	Therapist at age 26
Summary	33.4	12 (80%) Anglo	8 (53%) were involved before age 13	5 (33%) involved a parent-figure 2 (13%) involved exposure only	8 told a parent (53%) 5 (33%) successfully

*Reprinted by permission from Goodwin J, McCarty T, DiVasto P: Prior incest in abusive mothers. *Child Abuse Neglect* 5:1–9, 1981.
†Three percent (15) of the 500 women surveyed reported incest experiences.
‡A = Anglo, SA = Spanish-American.

Table 13–2*
Incest Victims in Six Populations of Abusing Mothers.† (continued)

No.	Age at Interview	Ethnicity‡	Age at Incident	Incident	Told Someone
Physical abuse mothers at psychiatric evaluation N = 20					
1.	21	A	17–18	fondling by stepfather	Mother "did not believe"
2.	28	A	10–15	intercourse with father	No one; brother knew
3.	27	A	9–10	fondling with uncle	No one
Sexual abuse mothers at psychiatric evaluation N = 20					
4.	27	SA	12–15	fellatio and attempted intercourse with stepfather	Mother "didn't protect"
5.	35	Indian	about 12	fondling with uncle	No one
6.	29	SA	12	attempted rape by father	No one
7.	26	SA	12–14	intercourse with uncle and mother's boyfriend	No one
Physical abuse mothers, unselected N = 27					
8.	22	A	10	stepmother—fondling and fellatio oral sex, then raped by stepfather	No one
9.	29	A	9–13	intercourse with father and older brother	Priest, police
10.	27	A	5	stepfather—"heavy petting"	Friend
11.	20	A	11	older brother—attempted seduction	Mother
12.	22	SA	7		Mother "didn't care"

No.	Age	Ethnicity	Age at incest	Description	Disclosure
Sexual abuse mothers, unselected N = 14					
13.	34	A	12	fondled by older brother	No one
14.	36	A	17	molested by uncle	Aunt
15.	23	SA	6	fondled and fellatio with uncle	No one
16.	31	A		brothers fondled me	No one
Mothers with a child who died of maltreatment N = 10					
17.	24	Indian	9-16	multiple intercourse with stepfather	No one
18.	26	A	6	intercourse with mother's boyfriend	No one
19.	32	A	10	fellatio with uncle	No one
20.	18	SA	9	fondling and intercourse with stepfather	No one
Mothers in a Parents Anonymous Group N = 9					
21.	28	A	11-12	raped by uncle, fondled by another uncle	No one
22.	34	SA	4	hanged and fondled by uncle	Yes—No one believed
23.	19	SA	9	fondled by grandfather	No one
24.	23	A	12	raped by stepfather	No one
Summary	26.4	14 (58%) Anglo 8 (33%) Spanish-American	21 (88%) were involved before age 13	0 (0%) involved exposure only 13 (54%) involved a parent figure	5 told a parent (21%) 1 (4%) successfully

*Reprinted by permission from Goodwin J, McCarty T, DiVasto P: Prior incest in abusive mothers. *Child Abuse Neglect* 5:1-9, 1981.
†Twenty-four percent (24) of the 100 women surveyed reported incest experiences.
‡A = Anglo, SA = Spanish-American, Indian = Navajo.

mothers in a Parents Anonymous group, 44%. The psychiatric evaluation was apparently no more likely to produce positive histories than was the questionnaire. The rates in groups 5 and 6 are somewhat higher than in other groups; these women were in a treatment rather than in an evaluation setting at the time they completed the Sexual Stress Questionnaires. Two mothers in the unselected incest group have recently described prior incest experiences to therapists and have stated that they could not admit to those experiences at the time they were given the Sexual Stress Questionnaire. It is likely that figures for all groups would be higher if subjects had been subjected to psychotherapy for a long period. However, even if those 19 abusive mothers who were in treatment are removed from the sample, the difference in incidence of prior incest between the abusive mothers and the normal women remains significant ($X^2 = 33.7$, $p < .01$).

According to these data, mothers of incest victims seem no more likely to have a history of incest than are mothers of children who are physical abuse victims. Eight of the 34 incest mothers (24%) and 16 of the 66 physical abuse mothers (24%) had experienced prior incest. Particular patterns of physical abuse may occur when the parent has been an incest victim. For example, of the 10 maltreatment deaths that were reviewed, genital mutilation was found in only one child at autopsy; both parents had been incest victims, the mother was involved with her father and the baby's father had been incestuously involved with his uncle.

The 24 incest victims in the abusive group differed from the women in the general population group who reported prior incest. Fewer of the victims in the abusive sample had told anyone. Only 5 of the 24 told a parent at the time, and 4 of these noted that they were not believed or protected. So, whereas 33% (5/15) of the general population victims were able to successfully tell a parent about the incest at the time, only 4% (1 of 24) of the abusive victims were able to do this ($X^2 = 6.0$, $p < .02$). In contrast to incest victims in the general population group who tended to have more education than did the overall sample, incest victims in the abusive group tended to have fewer years of schooling than other abusive mothers (10.7 years vs 11.6). Incest victims in the abusive populations were also more likely to have experienced incest prior to age 13 than were victims in the normal population ($X^2 = 5.6$, $p < .02$).

DISCUSSION

There is little statistical information about the number of childhood sexual experiences with an adult or with an adult relative in women in the normal population. Data on prior sexual abuse from the 500 normal women in this study compares well with previously published reports which find that 20% to 30% of adult women recall some kind of childhood sexual experience with an adult, and that in 3% to 12% of those incidents a relative was involved.[13-15]

Comparison of data from normal women with 100 mothers from abusive families indicates that the abusive women have an incidence of prior incestuous experiences eight times greater than that reported by women in the general population. This percentage is in the range of the highest incidences reported for delinquent women (15%) or psychiatrically symptomatic women (33%).[16] While the normal and abusive women did not differ in ethnicity or age, they did differ in education in that the normal group had on average two more years of education (13.5) than did the group of abusive mothers (11.6).

Prior victims in the two groups differed as follows: 1) significantly more incest victims in the normal group successfully reported the incident to a parent; 2) the incest victims in the abusive group were more likely to have been under 13 when the abuse began, and 3) the incest victims in the normal population seemed to have slightly more education (14.4 years) than the remaining normal women, while the incest victims among the abusive mothers averaged one year less education (10.6 years) than other abusive mothers. These data are consistent with the hypothesis that the girls who later became involved in child abuse suffered a more difficult incest situation and were able to cope with it less well.[17]

Because of the educational differences between the two groups, it might be argued that the differences are merely socioeconomic, with abusive mothers coming from a world where both paternal incest and child abuse are common. Several observations indicate this explanation is too simple: 1) the incest victims in the normal group actually had more education than nonvictims; 2) one of those victims in the normal group reported having sought psychotherapy when she became afraid of harming her baby; 3) the only case of genital mutilation[18] in the abuse group occurred in a family where both parents had been incest victims; and 4) in the cases reported below, where a clinical connection could be traced between prior incest and subsequent abuse, families of origin and procreation were in the middle or the upper middle class.

Clinical experience leads us to look for an explanation of the data in the individual's response to the trauma of an incestuous situation. As in other kinds of trauma, the victimized child uses the coping mechanisms that her personal experience, her family, and her society have provided to reconstruct herself after the disorganizing and conflicting experience. If coping mechanisms are few, the reorganized self may be more fragile and more vulnerable to disintegration under certain types of stress.[19] An example of vulnerability is that one of the prior incest victims in this study was forcibly raped, and only after that repetition of the original trauma, did she begin beating her 1-year-old daughter.

One of the consequences of unresolved trauma is the "coincidental" repetition of the trauma. The mother's repressed memories of her own abuse emerge as she unconsciously recreates a similar situation for her child, thereby allowing herself another chance to resolve her repressed conflicts.[10,11] This pattern is most clearly illustrated by case reports where the child's sexual abuse occurs at the same age as the mother's prior sexual abuse.[20,21] Another example of this projective identification from the parent to the child has been described in families where the parent of a delinquent child reveals a secret history of juvenile delinquency that may be almost identical to the child's pattern.[22] The parent can disavow a rejected aspect of herself by projecting it on the child ("She liked the incest; I did not.") and, at the same time, can vicariously relive it.[23]

The most commonly reported sequel of incest trauma is impairment of the ability to experience orgasm,[6,15,24] which occurs in 20% to 75% of incest victims. Frigidity in the mother and the cessation of marital intercourse has also been reported as a prelude to incest.[3,9,25] This sequence—victimization of the mother, consequent frigidity in the mother, victimization of the child—could be part of the link between incest victimization occurring in the mother and, subsequently, in the child. The husband's reaction to his wife's prior victimization is also important. One woman told her husband shortly after their marriage about her prior incest experience. He became obsessively preoccupied with what had happened to his wife and would become explosively enraged whenever he heard particular melodies that reminded him of his wife's incestuous father, a musician. Years later, he claimed that it was his sexual disgust toward his incest-victim wife that had led him to seek sexual gratification with his daughters.

Given the many hypotheses that "an incestuous model" in the parent[11] or an "incest carrier" predisposes to incest in the next generation, it was surprising to find that prior incest was no more common in mothers in sexual abuse situations than in physical abuse mothers. However, the intimate tenderness involved in parenting can be as intense, as overwhelming, and as physical as the intimacy of mating. The link between prior incest in the mother and subsequent physical abuse in her child may occur because sexually abused mothers feel as frozen and frustrated in expressing maternal tenderness[26] as they do in expressing sexual tenderness. Kaufman and co-workers[12] proposed a trigenerational model for incest: A woman who had had an ambivalent hostile relationship with her own mother marries a man who has been deserted by his own father,[27] and the combined efforts of both parents to receive nurturance from the daughter lead to her incestuous victimization. The present data indicates that there may be a fourth generation of incest: A victimized daughter desperate for control and terrified by tenderness who lashes out at her baby or neglects it when she feels out of control or unable to love.

Case Material

The sexualization, concealment, and fear of tenderness experienced by a prior incest victim trying to be a mother, are illustrated in the following case example.

Case 1 Amy, a 19-year-old housewife, called Parents Anonymous when her first baby, a son, was 2 months old. "I'm spanking my baby too hard. He keeps trying to attract me sexually. He squirms to get my attention and then has erections." She was afraid that other people might think her breast-feeding of the baby was sexual, and was secretive about all of her physical contacts with her baby. One week after her first call the baby sustained a skull fracture, which fortunately left no permanent damage. Treatment was begun. Amy felt that her body had been "marred" by the pregnancy. She was almost delusionally convinced that her husband was having an affair, despite his denials. Amy's mother had been a prostitute and Amy had a chaotic life before her natural father invited her to live with his family when she was ten. Shortly thereafter he initiated genital fondling with her which progressed to intercourse. At age 14, she reported the incest and subsequently lived in ten different foster homes. Individual psychotherapy centered on helping Amy to differentiate tenderness from sexuality. Amy had projected on her baby her own sense of having to "beg for love." She could not believe that anyone could ever love her for herself or that love could exist apart from a destructive, frightening sexuality. Her constant guilty daydreams about extramarital affairs had formed the nucleus for her conviction that her husband was being unfaithful. As therapy progressed she was able to fantasize nonsexual tendernesses in addition to the sexual affairs. She also became more comfortable with orgasm, which she had previously avoided because it made her feel out of control.

The experience of being out of control was described by another prior incest victim.

Case 2 Barbara, a 23-year-old housewife, sought psychotherapy after she left bruises on her 9-month-old son when she spanked him for opening a box. "I told him to stop touching it, but he wouldn't," she said. Barbara's father had begun fondling and licking her genitals when she was five, and the relationship continued for almost ten years until a younger sibling, also a victim, revealed the secret. Barbara said that she had tried not to have orgasm with her father but "had them anyway." At age nine, she had severely beaten her cat when it licked her in the ear. After delivering her baby, Barbara had moved out of her mother's house, "because she used to watch me breast-feeding as if there was something wrong with it." She had felt ashamed to talk with her husband about feeling out of control with the baby. Treatment centered around helping her remember and rework the incest experience, giving words to the instinctive feelings and responses she had experienced.[28]

In both of these cases the mothers experienced maternal tenderness as sexual, threatening, and shameful, and reacted with anger and frustration not only to their inability to consummate their tender feelings but also to their experience of tenderness as an imposed loss of control. The anger acted to turn off the threatening tenderness as well as to express the mother's frustration.

Lage and Marohn[29] have described several cases of women who concealed a pregnancy from everyone and then killed the baby at birth. In one case the woman had previously been involved in mutual genital fondling with her father, which had also been kept secret. Her therapists felt that the concealed prior incest had set the stage for the concealed infanticide by giving her the message, "Children are our possessions and we can do with them as we please," and, "Only appearances count." So long as the young mother continued to conceal and to rationalize at some level her father's sexual abuse of her, she continued to rationalize her own maltreatment of her child.

Some of the children of incest victims are physically abused by family members other than the mother. In the following case the mother was not the abuser, but her own prior sexual and physical abuse and her fears that she could not protect her children from a similar fate were part of the sequence of events that led to their being placed out of the home.

Case 3   Lisa was physically and sexually abused by her father from age six. When she was 12, she took her 18-month-old sister and ran away from home. She was afraid that something terrible would happen to her sister unless she got the baby away. They were caught and returned home. Lisa was severely beaten by her father. The next day the school reported her bruises to child protection authorities. A caseworker spoke with the father and decided to close the case. A few months later, the family home burned down and the baby that Lisa had tried to protect was killed. After the fire, Lisa's mother had a nervous breakdown and was institutionalized. Lisa has always wondered if her life would have been different had she been removed by child protection workers.

Lisa herself has had seven children by four different men. Each of the children has been removed from Lisa at around age 18 months. All have been permanently placed in other homes by age 12. It is Lisa's current husband who always is identified as the abuser. Child protection workers are repeatedly surprised by Lisa's failure to cooperate and by her deliberate breaking of rules at critical moments in her case. In other contexts she is a cooperative and reliable citizen.

This woman's unconscious wish that her own children be protected in the way that she and her own sister were not may have determined the paradoxically self-defeating behaviors that led to protective placement of the children in other homes.

CONCLUSIONS

The rate of prior incest was 24% in 100 mothers from abusive families and 3% in 500 normal women in the community. The rate of prior incest was no higher in mothers in incestuous families than in mothers in families where other kinds of abuse were substantiated. In some cases the working through of the prior incest experience can be crucial to restoring the ability to mother.[30]

The help of Robert Kellner, MD, and Richard Rada, MD, is appreciated.

REFERENCES

1. Steele BF, Pollock CB: A psychiatric study of parents who abuse infants and small children, in Helfer RE, Kempe CH (eds): *The Battered Child,* Chicago, University of Chicago Press, 1968.
2. Steele BF: Parental abuse of infants and small children, in Anthony EJ, Benedek T (eds): *Parenthood. Its Psychology and Psychopathology,* Boston, Little, Brown and Co, 1970.
3. Weiner IB: Father-daughter incest, a clinical report. *Psychiatr Q* 36:607–632, 1962.
4. Raphling DL, Carpenter BL, Davis A: Incest, a genealogical study, *Arch Gen Psychiatry* 16:505–511, 1967.
5. Summit R, Kryso J: Sexual abuse of children, a clinical spectrum. *Am J Orthopsychiatry* 48:237–251, 1978.
6. Meiselman K: *Incest.* San Francisco, Jossey-Bass, 1978.
7. Machotka P, Pittman FS, Flomenhaft K: Incest as a family affair. *Fam Process* 6:98–116, 1967.
8. Anderson LM, Shafer G: The character-disordered family, a community treatment model for family sexual abuse. *Am J Orthopsychiatry* 49:436–445, 1979.
9. Rosenfeld AA: Endogamic incest and the victim-perpetrator model. *Am J Dis Child* 133:406–410, 1979.
10. Brant R: *Manual on Sexual Abuse and Misuse of Children.* Boston, New England Resource Center for Protective Services, 1977.
11. Gebhard PH, Gagnon JH: *Sex Offenders. An Analysis of Types,* New York, Harper and Row, 1965.
12. Kaufman I, Peck AL, Tagiuri CK: The family constellation and overt incestuous relations between father and daughter. *Am J Orthopsychiatry* 24:266–279, 1954.
13. Finkelhor D: *Sexually Victimized Children.* New York, Free Press, 1979.
14. Landis JT: Experiences of 500 children with adult sexual deviation. *Psychiatr Q* (suppl) 30:91–109, 1956.
15. Herman J, Hirschman L: Father-daughter incest, families at risk. Read

before the Annual Meeting of the American Psychiatric Association, San Francisco, 1980.

16. Rosenfeld AA: Incidence of a history of incest among 18 female psychiatric patients. *Am J Psychiatry* 136:791-795, 1979.

17. Tsai M, Feldman-Summers S, Edgar M: Childhood molestation, variables related to differential impacts on psychosexual functioning in adult women. *J Abnorm Psychol* 88:407-417, 1979.

18. Slosberg EJ, Ludwig S, Duckett J, et al: Penile trauma as a sign of child abuse. *Am J Dis Child* 132:719, 1978.

19. Titchener JL, Ross WD: Acute or chronic stress as determinants of behavior, character, and neurosis, in Arieti S (ed): *American Handbook of Psychiatry,* vol 3. New York, Basic Books, 1974.

20. Rosenfeld AA, Nadelson C, Krieger M: Fantasy and reality in patient reports of incest. *J Clin Psychiatry* 8:159-164, 1979.

21. Brown BS: Clinical illustrations of the sexual misuse of girls. *Child Welfare* 58:435-442, 1979.

22. Johnson A: Sanctions for super ego lacunae of adolescents, in Eissler K (ed): *Searchlights on Delinquency.* New York, International Universities Press, 1949.

23. Zinner J, Shapiro R: Projective identification as a mode of perception and behaviour in families of adolescents. *Int J Psychoanal* 53:523-530, 1972.

24. Lukianowicz N: Incest. *Br J Psychiatry* 120:301-313, 1972.

25. Cormier BM, Kennedy M, Sangowicz J: Psychodynamics of father-daughter incest. *Can Psychiatr Assoc J* 7:203-217, 1962.

26. Offenkrantz W, Tobin A, Freedman R: An hypothesis about heroin addiction, murder, prostitution, and suicide: Acting out parenting conflicts. *Int J Psychoanal Psychother* 7:602-608, 1978.

27. Lustig N, Dresser J, Spellman S, et al: Incest, a family group survival pattern. *Arch Gen Psychiatry* 14:31-402, 1966.

28. Zetzel E: Therapeutic alliance in the analysis of hysteria, in *The Capacity for Emotional Growth.* New York, International Universities Press, 1970.

29. Lage G, Marohn R: Adolescent pregnancy as a threat to the organization of the self. Read before the Michael Reese Hospital Conference on Parenthood as an Adult Experience, Chicago, 1980.

30. Goodwin J, McCarty T, DiVasto P: Prior incest in abusive mothers. *Child Abuse Neglect* 5:1-9, 1981.

APPENDIX

The Sexual Stress Questionnaire

We would like to have you take a few minutes of your time to fill in this form. Its purpose is explained on the next page.

Some of you may not have experienced the kinds of upset we are asking about. However, please feel free to fill in the following pages if you would simply like to comment on these kinds of upsetting experiences.

There is no requirement that you fill out this form and you may refuse to do so simply by leaving it blank and returning it; however, any information you can give us will be helpful.

We are trying to understand more about the kinds of upsetting sexual events which happen to children. This study will help us to treat children who have been sexually victimized by helping us to understand how children cope with sexual events.

We would like you to describe any incident from your childhood that you thought was sexual that happened to you because as a child you had to give in to someone bigger. We are interested in any experience that happened before age 18 that either bothered you at the time or has left some sort of lasting memory. Examples are: being followed, being touched sexually, being asked by a grown-up to undress, being "flashed" (someone exposing themselves to you), "peeping Toms," obscene phone calls, being raped, or being beaten (in a sexual way).

All information is *anonymous* to insure confidentiality.
(Please fill in the blank or check the appropriate box.)
1. Your age: _____ Sex: Male ____ Female ____
2. Ethnicity: Anglo ____ Spanish-American ____ Indian ____
   Black ____ Asian ____ Other _____
3. Marital Status: Single ____ Divorced ____ Married ____
   Widowed ____
4. Highest grade completed: _____
5. Religion: Catholic ____ Protestant ____ None ____
   Other _____
6. What is your job? _____
7. Before age 18 were you ever in a sexual kind of situation as described above? Yes ____ If yes, please continue on the next page.
   No ____ If no, please return this form to the survey-taker.

EVENT NUMBER _____

7A. First, describe the event.
   1. How old were you? _____

154

2. What happened? _____
_____
_____
_____
_____

3. Where did it happen? _____
4. Who did it? _____
5. What time of day was it? _____
6. Was anyone drinking or drunk? _____
7. What happened after? _____
8. Did you tell anyone? _____

7B. Check the box that best describes how you feel or felt.

	How upsetting was the event immediately afterward?	How upsetting is the event to you today?	If this event were to happen again, how upsetting would it be?
Not at all Upsetting			
Mildly Upsetting			
Upsetting			
Quite Upsetting			
Highly Upsetting			
Extremely Upsetting			

14 Why Physicians Should Report Child Abuse: The Example of Sexual Abuse

Jean Goodwin
Carol Geil

Twenty years ago, the reasons why physicians should report child abuse were more clear than they are today. At the time that state laws were passed, which required the reporting of child abuse, this was clearly a medical advance. Prior to that, physicians simply had not been able to talk about the possibility that a child had been battered. It was hypothesized that there might be a genetic defect in some children which resulted in the triad of easy bruising, spontaneous subdural hematomata, and brittle bones causing multiple fractures.[1] Children's complaints of sexual abuse were explained away as fantasies, and children were chided by physicians for derogating their fathers.[2] Physicians, including pediatricians like C.H. Kempe, fought to make child abuse and neglect part of a civil juvenile code so that parents would not have to face criminal prosecution if they did admit that they had injured a child.[3] Once these laws made it safe for parents to talk about child abuse, physicians learned about an area of human experience which previously had been taboo.[4]

Today, physicians are much more familiar with the problems caused by the child protection laws than with the problems solved by those laws.

As in other medical breakthroughs, such as the development of anesthesia or the development of immunization, modern-day physicians have much experience with the damaging side effects of these treatments, but little or no experience in dealing with the catastrophes that the innovations were designed to prevent.

There are now those who say that the child abuse laws are too radical, that they infringe on parental rights to discipline and to educate their children, and that they infringe as well on the physician's right to a confidential relationship with the patient.[5] The child protection laws specifically exclude physician-patient confidentiality as a reason for not reporting. If physicians are mandated to report child abuse, should they also be required to give a Miranda-type warning[6] to each parent they interview? Physicians who report are protected from subsequent civil suit, and physicians who fail to report may be subject to a fine or a jail term. In New Mexico no physician has yet been fined for not reporting. However, courts have held physicians liable for damage which occurred to a child after the physician failed to report an abusive family situation.

Goldstein, Freud, and Solnit[7] have recommended severely limiting the jurisdiction of the child protection laws. They suggest that reporting be used only in cases in which 1) both parents have died or disappeared, 2) a caretaker has been successfully criminally prosecuted for a sexual offense against a child, or 3) a child is threatened by imminent death or serious bodily harm. In such cases they recommend that intervention should be vigorous and usually should result in placement of the child in an adoptive home. One problem in this plan is that a family would not be reported if the child were merely locked in a closet for days on end but had no bodily signs of injury. It is not clear that this system would simplify decision-making for physicians. Physicians have difficulty in making judgments about the imminence of death, even in more clear-cut diagnostic entities than child abuse. One can imagine the dilemmas that would be created if, for example, venereal disease were to be reported only if the case was imminently life threatening—to whose life? the lives of the patient's offspring? of the patient's contacts?—or if it resulted from a successfully prosecuted sexual offense.

In addition to these critics, there are those who say that the child abuse laws are not tough enough. This group argues that these laws, which provide for removal of the child from his parents, actually only punish the victim by sending the child into a dangerous impersonal world of foster care while allowing the parents to go unmolested. These advocates suggest that if children are to have equal rights, those who assault, murder, or rape children must face the same penalties they would face had they chosen a larger victim. They point out that law enforcement personnel are likely to do a better job of investigation than are caseworkers who have not been trained to interrogate suspects or to elicit confessions. Critics in this group, like psychiatrist Thomas Szasz,[8] suggest that making exceptions to the law on the grounds of emotional impairment in the parent-perpetrator can ultimately jeopardize the rights of the parent. Indeed, parents do at times face a double-jeopardy system: Legal action through the child protection laws and criminal prosecution as well.

Critics in both groups point to problems in the child protection system. Perpetual foster care in a series of different homes is not good for children.[9] Workers in state child-protective agencies are often untrained, overworked, and incapable of maintaining good communication with the referring physician. A report of child abuse can often cause as many family problems as it resolves; eg, when the adversary civil court system returns a child to the abusing parents to be punished for having "told on" them.[6] The frequency of reporting by physicians and families increases with the availability of helpful protective services. We have found that a change from a more sensitive to a less sensitive intake worker reduced sexual abuse reports by one-half in the first six months after the change.

In addition to all of these problems, there is conflicting evidence about whether reporting ultimately improves outcome for the child. In certain model programs, such as the sexual abuse treatment program in Santa Clara County, California, more than 75% of parents and children show measurable improvement, and recurrence of abuse is almost nonexistent.[10] Not all programs are this successful.

How, then, can the physician expose a family and himself to the stigmatization, stress, and risks of family separation which reporting implies? This chapter reviews five reasons for reporting child abuse:

1. To decrease morbidity for abused and neglected children
2. To generate accurate information about the incidence of child abuse and neglect
3. To routinize and destigmatize the process of reporting
4. To provide help for families who are otherwise unknown to and unhelped by social or psychiatric agencies
5. To increase physicians' influence with state social agencies.

The data and discussions are presented from the perspective of a psychiatrist (JG), who serves as a consultant to a protective service agency, and of a pediatrician (CG), who coordinates the treatment of abused children at a large county hospital.

1. Decreasing the Morbidity for Abused and Neglected Children

Some of the most discouraging data about child abuse and also about the preventive value of reporting are found in studies of battered babies. S. Smith[11] studied 134 battered babies reported to a child protection agency in Birmingham, England. Of those 134, 21 or 15%, died. Another 20, or 15%, suffered permanent neurological damage from the initial battering. Another study indicates that in 3% of children hospitalized for mental retardation, the handicap was caused by injuries inflicted by parents.[12] In another 21% of institutionalized children, physical abuse and neglect were judged to have contributed to the developmental retardation. In the Birmingham study, 60% of the babies were rebattered, despite the fact that the initial incident was reported. The critical missing factor here is, How many babies would have been rebattered, and how severely, had the initial incident not been reported? Another important finding in this study is that of the 134 battered babies, 60% had been diagnosed prior to the battering as having failure to thrive. What would have been the morbidity and mortality statistics had all of those children been reported at the time failure to thrive was first detected?

We now have some data on the effects of increased reporting on morbidity in sexually abused children. In Bernalillo County, New Mexico, in the five years from 1975 to 1980, the frequency of incest reports increased from 4 in 1975 to 125 in 1979. The number of reports approximately doubled in each successive year. In the first half of this time period, 39 families were reported. In four families a child victim had venereal disease, and in one family a victim was pregnant. In the second half of the five-year interval, there were 200 reports. The absolute numbers of children with either pregnancy or venereal disease remained the same despite an absolute increase in the county's population and more active case-finding. The combined frequency of these major complications in child victims decreased from 13% to 3% with increased reporting.

Is this decreased morbidity merely a reflection of a dilution of the serious cases by trivial unsubstantiated cases? We think not. Concurrent with the declining morbidity we have seen a decrease in the average duration of incest at the time of reporting and an increase in the percentage of reports of one-time-only incest rapes. This indicates to us that the increased numbers of reports reflect earlier reporting rather than an increase in trivial cases, and that it is the early case-finding that accounts for the decreased percentage of venereal disease and pregnancy now seen in victims.

In an earlier study of incest cases in the State of New Mexico which took place in 1976, we found that 10% of the reported cases of incest involved a pregnant victim. This 10% figure has been reported in many other studies[13] (see also Chapter 12) in settings where treatment for victims and families was not readily available. However, contemporary major treatment centers share our experience that fewer than 1% of the victims are pregnant in a setting where early reporting and treatment are emphasized.

In thinking about preventing morbidity, it is important to consider primary prevention for siblings as well as secondary prevention for the identified victim. The following is a case report of an incest situation in which a therapist decided for good reasons and in good faith not to report to child protection authorities. In this case the therapist's decision resulted in significant morbidity to a sibling.

Case 1   L was a 15-year-old girl, referred for psychotherapy when she placed a threatening note on her teacher's car. After a few months of psychotherapy she revealed to the therapist a four-year history of incest with her father. A family session was held in which the father admitted that he had made sexual advances to his daughter, but he repeatedly rationalized the advances by saying that he had "just been trying to show her what would happen if she were raped." The mother kept saying that she could not believe that it had happened. Individual therapy with the child continued and family sessions were held intermittently. Two years later, child protection authorities received a referral about the 12-year-old sister in the family. On investigation it was determined that the younger sister had been sexually involved with the father for about one year. The older sister had debated telling her therapist about her sister's initiation into the incest, but had rationalized not reporting by telling herself, "The trouble with my sister is that she likes it." In a family session at the child protection agency, the father admitted the relationship, but this time with emotion. The mother began treatment in a group of incest mothers. At the first meeting she left the group, sobbing and upset, saying, "I thought I had dealt with this, but I guess I really had not."

Could involvement of the younger sibling have been prevented had the therapist notified child protection authorities as soon as the first instance of incest was revealed? We have seen many other cases in which a protective service approach was taken only after another sibling, a neighbor, or another relative was approached sexually by the abuser. Some perpetrators have told us later in fathers' groups that the therapist's promise not to report the case never allayed their fear of being caught.

Failure to report not only gives the initial perpetrator time and anxiety enough to victimize another child, it may also give the victim time and opportunity to turn the passive experience into an active one by initiating sexual activity with a younger child. Burgess and co-workers[14] have described several cases in which a sexually abused latency age child dealt with the trauma by beginning to experiment sexually with a younger child or toddler. It is now generally known that many rapists and pedophiles have a history of sexual abuse in childhood.[15] What needs to be weighed by the physician deciding whether to report is that this evolution of sexual victim to sexual aggressor may occur within weeks or months and place this child's younger siblings and neighbors at risk for sexual abuse.

It is well to remember that morbidity in parents, as well as morbidity in children, can sometimes be prevented if the family is forced to receive medical evaluation. The following case is one in which reporting may have been instrumental in saving the lives of both parents.

Case 2   The R family was referred because all five children in the family, all of whom were under 4 years of age, were failing to thrive. Mr. R was alcoholic and Mrs. R had had a difficult hospital course with her last delivery, a twin birth. She had failed to keep postpartum medical appointments. Despite great anger and resistance in the parents, the children were removed. The removal triggered increased medical contact for the entire family. Mrs. R was diagnosed as having panpituitary insufficiency (Sheehan's syndrome) secondary to her most recent delivery, and replacement hormone treatment was begun. Mr. R entered an alcoholism treatment program where he revealed a detailed and dangerous suicide plan.

2. Determining the Incidence of Child Abuse and Neglect

In the State of New Mexico in 1976, homicide was the fourth leading cause of death for children aged 1 to 4, coming after accidents, anomalies and pneumonia.[16] Furthermore, it seemed as though the child death rate from homicide had increased in New Mexico from 11.1/100,000 population in 1973 to 19.6/100,000 in 1976. This had apparently occurred despite the initiation of several demonstration projects for the treatment and prevention of child abuse in New Mexico in that time period. However, a closer look at the statistics shows that the increase in homicide deaths was paralleled by a large decrease in accidental deaths. In 1973 the death rate for children aged 1 to 4 due to accidents was 74.6/100,000 population. In 1976 there were 33.2 deaths due to accidents per 100,000 population in that age group. Discussion with the state medical investigators indicated that what was happening in the state was that deaths, which would have been ascribed to accident ten years previously, were now being correctly diagnosed as instances of battering or homicide.

Intrafamilial sexual abuse or incest is another kind of child abuse in which incidence has been greatly underestimated. A survey of 500 normal women in the Albuquerque, New Mexico area showed that 15 of the 500, or 3%, had experienced intrafamilial sexual abuse prior to the age of 13.[17] As late as 1975, a major textbook of psychiatry estimated that the incidence of incest was one per million.[18]

The problem of proving that intervention in abuse/neglect families improves prognosis is made impossible by the fact that we lack a natural history of this condition before intervention was legally mandated.

Statistics now available indicate that any pediatrician in practice should be seeing cases of child abuse and neglect regularly. The best statistics indicate that 6 of every 1000 children will be battered; that figure increases to 3 in every 100 for children who have been residents of newborn intensive care units.[19] One out of 100 children will fail to thrive, some for environmental reasons,[20] and 3 of 100 children will be sexually abused. Only if all suspected cases are reported can the true incidence and spectrum of the problem be appreciated and accurate information be obtained about response to interventions and strategies for preventive intervention.

3. Making the Process of Reporting More Routine While Reducing the Stigma

Available evidence indicates that as the reporting of child abuse and neglect increases the percentage of substantiated cases decreases. In 1980 in Bernalillo County, only 25% of abuse/neglect referrals were substantiated. In 1975, 50% of reports were being substantiated. Even in substantiated cases, a child or children will be removed from the home in less than 5% of these cases. This means that out of 1000 referrals a child or children will be removed from the family in about ten cases. What this means to the individual physician is that it is highly unlikely that a particular child he or she refers will be placed in foster care. Child abuse is recognized well enough by the general public that families are often able to say that they understand why physicians must be concerned about the etiology of injuries in growing children. Parents often understand and appreciate the physician's concerns about the need for protection. As reporting has increased, self-referrals by parents have also increased; in 1980, 10% of reports were self-referrals. Even though a case may be officially considered "unsubstantiated," families referred are often families with problems, which the alert protective service worker may refer to other appropriate resources.

Sexual abuse is a particular instance in which physicians can become very worried about the effects on the family, especially on the offending father, if the sexual abuse becomes known. The myth of false accusations in incest remains active among physicians despite evidence that less than 5% of incest accusations are false.[21] The infrequent false accusations are readily detected. In addition, we have yet to see an instance of false accusation in which family treatment was not indicated. The physician may ask, "But even if the incidence were only 1 in 1000, would it not be tragic to have a father undergo the shame of an incest accusation and the associated court involvement if he were innocent?" These physicians may not understand how difficult it is to prosecute incest cases. We recently tabulated the court experience in 125 consecutive cases of substantiated sexual abuse in Bernalillo County. Only five persons were criminally charged among those 125 perpetrators. Of the five who were charged, only two were convicted. In both convictions there was physical evidence of sexual abuse in the form of photographs taken of the child by the perpetrator. Given this very low rate of convictions in substantiated (that is, substantiated by social workers) cases of sexual abuse, it is very unlikely that a false accusation of incest could lead to a conviction, at least not in this jurisdiction.

If one thinks about these false accusations from a medical rather than from a legal viewpoint, one can begin to imagine what dreadful family problems must be present before a child engages in an attempt to have her father jailed. A visit by a social worker who asks, "Is there a problem with your children?" is usually a helpful intervention for such disturbed families.

The sexual abuse area is one in which the move to recriminalize child abuse has been most active. In the model program in Santa Clara County, California,[10] fathers are routinely taken through the criminal court system to be sentenced to treatment. This is a unique situation because law enforcement and the courts are well coordinated to promote treatment rather than imprisonment of fathers. There is not the deterrent to reporting that there would be in a less ideal system which emphasized criminal prosecution at the expense of treatment approaches.

4. Providing Help for Families by Reporting Them

In 1972 in New York City, only 8 of 2300 reports of child abuse and neglect came from private physicians.[22] At present in Bernalillo County, about 1% of all referrals come from pediatricians in private practice.

Perhaps there is no need for reporting in the population that utilizes private practice medical care. Data from ten consecutive cases of fatal child maltreatment contradicts this hypothesis. Of these ten families, only four were receiving welfare or other social assistance and four of the families had incomes above $10,000 a year. Of the ten mothers, nine were either in the first three months' postpartum or pregnant at the time of the death of the child. Four of the five women not known to social agencies had been seen by a private pediatrician or obstetrician in the month prior to the child's death.[17] Of the ten child victims, four were under six months of age. Two of those four had been born prematurely and had been treated in a neonatal intensive care setting. These data clearly point to a role in child abuse prevention for the private pediatrician, as well as for the obstetrician.

However, child protection agencies also seem to have failed in prevention in these cases. Of the six children who were over six months of age at the time of their death, five had been previously reported to child protection agencies as being mistreated. This returns us to the question of whether reporting does actually reduce morbidity and mortality from child abuse.

On retrospective review, two families were found in which prior infant deaths had occurred, which were later judged to have resulted from the child maltreatment syndrome rather than from accidents. It may be that the chance to prevent battering of the next sibling was lost when those past deaths were misdiagnosed. Reporting may be more effective at preventing abuse for the younger siblings than for the victim who is reported. In some cases it may be a report of the abuse of the mother in her childhood that would have been necessary to preventively protect the children she later bears. The following is a case in point.

Case 3   At 16, *A* returned to live with her parents after bearing her stepfather's child. The stepfather beat and raped her, and she determined finally to tell someone about the incest situation. She told her story at a hospital emergency room but was not believed. She was judged to be "hysterical" and was sedated. Five years later, she left her ill 1-year-old son with her intoxicated, angry boyfriend. The child was sodomized and beaten to death.

Her failure to protect the child exactly mirrors her physician's failure to protect her. Of the ten mothers in our series of fatal maltreatment cases, four had been incest victims; none had successfully reported their plight. Since sexual abuse tends to occur in families with higher annual incomes than the average abusive family, these families are at risk for not being reported and for not receiving help.

Physicians other than pediatricians may have unique access to families in which child abuse is occurring. Psychiatrists may see these parents. Although fewer than 5% of abusing parents are diagnosed as psychotic, many are diagnosed as having personality disorder, alcoholism, or other substance abuse. Sexual dysfunction, depression, and suicide attempts are seen in the mothers of sexual abuse victims.[23] Psychiatrists who see these parents in times of crisis have an opportunity to detect child abuse.

Hysterical symptoms, particularly hysterical paralyses, have been reported in parents who are trying to defend themselves against abusing a child. Such parents may be seen in an emergency room where an alert physician may recognize the underlying danger of abuse.[24] Impending sexual abuse may also present with somatic complaints, as illustrated by the following case.

Case 4   A 42-year-old veteran demanded admission to a veteran's hospital complaining of back, leg, and stomach pain and saying that he felt he was going to die. Because his anxiety was so extreme, he was admitted. Each time that his symptoms abated enough to warrant discharge, he would develop a new series of complaints. "You can't send me home," he told his physician. A family session was held. The physician discovered that sexual relations had ceased between the patient and his wife and that the patient had been sleeping with his 14-year-old daughter.

Although actual sexual contact had not yet occurred, the patient feared that this was imminent. After four sessions of family therapy, the patient's somatic symptoms resolved and he felt ready to go home.

Emergency room physicians also treat childhood poisonings, burns, and other accidents which tend to occur in families where abuse and neglect are also risks. Some investigators have suggested that parents routinely be interviewed after accidents to assess their skills in protecting children. It is clear that "stress" may be a common factor in many injuries, accidental and nonaccidental.[25,26] Rape of a child, an occurrence that is also thought of as accidental, may also be more likely to occur in families in which "nonaccidental" incest rape is also a problem. One 8-year-old was brought in for examination three days after having been raped by a stranger. The child's alcoholic father had been adamant in his refusal to allow the rape to be reported. On examination the child admitted that she had been having intercourse with her father for several months prior to the rape.

Physicians can become involved by parents as co-perpetrators of certain kinds of child abuse. Munchausen's syndrome by proxy has been described by pediatricians.[27] In this syndrome, a mother simulates an obscure disease in her child and has the child continuously evaluated and reevaluated medically. One death from this syndrome has been reported; a mother who was simulating hypernatremia in her infant miscalculated and administered more sodium than her child could survive. In the sexual abuse area we have seen disturbed mothers who take their children to different physicians to have pelvic examinations which the mother insists on observing. The mother may then repeat the "pelvic examination" at home and this becomes a part of the abusive sexual behavior. Nineteenth century cases in which fathers and physicians collaborated to devise inspections and punishments to prevent children from masturbating probably represent another instance of the cooperation of the professional in the perpetration of sexual abuse.[28]

5. Reporting Increases the Physician's Influence with Child Protective Agencies

Most professionals agree that in severe abuse situations treatment is not a one-person job. We recently reviewed the first nine months of treatment in a family in which sexual abuse had occurred. Thirty-two different agencies were involved with the family in that nine-month period. Why so many different agencies? There were three incest victims in the family and two brothers who were being physically abused. One of the incest victims had become pregnant by the father and needed support in relinquishing that baby; another was severely depressed; the third was involved in prostitution and drugs and kept running away from home and from alternate placements. Both physical abuse victims required medical care and special educational placement. The father was unemployed; the family home burned down; the mother needed birth control counseling; and so forth. Crisis intervention in such a family is an almost daily necessity.

The question for the physician is, "How can I find the help I need?" It is also clear that the problems involved are exceedingly complex and that recognition and reporting are just the first steps in helping the family, although extremely critical ones. It is important for the physician not to consider protective services as only a resource to which he or she refers families, but to realize that he himself should be an important resource to the protective service worker, because of both his medical expertise and his relationship with the family. An ongoing collaboration which involves the family, the physician, and the protective service worker serves the best interests of the child. Perhaps the best incentive to continued reporting by physicians is the experience of participating in a constructive, positive response to the needs of an abusive family which results in adequate protection of the children.

Physicians with a good working relationship with protective services may help to promote better assessment of the health needs of children already in foster placement, such as maintaining growth charts or immunization records. The physician is also in an ideal situation to work cooperatively with protective services concerning high risk families. For example, a mother had had a previous infant removed to foster care because of failure to thrive and multiple fractures. When she became pregnant again, her private pediatrician was alerted by her protective service worker that this mother would need extra support and monitoring. In this case the mother was successfully able to nurture the second child.

DISCUSSION

Physicians usually have good reasons for not reporting a case of child abuse. For example, when a child complains of sexual abuse, the physician is confronted with a host of worries. Is the child telling the truth? How can the family be confronted? What sort of a forensic examination is required? What legal involvements will occur? Will the family be separated? Will protective service involvement simply make things worse? Might this be "normal" behavior in the family culture? In our experience many of these problems are resolved by reporting, and few are resolved by not reporting. By reporting, the physician gains allies and information. Child and family-oriented worries are given priority: Does the child feel supported and protected? Is she at risk for gonorrhea? For pregnancy? For physical abuse? For neglect? Are there other

166

family problems? Are other children at risk for sexual abuse by the perpetrator? Are all family members receiving adequate medical care? Does the family have support from extended family, schools, jobs?

As physician and caseworker collaborate, they may effectively challenge in each other untested assumptions about intrafamilial sexual abuse, ie, that children lie about incest, that mothers are never perpetrators, that only daughters are victimized, that the children do not mind being abused, that the children can never return to live with the perpetrator, that natural fathers are never perpetrators, that gonorrhea is transmitted through the bed sheets. It is only because of recent efforts to obtain thorough and accurate reporting that we are beginning to be able to evaluate critically these assumptions.

Increased reporting will inevitably lead to a greater percentage of reported cases that cannot be substantiated. Similarly, more extensive screening of the contacts of patients with venereal disease would be expected to yield a higher percentage of contacts with negative cultures, as well as yielding positive diagnoses in cases which otherwise would have gone undetected. The "unnecessary" bother to the "false-positive" families is horrifying only in the context of our unrealistic expectations that parents should be flawless. Most patients will understand the need for further diagnostic tests when there is a positive test for syphilis and will understand that there is a possibility that syndromes other than syphilis, or that a laboratory error, caused the positive test.

The need for further testing in cases of incest accusation can be explained along similar lines. The disrupted families that are reported because of intrafamilial sexual abuse are always quick to charge that the state is "killing" them through its intrusive intervention. The children and the families who are actually killed through the "kindness" of nonintervention will be more difficult to detect. Systematic reporting and follow-up will be necessary if we are to adequately weigh the relative risks.

REFERENCES

1. Caffey J: Multiple fractures in long bones of infants suffering from chronic subdural hematoma. *Am J Roentgen* 56:163-173, 1946.

2. Butler S: *Conspiracy of Silence: The Trauma of Incest.* San Francisco, New Glide, 1978.

3. Kempe CH, Silverman FN, Steele BF, et al: The battered child syndrome. *JAMA* 181:17-24, 1962.

4. Blumberg M: Treatment of the abused child and the child abuser. *Am J Psychotherapy* 31:204-215, 1977.

5. Rosenfeld AA, Newberger EH: Compassion vs. control: Conceptual and practical pitfalls in the broadened definition of child abuse. *JAMA* 237:2086-2088, 1977.

6. Terr LC, Watson AS: The battered child rebrutalized: Ten cases of medical-legal confusion. *Am J Psychiatry* 124:1432–1439, 1968.

7. Goldstein J, Freud A, Solnit A: *Before the Best Interests of the Child.* New York, Free Press, 1980.

8. Szasz T: *The Myth of Mental Illness: Foundations of a Theory of Personal Conduct.* New York, Harper & Row, 1974.

9. Goldstein J, Freud A, Solnit A: *Beyond the Best Interest of the Child.* New York, Free Press, 1980.

10. Giaretto H: Humanistic treatment of father-daughter incest, in Helfer R, Kempe CH (eds): *Child Abuse and Neglect: The Family and the Community.* Cambridge, MA, Ballinger, 1976.

11. Smith SM, Hanson R: One hundred-thirty-four battered children: A medical and psychological study. *Br Med J* 3:666–670, 1974.

12. Buchanan A, Oliver JE: Abuse and neglect as a cause of mental retardation: A study of 140 children admitted to subnormality hospitals in Wiltshire. *Br J Psychiatry* 131:458–467, 1977.

13. Maisch H: *Incest.* New York, Stein & Day, 1972.

14. Burgess AW, Groth AN, Holmstrom LL, et al: *Sexual Assault of Children and Adolescents.* Lexington, MA, Lexington Books, 1978.

15. Hanmer EF: Symptoms of sexual deviation: Dynamics and etiology. *Psychoanal Rev* 55:5–27, 1968.

16. *Selected Health Statistics 1977.* Santa Fe, New Mexico: Health and Environment Department, 1977.

17. Goodwin J, McCarty T, DiVasto P: Prior incest in abusive mothers. *Child Abuse Neglect* 5:1–9, 1981.

18. Rush F: *The Best Kept Secret: Sexual Abuse of Children.* New York, Prentice-Hall, 1980.

19. Chadwick DL, Henderson RW, Dean DJ: The incidence of abuse and neglect in infants discharged from a neonatal intensive care unit. *Clin Res* 26:179A, 1978.

20. Koel B: Failure to thrive and fatal injury as a continuum. *Am J Dis Children* 118:565–567, 1969.

21. Goodwin J, Sahd D, Rada R: Incest hoax: False accusations, false denials. *Bull Am Acad Psychiatry Law* 6 (3):269–276, 1979.

22. Helfer RE: Why most physicians don't get involved in child abuse cases and what to do about it. *Children Today* 4:28–32, 1975.

23. Goodwin J. Suicide attempts in sexual abuse victims and their mothers. *Child Abuse Neglect* (To be published).

24. Mogelniecki R, Mogelniecki NP, Chandler JE, et al: Impending child abuse: Psychosomatic symptoms in adults as a clue. *JAMA* 237:1109–1111, 1977.

25. Martin HL: Antecedents of burns and scalds in children. *Br J Med Psychol* 43:39–47, 1970.

26. Rogers D, Tripp J, Bentovim A, et al: Non-accidental poisoning: An extended syndrome of child abuse. *Br Med J* 1:793–796, 1976.

27. Meadow R: Munchausen syndrome by proxy: The hinterland of child abuse. *Lancet* ii :343–345, 1977.

28. Williams G, Money J: *Traumatic Abuse and Neglect of Children.* Baltimore, Johns Hopkins Press, 1980, pp. 411–414.

15 Cross-Cultural Perspectives on Clinical Problems of Incest

Jean Goodwin

Like the blind men with the elephant, anthropologists and psychiatrists have traditionally grasped at different ends of the problem of incest. Anthropologists try to understand the rules that cultures develop about incest. Psychiatrists try to restore to normal functioning those individuals who have broken those rules.

This chapter will describe six clinical *problems* in the treatment of incest victims and their families:

1. Hysterical seizures developing after an incest event
2. Suicide attempts in incest victims and in other members of their families
3. Runaway incest victims
4. How incest operates as a defense against loss
5. Subsequent maternal failure in women who have been incest victims
6. How to talk with children about incest in a nonthreatening way.

Clinical aspects of these problems have been discussed in previous chapters. This chapter will focus on the cross-cultural and folkloric data which have been critical to understanding these clinical problems.

In the process of trying to understand these clinical problems in a cross-cultural context, I have developed the hypothesis that clinicians like myself, together with storytellers and rule-makers in many different societies, have been observing a single set of symptoms that characterize incest victims and their families. Most of the cross-cultural data referred to here comes from S.K. Weinberg's 1955 book, *Incest Behavior,*[1] which reviews beliefs about incest from 11 different cultures. These data are limited and somewhat dated, but are unbiased in that they were not originally selected to support the hypothesis that the punishments and consequences of incest reported in these cultures are congruent with the psychological symptoms that American clinicians observe in incest participants. Western folk beliefs about incest will be drawn from Greek mythology and from the medieval cycle of legends about fathers who propose marriage to their daughters; this tale is typified by the Grimms' fairytale *Thousandfurs.*[2]

1. Hysterical Seizures Developing After an Incest Event

My first exposure to the clinical association between hysterical seizures and incest was several years ago when as a psychiatric consultant I saw a young Navajo boy. The clinical question at that time was whether the boy's seizures were "real" or hysterical. When I consulted a psychiatrist who had worked on the Navajo reservation, he advised me to ask the boy whether he had experienced incest and whether he was considered to be a witch. The boy's affirmative answers to these questions opened the door to a therapeutic relationship that controlled his seizures. As the Navajo see things, seizures, witchcraft and incest are inextricably linked. Any child who has organically-based seizures will be *assumed* to have experienced incest and will be compelled to produce hysterical seizures as well in order to confirm his reputation as a witch, so that he can have at least one weapon with which to intimidate the peers who are tormenting and avoiding him.

Several years later, I was surprised to find a similar constellation of symptoms in an Anglo-American teenage girl who had her first hysterical seizure after she had run away from home two weeks after her natural father had intercourse with her for the first time. I was intrigued enough by the parallels in the two cases to review the records of 12 consecutive psychiatric admissions for hysterical epilepsy.[3] Four of these 12 patients reported prior incest. Only one of the four was Navajo. On reviewing a previous study from Canada that reported on 25 cases of hysterical seizures, I found that two of the women in that sample had reported a prior incest experience to a neurologist in a context where there was no theoretical suspicion that incest and hysterical seizures might be causally connected.[4]

One could explain the connection between incest, seizures, and witchcraft among the Navajo as the result of cultural programming, but how to explain similar connections appearing in Anglo-American teenagers in the late twentieth century?

Incest has been connected with witchcraft in several areas of Western folklore. Incest was said to occur as part of the witches' sabbath.[5] The product of mother-son incest was reputed in various parts of Europe to have powers as a witch, magician, or vampire.[6] Anne Boleyn, wife of Henry VIII of England, was convicted as a witch in part because incest had been proved against her.[5] Anglo-Americans and Navajos are not the only cultures with traditions linking incest and witchcraft. Two of the 11 cultures reviewed by Weinberg make similar connections. The Mojave Indians say that most shamans have experienced incest, and the Wayao of Africa commit incest in order to gain magical powers.[1]

Folklore connections were also made between incest and seizures. Galen, the second century Greek physician whose opinions became dogma during the Renaissance, taught that seizures were the result of premature intercourse in childhood; that is not in fact too distant from Freud's hypothesis that an hysterical seizure repeats a traumatic event.[7] The Navajo remedy for seizures is to subject the sufferer to the Moth Way chant, a ceremony that retells the story of a disastrous cultural experiment with incest.[8] Since the thirteenth century, European seizure victims have been advised to make a pilgrimage to the Church of Saint Dymphna at Gheel (or Geel) in Belgium. There the epileptic reviews, on prescribed daily circuits of the church, the story of a young princess who fled from her father's sexual advances (see Appendix I). In both of these healing rituals, the review and the reworking of an incest story is the central action. This treatment might work as an efficient "shotgun therapy" for seizures in much the same way that penicillin works in upper respiratory infections. For the minority of cases that are curable, the prescribed treatment will be curative. For the majority of cases where neither an incest experience or a bacteria has had etiological importance, the prescribed treatment will have nonspecific beneficial effects. Even though the majority of seizures are probably not incest-related, the seizures that can be cured without modern medicines may well be responsive to an incest story. Patients who were not incest victims might respond to the stories as well because of their impact on unconscious oedipal conflicts, their symbolic impact in creating a liminal situation where realities can be reversed to make regeneration seem possible, or because of less specific placebo effects. In both European and Navajo cultures other mental disorders, including psychoses, and possession states, are treated in the same way as epilepsy.

These observations led me to the following hypothesis: Hysterical epilepsy is one of a definable spectrum of responses to the experience of incest which have been observed by various cultures and which can be deduced from the cultural lore about the consequences of incest.

Hysterical epilepsy is a particularly natural symptom choice for an incest victim. The hysterical seizure repeats movements related to sexual stimulation as well as movements that are related to resisting a sexual assault.[9] During a seizure the patient is able to terrify others, rather than being the one terrified as she had been during the sexual attack. Incest must be kept secret, but the hysterical seizure attack, which symbolizes the incest, may take place in public, releasing some of the tension of the secret. One of our patients repeated the phrase, "I promise," during her hysterical seizures. Therapeutic analysis helped her to recall that her brother "made me promise not to tell" after each episode of fondling. Incest victims often pretend to be asleep during the sexual event and the adult participant, especially if he is alcoholic, will often claim to have no memory of the sexual attack. The feigned sleep and the feigned amnesia that accompany the hysterical seizure repeat these defenses against acknowledging the incest secret.

Other types of dissociative symptoms have been reported in incest victims including multiple personality, and a trance-like withdrawal from unpleasant realities.[10] The dissociated incest victim and those around her often decide that since she is not in contact with ordinary reality, she must be in touch with some more powerful reality. Also, since hysterical seizures and related symptoms such as possession states are easily treated by hypnosis, the incest victim is likely to become the patient or disciple of a hypnotist or shaman who may then train the victim to become a practitioner. This is one possible life history that would link the incest experience to the subsequent hysterical seizure, and then to the eventual identification as a witch or a healer.

2. Suicide Attempts in Incest Victims and Other Family Members

When I began to collect cases of hysterical seizures in incest victims, I was surprised to find that all six of these teenagers had either threatened or attempted suicide.[3] My acquaintance with the Navajo folk beliefs had not prepared me for suicide attempts, but only for seizures and witchcraft. I went back to my friend, the psychiatrist who had worked among the Navajo, and asked him about suicide. I was reassured to learn that the Navajo had again anticipated my clinical observation. The Navajo say that the act of incest plants a moth into the brain. As this moth matures, it will drive the incest offender into the fire just as a moth flies into the fire. The belief is linked to the Moth Way legend which tells of how delightedly the moth people welcomed a plan to marry their daughters to their sons so that no one would ever need to leave home. However, during the wedding ceremony all the moths flew into the fire. The implication is that the impulse to commit incest is as self-destructive as the impulse to fly into the fire. Several cases have been reported in which Navajo incest victims have actually fallen into the fire in their hogan during an hysterical seizure and have been seriously burned.[8]

In a brief follow-up of 201 urban Anglo-American and Spanish-American families where incest had occurred, I found subsequent suicide attempts in 11 of the families. Of the 13 suicide attempts that occurred in these 11 families, five occurred in mothers and eight in daughters.[11] Previous studies have also reported suicide attempts in perpetrators; in a study done in Germany, 3% of incarcerated incestuous fathers killed themselves in prison.[5] In our sample the three mothers who made suicide attempts in the first week after the incest accusation had all been incest victims themselves. They also had serious psychiatric diagnoses and substance abuse problems. These three conditions combined made it impossible for them to cope with the incest accusation. The two mothers who made attempts at suicide later did so at a point when they felt they were being forced to choose between husband and daughter. The suicide attempts seemed to express the frustration these mothers had at feeling forced to choose the daughter; the attempts also gave them an excuse to retreat from that mothering choice. Neither of these mothers was able to return to successful mothering of her daughter, and both of the daughters later attempted suicide themselves. All eight of the daughters who attempted suicide were between 14 and 16 and had been involved in incest with the father-figure in the family. None of their families had remained intact after the disclosure of the incest. The mothers had actively blamed and disbelieved these eight victims.

The Western cultural experience gives us some warning that suicide attempts may be a problem in incest families. In the Oedipus story, the "victim" Oedipus plucks out his eyes in a self-mutilating gesture; the "perpetrator" Joscasta commits suicide by hanging herself, and an "uninvolved sibling daughter" Antigone ultimately hangs herself. In the story of Phaedra's attempted seduction of her stepson, she too kills herself.[12] In the series of medieval legends and romances which describe a daughter's flight from an incestuous father, the daughter often mutilates herself to discourage the father by cutting off her hands or breasts.[6] In other versions the heroine commits suicide, commonly by drowning, to escape incest.

The cross-cultural experience is similar. In 5 of the 11 cultures described by Weinberg, suicide was forced on incest participants.[1] It was second only to banishment in frequency of use as a punishment for incest.

Is there some common psychodynamic factor that explains why, like Oedipus and other legendary figures, modern-day teenage incest victims harm themselves? Is it the same factor that made the Tikopians and Gilbert Islanders decide that it was a workable punishment to ask incest participants to canoe out into the Pacific ocean? Or that made the Greeks and Romans decide that incest partners would take their meaning if they sent each a sword? The Murngin of Australia ask the incest participants to walk into enemy territory where they will certainly be killed.[1]

Sexual guilt is the major theme of the Oedipus story. Certainly, in the victimized teenagers who attempted suicide, the mothers' blame and disbelief, and the chaos that their accusations had loosed upon their families were constant reminders of the price that had been exacted for their sexual activities. In addition, 4 of the 8 made attempts immediately after a sexual experiment with a boyfriend, eg, after a first experience with breast-petting.[11] It may seem logical to attack one's body if that body seems capable of causing so much devastation. All five of the mothers who attempted suicide in my study had been sterilized either surgically or through repeated bouts of gonorrhea. Other studies have shown that hysterectomy in the mother is present with significantly greater frequency in incest families than in the general population. Sixty-five percent of incest mothers have had hysterectomies.[13] This family experience of castration may act to reinforce the family's belief that sexuality is dangerous and that those who have yielded to it will inevitably be mutilated or killed.

Another theme in the Oedipus story and in the lives of my patients is the failure of the child's desperate attempt to keep the family from disintegrating. The tragedy in these stories is that it is the very thoroughness and desperation of the attempt that assures failure. Oedipus thought that by leaving home he was taking the only possible course that would avoid for him the loss of his father; unknowingly, he killed his father on the journey. The eight incest victims in my sample had made an unconscious decision that the only way to keep their mother, and to keep their father for their mother, was to satisfy the father's sexual needs. Yet it was that very sacrifice which led to the father being banished from the home and to the mother turning against the daughter. For a child whose self-esteem is based on her loyalty to the family and on her competence in solving problems to meet her family's needs (as did Oedipus when he bested the Sphinx), this failure is devastating.

A third motive for suicide in these children is that they, like Oedipus, are afraid that if they are allowed to live they might become dangerous and harmful to the parent who has abandoned them. In my series, mothers and daughters were enmeshed in hostile relationships with each other and with other women. The daughter-victim is often afraid even to ask the mother for help, much less to express anger at her. She is afraid this will make the mother withdraw even more, or if the mother is physically ill as she is in 20% of incest familes,[5] the child is afraid that her anger might be the final blow which kills the mother. So as the child sustains more rejection and blame from the mother, she has no outlet for her anger except to turn it against herself. A Lithuanian folk ballad describes a mother who exposed to the ocean her infant sons in a small boat. When they unexpectedly returned alive as adults, she proposed to marry one of them.[6] However, rather than protecting her as

Oedipus had done, the sons killed the mother. In clinical practice as well as in folklore, the anger of the victimized child will occasionally erupt as homicide rather than as the more usual suicidal behavior.[9]

3. Runaway Incest Victims

Of all female teenagers who run away, between 30% and 50% are incest victims.[14] All six teenage incest victims with hysterical seizures and suicide attempts that I and my co-workers have described had also run away from home.[3] Of the eight teenage incest victims with suicide attempts but without seizures, four had also run away from home.[11]

One of the major problems in treating teenage incest victims who can no longer manage or be managed in the family is that these children run away from placements as well as from their homes. In one family the eldest daughter-victim reported the incest and then ran away from placements back to her home 12 times during her teenage years. On the last occasion, she had become 18 years of age and could no longer be removed by child protective authorities. However, when this girl's younger sister reported incest that had now shifted to her, the younger sister agreed to testify in criminal court against her father and he was sent to jail. The mother in the family was so angry with this daughter that she would not allow her to return home. In the first year after her report the child ran away from 13 different placements.

Working with this family gave me ample opportunity to contemplate the various meanings of running away. Running away was certainly this family's principal strategy for coping with problems, although this was usually done by denial, psychosis, or intoxication rather than literally by running with the feet. Also, in this family the child's admission of the incest was treated as a running away, as an abandonment of the family. The only way to undo this was to run away again. Furthermore, with her father in prison, it seemed that the younger daughter was unwilling to let herself become more comfortable in a placement than was her father. In fact, when he was injured in a fight in prison, the daughter attempted suicide. It was as though she felt, like Camus, that if her friend were in prison, she too should be sleeping on the floor.[15] Another process which seemed to be taking place was that this child was growing so rapidly during the year in which she had her first opportunity to live with normal families, that she would outgrow a placement quite rapidly. With each new placement, her behavior problems decreased and her strengths increased, so that each new set of parents could begin by treating her more as a normal adolescent. It was almost as though she had substituted the question, "Where will I be?" for the more usual adolescent question of, "Whom will I become?" As with many adolescent incest victims, the storm seemed to ease after exactly one year. She chose a rather Spartan placement supervised almost entirely by peer counselors, completed the program there, and is now working. Her solution seemed to satisfy her need for a prison-like existence and for a placement in which she would not betray her parents further by substituting better parents for them.

Our Western mythology tells us that incest victims wander. Oedipus wandered out into the desert. Hippolytus, after being sexually approached by his stepmother, got into his chariot and fled so blindly that his journey ended in his being trampled under the feet of his horses.[12] Saint Dymphna set sail from her home without knowing how to navigate or steer (see Appendix I).

If one looks at Weinberg's cross-cultural sample, banishment is the incest punishment most commonly prescribed for both perpetrator and victim. In the 11 cultures described by Weinberg, seven mentioned banishment.[1] Ostracism can substitute for banishment in some cultures. This review is a reminder that when we speak about an incest taboo, we are using a word which means "to set apart."

American social workers seem to be following in the grand tradition of banishment and ostracism of incest participants. A typical case plan involves banishing the offending father to prison, banishing the child to a foster home, and banishing the mother and the remaining children to a wasteland of poverty and ostracism.

What is remarkable is that even when social institutions make every effort to keep families together and integrated into the social system, individual family members manage to taboo, ostracize, and banish themselves. Other cultures do not make a distinction between perpetrator and victim. Whoever breaks the taboo is punished, regardless of sex or age. Clinically, in our society children and adolescents who have been involved in incest can at times attain for themselves, through suicide attempts and runaways, a punishment equivalent to that meted out to the offender.

An extreme example of this is the Cinderella syndrome, a pattern of simulated neglect in children who had previously experienced actual abuse. Several years ago, we observed two cases in which 9-year-old incest victims dressed themselves in rags, claimed they had to do all the chores and that their adoptive parents favored their siblings.[16] Because of this extreme behavior, these children were referred to a protective service agency and eventually had to be placed in another home. Both of these girls had been physically and sexually abused in their original homes. Instead of being banished, however, they had been taken in by relatives dedicated to parenting them.

It is instructive to recall that the fairytale *Cinderella* is closely related to the series of tales such as *Thousandfurs* and *The Legend of Saint Dymphna,* that describe the flight of a daughter from her incestuous father who had chosen the daughter to replace her dead mother. Almost inevitably this heroine, although rescued by a prince who marries her, encounters a new series of problems with a stepmother or mother-in-law who treats her like a criminal or witch, often threatening to have the heroine burned at the stake.[17] These difficulties with the new mother-figure always precipitate a new cycle of running away by the heroine.

Despite the best efforts of the incest victim and of the adoptive parents, the banishment prescribed in the old myths took place in the cases I and my co-workers described. It took place in the form of both the child's Cinderella fantasy, which brought about literal removal, and severe scapegoating of the child, which had created a psychological banishment.

One of the principal dynamics at work in these cases was the child's need to preserve a good image of the original parents despite the physical and sexual abuse. These children displaced their anger and hurt from the past into the present in order to cling to the image of an idealized past mother. This seemed necessary in order for them to hope for something good in the future. The price they paid was that they had to keep running from the frightening parental figures that their displacement created in the present. The Cinderella child abandons her new family in a blaming way, just as she imagines that her natural mother abandoned her by dying. By recreating and justifying the event, the child avoids feeling the hurt and the loss of that abandonment.

In my clinical examples both patients who produced Cinderella syndromes had experienced the death of a mother, in addition to incest. Like Oedipus with his father, they suffered the anxiety that their sexual experiences had somehow contributed to the mother's death. The treatment for these children was to complete their mourning for the lost mother. In both of their adoptive families, certain family members had been so outraged and ashamed of the child's original mother that the child had not been allowed even to speak of this person.[16]

In the Grimms' version of the Cinderella story, Cinderella waters a tree with her tears each day as she mourns for her dead mother. It is this tree that ultimately produces dresses and shoes for the prince's ball and the other attributes necessary for Cinderella to form successful relationships.[2]

Watering a tree with one's tears may be the most apt metaphor for the kind of therapeutic grieving necessary in any incest victim who runs away. Like other melancholics, the teenage incest victim who runs away is often making a symbolic statement that it is she who has committed the crime of abandonment, not the parents who are guilty of abandoning her. By simulating neglect, the younger Cinderella runaways are coming closer than do the adolescent runaways to stating that they are running away in order to find the good parenting that they need. However, the Cinderella child is usually unaware of how her own psychological flight from grieving for the dead mother and from feeling grief about the frightening incest experience have perpetuated her difficulty in forming the new attachments which would provide the mothering she seeks.

4. How Incest Operates as a Defense Against Loss

The phenomenon of runaways in incest victims becomes even more puzzling when one becomes sufficiently familiar with incest families to understand that separations are avoided and viewed as highly dangerous in these families.[18] These are families in which daughter-victims are not allowed to date, mothers are not allowed to have jobs outside of the home, and children who run away almost inevitably allow themselves to be caught in a way that binds them even more tightly to the home.[19]

In fact, one of the clinical interpretations of the runaways which occur in these families is that they are counterphobic; that is, the family fears of separation are so extreme that the child is too afraid to take the usual gradual steps to leave home and so, like Hippolytus, must blindly run.

Since separation is the major fear in these families, many clinicians have felt that the incest itself must be functioning to abate that fear of separation. It is clear that in some families an incestuous relationship acts directly to prevent divorce in the parents. In more than one half of incestuous families the mother is refusing sex to her husband at the time the incest starts.[20] The incest relationship provides the sexual outlet for the husband while at the same time binding him more closely to his wife because he feels he has to atone for his guilty secret. The wife's discomfort is eased as her daughter moves into a more mothering role.

These families are not only wary of the daily separations and losses that are the normal human circumstance, but they become panicked when they must face a real threat of death. Again and again one hears in the family history that it was an accident, an illness, or a death in the family which immediately preceded the initiation of incest. I have seen three families in which the incestuous relationship began after a child had been seriously injured in an automobile accident. In two of these cases, the parent began sexually fondling the child while the child was ill in the hospital. Another very typical family history is that the sexual abuse began immediately after the mother's hysterectomy or the father's vasectomy. Again, it is common for sexual abuse between father and daughter to begin while the mother is still in the hospital recovering from the hysterectomy.

Western mythology and folklore give us some clues that a family tragedy can precipitate incest. The name Oedipus means "clubfoot," and the death by exposure of such a child would have been routine. Perhaps it was this child's deformity which was the first unmanageable loss in the family of Laius and Jocasta. Of course, it was the death of Laius which immediately preceded the onset of the incest. In the biblical story of Lot and his daughters, that family had just experienced the loss of their home and their city, plus the turning of the mother into salt.[21] In Grimms' fairytale, *Thousandfurs,* the king asks his daughter to be his wife after her mother dies tragically.

When we look at the cross-cultural data, incest emerges more concretely as a literal antidote against death. The Murngin of Australia say that the corpses of incestuous progeny do not rot.[1] The Malawi of South Africa say that if one has intercourse with one's sister, one becomes bulletproof.[5] Another South African tribe allows a father to have sexual relations with his daughter only immediately before he goes out to hunt the dangerous hippopotamus.[22] Among the Dierri in Australia, incest is allowed only immediately before battle.[5] In Black America, one sometimes hears the belief that incest will cure venereal disease; in the Middle Ages incest was thought to be a cure for bubonic plague.[6]

What is at work here? How is incest a remedy for death and other kinds of loss? It must operate against loss in some more basic way than simply by shoring up a failing marriage.

It has been postulated that the continuing lure of infanticide for human beings has to do with the fact that infanticide undoes the aging process.[23] Hercules, for example, killed his wife and all his children in the process of attaining heroic powers. As soon as one has children, one is confronted with the fact that someday one will be dead and one's child will be living in one's place. By killing one's children, one makes a symbolic statement that no such replacement will be required. Infanticide was often performed ritually in ancient times to ensure the undying strength of the parental generation: The walls of Jericho were strong because the bodies of the king's first- and last-born sons were part of the foundation; until the 1600s, dykes in Europe were similarly strengthened.[24]

Is it possible that incest could provide another symbolic opportunity to turn back the clock? It is said that Cardinal Richelieu sucked milk from his daughter's breast in order to prolong his life.[5] His death at age 57 is a dubious advertisement for this technique; although given the lethality of his physicians as documented by a contemporary patient, Moliere, Richelieu may not have fared too badly.

However, there is a certain logic to the idea that if one has sex with one's own daughter, one will never move into the older generation. No one will ever leave the family of origin to seek a mate, so the father will never be reminded by an empty nest that he is getting older and closer to death. There will never be a need for the entry of a young son-in-law to challenge the father's authority or to remind him that there exists a younger generation. If the father continues to conceive children with his daughter, even after his wife's menopause, he need not be reminded that time is passing and that he needs to reassess his priorities as he moves into a new developmental stage.

In mythology there are several legends, such as the myths about the

House of Tantalus, in which incest is linked with the ritual killing and subsequent cannibalism of children. In the New Guinea Arapesh, shamans boast that they have experienced both incest and cannibalism.[25] One anthropological theory suggests that incest became taboo because it was part of a magical ritual leading to immortality that was not allowed to ordinary persons.[26] This primordial resurrection rite may have prescribed ritual incest between adolescent brother and sister followed by ritual murdering and cannibalism of the male, with the subsequent child of the brother-sister mating representing the magically revived king. The Isis/Osiris myth is only one of many African beliefs that link the practice of incest to the attainment of immortality. Isis retrieves the fragments of her brother/husband's body and restores him to life. It has been suggested that the epidemic of brother-sister marriages in Egypt during the Roman occupation in the first two centuries after Christ was connected with the democritization of embalming, which stimulated even commoners to attempt the pharaonic recipe for immortality: Brother-sister marriage followed by the embalming rituals after death.[27]

In one way these are logical conclusions. The Navajo, however, would say they make as much sense as a moth's flying into a flame. Mythology and fairytales are an unending source of good advice about the folly of both infanticide and incest as techniques for attaining immortality. They consistently remind us that rearing a healthy child is the only route to immortality that exists in reality.

5. Subsequent Failure of Mothering in the Incest Victim

In a survey of 100 abusive mothers, I and my co-workers found that 24% of these women had been incest victims in childhood[28] vs. a 3% prevalence of prior incest in 500 normal women in the same community. Mothers of sexually abused children were no more likely to have experienced incest than were mothers of physically abused children.

Children who have been sexually abused often express overt worries that they will somehow fail as mothers. Asked if they will ever have children, the usual answer is no. Often they go on to say that they are worried that something was broken inside them by the incest so that they cannot have children. It seems that these same children, as adults, reproduce at higher fertility levels than the general population.[29] Perhaps this occurs in part because they are challenging their own fears about sterility.

Two of the 11 cultures reviewed by Weinberg predicted sterility and the inevitable extinction of the family as sequels of incest.[1] The Mojave Indians say that such a family will inevitably become extinct. The Tikopia of Melanesia say that incest offenders will become barren or their offspring will die. The Tanala of Madagascar also say that incest will lead to sterility.[30]

There are some indications from Western mythology that incest participants do not reproduce efficiently. In the Oedipus story, his sons slay each other and his daughters are condemned to death for insisting that the bodies of their brothers be buried. Legends in South America and Borneo describe how brother and sister must mate to populate the earth; however, the first child born to the couple is a dog.[26,31] Many stories in the *Thousandfurs* or *Catskin* cycle tell how the young incest victim is falsely accused of having borne a "monster" and is then condemned to death.[17] Often in folklore the fertility and prosperity of the entire land is endangered by a breach of the incest taboo. The Ashanti of Africa say that unless incest participants are killed, crops will refuse to bear fruit and children will cease to be born. It is only after his kingdom is struck by a plague that Oedipus realizes that his marriage to Jocasta is incestuous. French peasants say that horses will die, orchards will become barren, and flocks will be devastated by disease if the taboo is violated.[26] In the King Arthur legend the kingdom of Camelot is destroyed by Mordred, Arthur's son/nephew, born of an incestuous mating between the King and his sister.[6]

A clinician observes many obstacles to successful reproduction for the incest victim. She cannot reproduce if she dies, either from perineal damage secondary to premature intercourse, from complications of a premature pregnancy, or from suicide. Since 40% of incest victims become promiscuous, the risk of venereal disease which might impair fertility is increased. Frigidity, homosexuality, and psychosomatic disorders have all been reported as sequels to incest. Any of these might impair fertility by interfering with mating (see Chapter 12). Twenty percent of incest victims have been reported to have experienced severe depression.[32] If this occurs postpartum, the depression could interfere with the maternal nurturing necessary to the survival of the child. Our data indicate that the incest victim is at higher risk for battering her child. Four of ten mothers of children who had died from physical abuse were incest victims.[28] This is still another kind of reproductive failure. Genetic obstacles become a factor if the incest victim conceives by a consanguineous partner. The offspring of such a first-degree mating has less than a 50% chance of surviving and being normal. The "animal" children of folklore, born of incestuous matings, may represent deformed children.

It is likely, however, that the psychological obstacles to mothering have been most often observed in incest victims in different cultures. In medieval incest legends like Manekine (see Appendix II), the heroine's children are often described as in grave danger of being killed or abandoned.[17] Incest victims may not have experienced good mothering because of the neglect that usually precedes the incest event. They also have difficulty allowing themselves to experience physical sensations that accompany sexual and maternal love. As many as 85% of incest victims react to the incest experience with aversion to sexuality and with frigidity.[29] The mothers who batter their children often complain that the experience of breast-feeding and physical contact with the young infant is overwhelmingly close to sexual feelings. One such woman actually became convinced that her newborn son was trying to seduce her when he had erections while urinating.[28] The early sexual exploitation, which has made sexuality unmanageable, can also make mothering an intolerable experience which the mother turns off by becoming full of rage and physically abusive.

Some incest victims do not themselves abuse their children, but rather fail to protect the child from abuse by a husband or boyfriend. This failure to protect the child is linked to an inability to protect herself. More than one third of women who have been multiply-raped are incest victims.[33] Case examples are extreme. One incest victim literally froze when an intoxicated stranger began fondling her breasts; after struggling for weeks with the problem of what she might have done to stop him, she decided that she might have crawled under a table. The nonverbal techniques for signaling a sexual negative seem to be undeveloped in these women. Most victims still rationalize at some level the bizarre, exploitative, tyrannical actions of their fathers, and have difficulty even in recognizing, much less in resisting, such behaviors in their husbands.[28]

The Kalahari Bushmen of South Africa provide an instructive contrast to these sexually abused mothers who neglect, batter, and fail to protect their infants. In two decades of intensive anthropological studies of several hundred Bushmen, no instance of child abuse has been found. Infanticide of deformed infants is practiced. This is neither sociologically nor psychologically classifiable as child abuse. The Bushmen provide an almost absolute contrast to the abused and abusive parents who have unrealistic expectations of their children (based on their own memories of having themselves been prematurely thrust into a parental role), who lack any support from their parents or other adults, who have forced themselves into early pregnancies to prove their fertility, and who have experienced violence and incest in their own childhoods.

The Bushmen believe that children are incapable of even the simplest constructive activity and discourage children from any action that might be construed as work—gathering nuts, carrying them, cracking them. Girls are never asked to care for younger children.[34] In Bushman culture, social pressure would make it impossible for a girl to assume a maternal role. A number of adults are always closely present monitoring the activities of the children. Mothers are often heard to repeat a common Bushman idiom, which translates loosely as, "Get this child off my hands." At that point, a nearby adult assumes responsibility for the child. Low lean body mass, which delays menarche and suppresses later menstrual cycles during times of stress, and prolonged breast-feeding, allow women to economize maternal investment. The average interval between children is over four years. There is a strong cultural sanction against the physical expression of aggression which extends to children as well as to adults. Children are neither spanked, threatened, nor isolated. Misbehaving children are removed from the situation and distracted. Scolding is reserved for emergencies. Tantrums are ignored.[35]

What is also pertinent to this discussion is that secret sexual liaisons are an impossibility among these groups of Bushmen. The Bushmen live in open huts, clustered very closely together. They are all expert trackers, so that any couple who tried to sneak away from the settlement would leave behind signs which could literally be read like an open book. Genetic studies indicate that all children in these groups were fathered by the socially recognized father (Henry Harpending, personal communication).

One way to interpret this analogy between Bushman culture and our own society is that if we are to eliminate child abuse, we may need to give up our unrealistic expectations of children, provide constant support for parents, find ways to economize maternal investment, and develop strong sanctions against violence. It may also be necessary to eliminate the incestuous acting out that can lead to subsequent impairment of mothering in the victim.

6. How to Talk with Children About Incest

Many parents and pediatricians come to me saying that they suspect that a child has been sexually abused, but that they are afraid to talk with the child about it directly. Some are afraid of "putting ideas into the child's head." They have been conditioned by the Freudian myth to believe that children cannot distinguish incest fantasies from an actual sexual experience.[36] Others have tried to talk with the child about a possible sexual contact, but have found the child most unwilling to discuss sex and not possessing an adequate vocabulary to do so.

Some therapeutic stories have been written about incest, movies have been made, games have been invented—all in the effort to provide tools for talking with children about sexual abuse.[37]

What seems to have been forgotten in this effort is the incredible wealth of incest stories to be found in the mythology and folklore of our own and every other culture. Montaigne suggested that these folktales contain the best arguments ever devised against incest.[26] In this chapter I have already mentioned Oedipus, Phaedra, Lot, Isis and Osiris, and the fairytales of the Thousandfurs cycle. I have recently retold in English the story of the seventh-century Belgian saint, Dymphna, who rejected her father's proposal of marriage and was beheaded by him after having made a valiant attempt to run away. This story and *The Story of the Princess of Hungary,* based on legends from the twelfth and fourteenth centuries, are included as appendices to this chapter.

Incest stories which have survived for centuries provide multiple metaphors about the incest experience. Not only do these stories open up the topic of incest in a simple and nonthreatening way, but they communicate the variety of responses to the sexual abuse experience. The story of Oedipus describes the willingness to sacrifice all to save the family, the suicidal despair, the sexual guilt, the self-banishment, and the fear of reproductive failure that haunt the incest victim. The story of Phaedra's attempted seduction of Hippolytus illustrates the special incestuous temptations of stepparents and the dangerous blind panic that characterizes the runaways of incest victims. The story of Lot illustrates the importance of castastrophic loss, paternal alcoholism, and family isolation as precipitants of incest. The fairytale, *Thousandfurs,* catalogues the techniques that incest victims use to defend themselves from further sexual trauma: The victim runs away, pretends to be a beast and tests her prince, tempting him to reject or abuse her.[2] The story of Dymphna focuses on the victim's determination to save her own mind and to heal her demon-possessed father and shows how this becomes transformed into an identification as a healer (see Appendix I). This legend is also helpful in providing, in the person of the monk Gerebernus, a model for the therapist working with an incest victim. Other related tales, such as Manekine (*The Story of the Princess of Hungary*), and *Cinderella,* show how the incest victim projects her resentment of her neglectful mother onto other women and how this can lead to repeated runaways unless the girl allows herself to feel the hurt at being abandoned by her parents and can resolve this. Stories in this cycle usually end with the heroine later meeting the incestuous father accidentally and forgiving him. Stories of this type also show how self-mutilation is attempted by the victim in an effort to discourage the father's sexual interest. For example, one heroine cut off her hand so her father would not kiss it. In these stories is also the fear of having a monster-child who must be destroyed, which persists as long as the heroine has not resolved her guilt about the incest experience. The heroine may be struck dumb so that she literally cannot speak about what has happened; some stories end with the heroine's powers of speech being restored at the same time as her dead children are returned to her (see Appendix II). The speechlessness and mannequin-like qualities of these heroines recall the clinical descriptions of incest victims trying to function despite massive repression and occasional dissociation.

Many different strategies can be used to integrate these folktales into the treatment of victims. For example, one preadolescent girl was preoccupied with negativistically refusing school and had refused to talk about her father-daughter incest experience. She finally disclosed that she was afraid that if she went to school a particular classmate would tear out her eyes. "There is a story about that," I said, and told her the story of Oedipus. As we tried to understand why Oedipus would have plucked out his own eyes, she began to talk for the first time about her feelings of guilt about the sexual relationship with her father.

With younger children one can simply offer to tell a story during a play therapy session and the child can then act out with puppets or make drawings about parts of the story. Sometimes children will bring in their own story material which can be used in this way. A 7-year-old whose mother had disbelieved her accusations of incest played out the story of Jesus healing the blind man repeatedly in play sessions with her mother. At times she healed her mother's blindness; at other times she reversed roles and asked her mother to heal her.

Reading *Thousandfurs* can be a helpful exercise for use in groups of adolescent and adult incest victims. In this tale the princess runs away from her incestuous father, disguising herself in a coat made of many furs. She is tracked down by the hunting dogs of a neighboring prince whom she eventually marries. Incest victims who read this story predictably misunderstand it as follows: They believe that it is the girl's father who has tracked down the heroine, and that it is this incestuous father who eventually succeeds in carrying out his wish to marry the daughter. This misunderstanding of the story is a helpful way to begin group discussion of the continuing impact of the incest experience on current relationships with men.

Can such stories be used in prevention and case identification? Appendices I and II are brief versions of two medieval legends in the Thousandfurs cycle: *The Legend of Saint Dymphna* and *The Story of the Princess of Hungary*. We are beginning to use these stories both in treatment groups for incest victims and in rape prevention sessions for grade school and for junior high school children.

SUMMARY

It is likely that most professionals in our culture know less about incest than the average Navajo. In our culture the suppression of sexuality, the patriarchal emphasis, and the supreme value placed on privacy have led to a "conspiracy of silence" about incest. Clinical experience, tradition, and cross-cultural data indicate that incest may lead to a relatively fixed set of symptoms which have been observed in many different cultures and times. Informants have been telling anthropologists for centuries that the reason for the incest taboo is that incest does not work out well.[38] Anthropologists have tended to reject this explanation as simplistic and to search for deeper meanings to the incest taboo. However, clinical data from our own culture support this simple contention. These clinical data also lead us to believe that incest between first-degree relatives is common enough so that each generation in each culture will have the experience of a new series of disasters which will confirm the wisdom of the incest taboo.

My thanks to Patricia Draper, PhD, Joan Koss, PhD, and Julie Taylor, PhD, for reviewing early drafts of this chapter.

REFERENCES

1. Weinberg SK: *Incest Behavior.* New York, Citadel Press, 1955.
2. Manheim R (translator): *Grimms' Tales for Young and Old.* New York, Doubleday, 1977.
3. Goodwin J, Zouhar M, Bergman R: Hysterical seizures: A sequel to incest. *Am J Orthopsychiatry* 49:698-703, 1979.
4. Standage K: The etiology of hysterical seizures. *Can Psychiatr Assoc J* 20:67-73.
5. Maisch H: *Incest.* New York, Stein and Day, 1972.
6. Brewster BW: The incest theme in folksong. *Folklore Fellows Communications* 80 (212):1-36, 1972.
7. Temkin O: *The Falling Sickness.* Baltimore, Johns Hopkins Press, 1971.
8. Proskauer S: Oedipal equivalents in a clan culture: Reflections on Navajo Ways. *Psychiatry* 43:43-50, 1980.
9. Ginsberg EL, Hebeler J: Counter-violence counseling. Read before the Third International Congress on Child Abuse and Neglect, Amsterdam. April 21-25, 1981.
10. Silber A: Childhood seduction, parental pathology and hysterical symptomatology: The genesis of an altered state of consciousness. *Int J Psychoanal* 60:109-116, 1979.
11. Goodwin J: Suicide attempts in sexual abuse victims and their mothers. *Child Abuse Neglect* (To be published).
12. Aldington R, Ames D (translators): *New Larousse Encyclopedia of Mythology,* ed 13. London, Hyman, 1977.
13. Fine S: The teaching, service and research components of a university sexual medicine clinic for children. Read before the Third International Congress on Child Abuse and Neglect, Amsterdam. April 21-25, 1981.
14. Kempe CH: Sexual abuse, another hidden pediatric problem. The 1977 C. Anderson Aldrich Lecture. Pediatrics 62:382-389, 1978.
15. Camus A: in Thody P (translator): *Notebooks, 1935-1942.* New York, Modern Library, 1965.
16. Goodwin J, Cauthorne C, Rada R: The Cinderella syndrome: Children who simulate neglect. *Am J Psychiatry* 137:1223-1225, 1980.
17. Cox MR: *Three Hundred Forty-five Variants of Cinderella, Catskin and Cap o' Rushes.* London, Folk-lore Society, 1892.
18. Bethscheider JL: *A Study of Father-Daughter Incest in the Harris County Child Welfare Unit,* thesis. Sam Houston State University, Houston, 1972.
19. Gutheil T, Avery NC: Multiple overt incest as a family defense against loss. *Family Process* 16:105-116, 1977.

20. Kroth JA: Family therapy impact on intrafamilial child sexual abuse. Read before the Second International Congress on Child Abuse and Neglect, London, September, 1978.

21. Rosenfeld AA, Nadelson CC, Krieger M, et al: Incest and sexual abuse of children. *J Am Acad Child Psychiatry* 16:327–339, 1977.

22. Forward S, Buck C: *Betrayal of Innocence*. New York, Penguin, 1978.

23. Muslin H: On the resistances to parenthood. Read before the Michael Reese Hospital Department of Psychiatry Conference on Parenting as an Adult Experience, Chicago, March 7–8, 1980.

24. Montag BA, Montag TW: Infanticide. A historical perspective. *Minn Med* 62:368–372, 1978.

25. Tuzin D: *The Voice of the Tambaran: Truth and Illusion in Ilahita Arapesh Religion*. Berkeley, CA, University of California Press, 1980.

26. Raglan Lord: *Jocasta's Crime: An Anthropological Study*. London, Methuen, 1933.

27. Middletown R: Brother-sister and father-daughter marriage in ancient Egypt. *Am Soc Rev* 27:603–611, 1962.

28. Goodwin J, McCarty T, DiVasto P: Prior incest in abusive mothers. *Child Abuse Neglect* 5:1–9, 1981.

29. Meiselman KC: *Incest*. San Francisco, Jossey-Bass, 1978.

30. Kardiner A: *The Individual and His Society*. New York, Columbia University Press, 1939.

31. Canal Feijoo B: *Mitos Perdidos*. Buenos Aires, Compania Impresora, 1938.

32. Lukianowicz N: Incest. *Br J Psychiatry* 120:301–313, 1972.

33. Miller J, Moeller D, Kaufman A, et al: Recidivism among sex assault victims. *Am J Psychiatry* 135:1103–1104, 1978.

34. Draper P: !Kung women: Contrasts in sexual egalitarianism in foraging and sedentary contexts, in Reiter R (ed): *Toward an Anthropology of Women*. New York, Monthly Review Press, 1978.

35. Draper P: The learning environment for aggression and anti-social behavior among the !Kung, in Montagu A (ed): *Learning Non-Aggression*. New York, Oxford University Press, 1979.

36. Goodwin J, Sahd D, Rada R: Incest hoax: False accusations, false denials. *Bull Am Acad Psychiatry Law* 6 (3):269–276, 1979.

37. Holley KC: *Sexual Misuse of Children: Tools for Understanding*. Tacoma, WA, Pierce Country Rape Relief, 1978.

38. Burton RV: Folk theory and the incest taboo. *Ethos* 1 (4):504–511, 1973.

The Legend of Saint Dymphna

Once upon a time a beautiful Princess lived on an island where her mother and father were Queen and King. The name of this princess was Dymphna, and from her birth she had been an amazing child, in beauty, sweetness, and cleverness.

Dymphna's father, King Coninck, was a cruel man and a pagan. As Dymphna grew older, she understood that the Queen disagreed with the King about many things. For one thing, the Queen was a Christian, and Dymphna too began to learn Christianity from the hermit Gerebernus who lived in a hut in the forest.

One day the Queen became ill. On Christmas Eve, just before she died, she called Dymphna and Gerebernus to her and said, "My daughter, I am no longer able to keep you under my protection. You must make your own decisions now. Gerebernus, try to guide her, with God's help." After that, the Queen died.

On losing his Queen, King Coninck sank into a black chagrin, becoming more and more cruel and more strange than ever. His counselors, trying to cheer him, suggested that he seek a new Queen. And so he sent his soldiers throughout the land searching for someone worthy to be his Queen, someone as beautiful, as sweet, and as clever as was his dead wife. Alas, no such person could be found. When his messengers returned, the pagan King's mood became even blacker. Then a demon spoke to him. "What you seek is near you," said the demon. King Coninck, glancing up, saw his daughter, Dymphna. "There is the living image of your dead wife," the demon said. "She alone is worthy to be Queen of Ireland."

The next day he asked Dymphna to be his wife. When she refused he thought, "She says this because she is shy, still a young maiden. She will come around to my view soon enough. It is the only reasonable thing we can do, now that the Queen is dead."

Each day Coninck made his proposal anew, at times stroking her body and using sweet flattery, at other times explaining why his way was right, and at other times shouting, threatening, and waving his sword in a rage.

At last Dymphna could bear it no longer, and went to the hermit Gerebernus for advice. "I wish my mother were here," she said. Gerebernus thought for a long time and, at last, he said, "There is no way out except to run. All I can offer to do is run with you." The hermit told Dymphna that to gain time, she should ask the King to give her 40 days in which to make up her mind about the marriage.

When Coninck heard this, he was overjoyed. He showered Dymphna with presents, and gave her dozens of fine silk dresses. "I will often be away from the castle," she told him. The King imagined that she was preparing for the wedding feast. In reality, she was preparing to fly.

One day she went out on her white horse and did not return. She met Gerebernus and an old couple who had been friends of her mother. They ran their horses as far as the sea where Gerebernus had a boat ready. "My Princess," he said, "I do not know how to navigate, so I cannot tell you where this boat will take us. Do you still want to go?" Dymphna nodded and got into the boat. It was very cold and the sea was full of storms.

It was not until several days had passed that the servants in the castle dared to tell Coninck that his daughter had disappeared. First, he had his soldiers search for Dymphna throughout his own kingdom. When he found that Gerebernus too was missing, Coninck decided that it was Gerebernus who had caused all of his troubles. "This hermit turned my wife against me, and probably poisoned her in the bargain. Now he has turned my dear Dymphna against me, and has taken her away." Coninck gathered a large army and began to search for Dymphna through all Ireland and then across the seas.

Miraculously, Dymphna's boat reached shore at the busy port of Antwerp, in Belgium. People came to stare at the old hermit and at the beautiful princess who wore torn, sodden, silken rags. She bought food for her friends with the Irish coins she had with her. Because she was beautiful, merchants "sold" her the food, even though her Irish coins had no value in Antwerp. "Let us keep going," said Gerebernus. "There are too many people here."

They walked for many days into the forest. After a long while, they came to a shrine dedicated to Saint Martin in a lonely place with only 15 houses nearby. The village was called Gheel (or Geel, pronounced like a *gale* of wind). Gerebernus liked Saint Martin, so they stopped and built a hut near the shrine. They lived there in peace for about three months.

Meanwhile Coninck and his soldiers searched for Dymphna, moving out in ever-widening circles from Ireland. In Antwerp, the King heard of the beautiful girl and the hermit who had arrived in a boat. Coninck sent his men to comb the countryside for more news.

It was Coninck himself who sat down to dinner one night at the Inn at Gheel. "Oh, I cannot take this kind of money from you," said the woman who had served him. "I take these from the girl who lives with the hermit in the forest, but only because she is mad. I do it out of charity. Mad as a hatter she is, but lovely. Why, she says her father wants her to be his wife. She imagines it all, of course. She tells me that we must keep all this a secret. Poor girl. She believes, in her madness, that her father is still searching for her."

Coninck drew his sword and ran toward the hut in the forest. His soldiers followed. The woman at the Inn was left holding another one of those strange unlucky coins.

It was the end of May now, and warm and light in the evenings. Gerebernus saw the soldiers coming and went to the door, hoping to shield Dymphna from them.

"You are the enemy," said Coninck, seeing Gerebernus. "I will kill you and be free."

Dymphna came to stand at the side of her confessor. "Please, for the love you have for me, do not kill him."

"And what will you do for me if I spare your friend?" Said the King, reaching out to fondle her breasts. "What little favor will you do for your father then?" Gerebernus pushed the King away. "The time has come to speak plainly, my King. No pacts with the devil are allowed. What you have proposed violates all rules of man and God."

The King spoke again. "Will you have me, Dymphna? In exchange for his life?"

"Never," said the Princess. King Coninck nodded, and a dozen spears pierced Gerebernus at the same moment.

"Now, my daughter," said the King, "Will you be Queen of Ireland now?"

"Never," said Dymphna.

As always, the passionate lust of the King was very near to becoming a passionate rage. "You will be Queen of Ireland, or you will die," he said.

"My father," she answered, "I simply cannot."

He nodded as before, but this time no soldier moved. He lifted his chin, his eyes blazing. Still, nothing happened. At last, one soldier walked over to Dymphna. He raised his sword. Then he let it fall again. He could not kill her.

Coninck strode over to where she stood. With his own sword, he cut off the head of his daughter.

Dymphna was surprised to find that after all of that, she was still thinking. Coninck had done all he could to stop her thinking, but even this last had not succeeded. She was going upward, very fast, and Gerebernus was with her. She stretched out her arm to hug her mother. "Dear Mother," said Dymphna, "Soon we will be together, but now I must find a way to bring Father with us."

Dymphna pointed down to where her father, the King, was trampling and hacking at what he could see of Dymphna and of Gerebernus. His demon had now gained possession over his self. Coninck slavered and howled, trotted in circles, and kept spinning his sword above his head. His soldiers backed away from him in horror.

Dymphna, who was learning to fly with more control now, glided down to hover behind the woman at the inn. "What have I done?" The woman began to think. "I thought she was just a mad, silly girl, but she was fighting for her life. How can I make up for what I have done?" Just then King Coninck came wandering in. Coninck howled at the door, then fell to the floor and settled down to writhing like a snake, and hissing. The woman at the inn went to him. "Perhaps I can care for this poor creature. He is guilty of much, but so am I. I will try to give him the care that I did not give to his child. This one I will treat as one of my own family, not as someone to ridicule or to point the finger at, but as someone who truly belongs with us."

Dymphna saw clearly now the demon riding upon her father's back. It looked like a small dragon with horns. She was amazed that she had never seen it before. She took the sword from her father's hand. The demon knew that she had recognized him and ran to hide under the bed. Coninck collapsed into the arms of the innkeeper. Dymphna kept stalking the demon. She hunted him for nine days before she caught him and stabbed him to death with her father's sword.

All this happened almost thirteen hundred years ago. Still today, if you see a picture of Saint Dymphna, she will be holding her father's sword and standing on the head of a vicious-looking demon. Gerebernus became a saint too, and now he has long conversations with his friend, Saint Martin, every day. In memory of Saint Dymphna, today the families of Gheel still take in those who are possessed or deranged and help them to get well. Dymphna still helps to heal such people, as she healed her father. It is said that madness can be cured if one stays for nine days in Dymphna's church. Today, fathers still make passionate, demonic proposals to their daughters, and the daughters must try to find a way to say no. This is about as easy as sprouting wings. Dymphna and Gerebernus still wonder if they could have found a simpler way to do it.

SOURCES

Bogaerts Felix: *Dympne d'Irlande. Legende de Septieme Siecle.* Anvers, L.J. de Cort, 1840.

Janssens G: *Sainte Dimphne. Patronne de Gheel.* Lierre, J. Van In, 1894.

Geel: A Changing Tradition. A color film produced by the University of California Extension Media Center, Berkeley, 1973.

APPENDIX II

The Story of the Princess of Hungary

Once upon a time there was a princess so bonny and bright and gay that she was called Joy. Everyone said she was the exact image of her good mother.

One day the princess's mother, the Queen, became ill. The King stayed by the Queen's bedside and swore that he would never leave her. As the Queen lay dying, she made him promise that he would never remarry unless it was to someone who had the Queen's own golden hair, the Queen's own sea-blue eyes, and the Queen's own flame-red lips. The King promised, and the Queen died. However, he was so overcome by grief that he did not even think of marrying for many months. Then his barons began to mutter that the King had no son. The barons insisted that he take a wife. However, the King could find no one in the land as beautiful as his dead Queen, and he was determined to keep his promise.

One day, while Joy was playing chess with her father to cheer him, the King looked at his daughter in a new way. He saw that she had the Queen's own golden hair, and the Queen's own sea-blue eyes, and the Queen's own flame-red lips. He caught up her small hand, kissed it, and begged his daughter to marry him. Joy replied by taking up her father's sword with which she cut off her own left hand even as the King held it to his lips.

Enraged, the King tossed Joy's severed hand over his shoulder, where it fell into a stream. He ordered that his daughter be burned at the stake immediately. However, the court jester loved Joy and could not bear to see her hurt any further. So he made a mannequin or dummy so that it looked exactly like the princess. He tied the mannequin to the stake to be burned, and he spirited the real princess away to a small boat. The princess had lost her power to speak, and her eyes held only a cloudy emptiness. As the court jester set her adrift in the cold sea, he said, "I am afraid it was Joy that was burned today. I fear it is only the mannequin that I have saved." From that day, the princess was called Mannequin or Manekine.

When her boat cast her up on the coast of Scotland, everyone who saw her was struck by her sad loveliness. The King came to see for himself this silent, one-handed beauty, and he fell in love with her at once. Despite the muttering of his mother, who was sure that Manekine was a witch, the King and the castaway were married. However, before their child was born, the King had to leave on a crusade.

Manekine had a beautiful baby boy and wrote to the King to tell him of their joy. However, her mother-in-law intercepted her letter, and replaced it with one saying that the Witch-Queen had borne a monster and that both must be burned at the stake. The King was troubled when he received this letter but wrote back saying that he would come back immediately and that nothing should be done until his return. However, Manekine's mother-in-law intercepted this message too, and replaced it with a letter that ordered that Manekine and her son be burned at the stake.

Now Manekine had been burned at the stake once before, so she remembered how it could best be done in order to survive. She made two mannequins, one to resemble herself, and one to resemble her baby; she tied them to the stake, and she fled with her baby out to sea in a small boat.

This time the sea took them to Rome. There Manekine became a beggar to get food for her starving baby. Despite all her struggles, the baby died of hunger.

One day Manekine was sitting in her rags beside a fountain. On a balcony above her, she heard two men talking as they ate. Both were pilgrims who had come to Rome asking forgiveness. The older man was doing penance for having desired his own daughter for his wife and for having killed her when she refused him. The younger man was asking forgiveness for having abandoned his young wife to the cruelty of his mother. He had not been able to return in time to prevent his mother from killing his wife and child, but he had had his mother burned at the stake when he learned the truth.

Suddenly, Manekine realized who these two men were. Her voice was restored to her and she uttered a shout of recognition. Her father and husband came running down; they recognized her at once because of her missing left hand. Then the two men knew each other as well, for Manekine had never told her husband that her father was the King of Hungary, and her father had never dreamed that his daughter would be married to a King. "I forgive you both," said Manekine, and with those, her first words since her father's unnatural proposal, a miracle occurred. Her left hand flowed into the fountain and flowed up to Manekine where it joined smoothly to her arm. The hand must have been flowing down from Hungary from that first moment when her father threw it into the stream. Then Manekine heard splashing sounds from the fountain. She turned around to see her young son, no longer a baby now, but standing in the water and holding out his arms to his mother.

SOURCE

Cox MR: *Cinderella: Three Hundred Forty-five Variants of Cinderella, Catskin, and Cap o' Rushes.* London, Folk-lore Society, 1892.